A Weapon in the Struggle

Edited by Andy Croft

A Weapon in the Struggle
The Cultural History of the Communist Party in Britain

Pluto Press
LONDON • STERLING, VIRGINIA

First published 1998 by Pluto Press
345 Archway Road, London N6 5AA
and 22883 Quicksilver Drive,
Sterling, VA 20166–2012, USA

British Library Cataloguing in Publication Data
A catalogue record for this book is available from
the British Library

ISBN 0 7453 1209 8 hbk

Library of Congress Cataloging in Publication Data
A weapon in the struggle: the cultural history of the Communist Party
   in Britain/edited by Andy Croft.
      p.   cm.
   ISBN 0–7453–1209–8 (hardcover)
      1. Communist Party of Great Britain—History. 2. Communism—Great
Britain—History. 3. Great Britain—Politics and government—20th
century.   I. Croft, Andy.
HX244.W43   1998
324.241'0975—dc21   98–24912
                                                                CIP

Designed and produced for Pluto Press by
Chase Production Services, Chadlington, OX7 3LN
Typeset by Stanford DTP Services, Northampton
Printed in the EC by T.J. International Ltd, Padstow

Contents

Introduction

> I was asked in 1953 to take a weekend school on the theme 'Culture is a weapon in the fight for socialism'. Thinking out what I would say, I felt that the theme stated no more than a half-truth. At the school I said that culture, as Caudwell had written of poetry in *Illusion and Reality*, heightens our consciousness of the world we want to win and our energy to win it. In this sense it was true that culture is a weapon in the fight for socialism. But the truth depended on recognition of the greater truth that socialism is a weapon in the fight for culture. For our final aim was not the establishment of a political and economic structure, but the heightening of human life. Without this recognition, the slogan became a perversion of the truth, since it degraded culture into a means to a political end. (Alick West, *One Man in His Time*)

This book takes its title from a slogan used by British communists at the height of the Cold War to define their attitude to cultural activity. There is a touching earnestness about the idea of culture as a weapon in political struggle; the thought that art and politics might be usefully and actively related seems unbelievably quaint in an age where both are more usually considered unconnected objects of private and passive consumption. But there is also a grisly vainglory here, an expression of the self-consciously embattled spirit in which the Communist Party conducted its cultural life, distorted by a slavish and idiotic devotion to imported Soviet examples, and a would-be military model of cultural organisation. And it is hard to think of a more self-defeating metaphor, as of course the enemy always had rather more divisions on the cultural front than the British Communist Party could ever deploy.

Yet the Party's artistic life was not always as reductive or as grim as its pronouncements on the subject. For all the talk of culture as a 'weapon in the struggle for socialism', the Communist Party also contained another, utopian, sense that socialism was a weapon in the fight for an enriched and democratic human culture. Delegates to the Party's 1952 Party Congress, for example, after voting against 'the Americanisation of Britain's cultural life' and 'reactionary films and debased literature and comics' were treated to a concert at which, between readings from Dickens and poetry from the Trinidadian communist Peter Blackman, the pianist James Gibb played Beethoven, John Goss sang Vaughan Williams' *Hugh the Drover*, the WMA Singers performed some English folk songs, the Birmingham Workers Choir sang an 'eighteenth-century medley', while Alan Bush conducted part of his opera *Wat Tyler* and Unity Theatre provided some Old Time Music Hall. It was, to say the least, a contradictory organisation which by day endorsed the attacks in the Soviet Union on Shostakovitch and Akhmatova, and in the evening found relaxation and pleasure in such a jolly and idiosyncratic repertoire. Because the Communist Party never resolved this contradiction it was arguably condemned to failure. But it was also out of this contradiction that British communists made much of their most lively and entertaining art, some of which at least deserves to survive that failure.

There is another contradiction which needs to be considered here. The arts have long been an easy target for anti-communist historiography. Few aspects of communist history have attracted so much attention as its cultural record, yet almost nothing is known about the specific cultural histories of the British Communist Party. The appalling treatment of artists in the Soviet Union, China and the People's Democracies was always enough to suggest that communists could not be trusted with the imagination. Because communism in the Soviet Union appeared to prove itself the historical enemy of creativity, historians have been saved the trouble of examining what this meant for communist artists a long way from Moscow.

These essays attempt to unravel both contradictions by considering some of the achievements and failures of communist artists who, though mostly forgotten now, once had an extraordinary impact on British cultural life, out of all proportion to the Party's political influence (which was itself out of proportion to its size). Together they represent a kind of tentative outline history of some of the ways in which the Communist Party tried to intervene in British cultural life – in painting, theatre, music, poetry, fiction, criticism, film, song and even historical pageants – and of some of the ways in which individual artists tried to play their part in the life of the Communist Party.

There are many obvious omissions here, to which I hope this collection will encourage others to attend – the work of Caribbean communists like Claudia Jones in establishing the Notting Hill Carnival, the influence of actors and writers from Unity Theatre on the development of TV drama, the role of Reggie Smith, Ewan MacColl and Charles Parker in shaping British radio drama, the involvement of London communists in the first London *mela*. There are many individuals whose work is not discussed here, but whose distinguished careers also need to be assessed one day – the Lutenist Diana Poulton, for example, who was also manager of the Party publishers Lawrence & Wishart; Montagu Slater, head of film scripts at the Ministry of Information and librettist of Britten's *Peter Grimes*; sculptors like Lawrence Bradshaw and George Fullard; the polymath Jack Lindsay, author of over 160 books; the film-maker (and table tennis champion) Ivor Montagu; Thomas Russell, secretary of the London Philharmonic Orchestra. And no assessment of the Communist Party's contribution to British cultural life will be complete without some account of the role of communists in local Workers Theatre Movement (WTM), Workers Music Association (WMA) and Unity groups (in 1949 the amateur People's Theatre in Newcastle performed the *world* premiere of O'Casey's *Cock a Doodle Dandy*), in Left Book Club groups, in Glasgow Unity Theatre, in the wartime Army Bureau of Current Affairs (ABCA) and the Council for the Encouragement of Music and the Arts (CEMA).

Although for reasons of space these essays do not go much beyond 1956, this is not to imply that the departure of so many of its most distinguished artists that year left the Party short of cultural energy or ideas. A fuller account of communist cultural initiatives would have to include, for example, the evangelical promotion of children's poetry by communist teachers inside NATE and ILEA in the early 1970s (when Chris Searle was sacked for publishing a book of poetry by children from a secondary school in Stepney), the work of Buzz Goodbody and Colin Chambers at the RSC, the role of communists in setting up the Federation of Worker Writers and Community Publishers, the impact of magazines like *Artery*, *Fireweed* and *Red Letters*. As late as 1977 the Party was able to attract 11,000 people to Alexandra Palace for the People's Jubilee. If thereafter the Party never regained the cultural authority it had once enjoyed, it nevertheless continued to engage the loyalties of distinguished and well-known figures like Tilda Swinton, Sally Hibbin, Dick Gaughan and Ken Currie.

This book therefore represents only the beginnings of a discussion about the particularities – and the peculiarities – of British communist cultural history. It may be that the cultural legacy of the Party will prove – together with its anti-colonial work and its role in the trade unions – its most important and enduring contributions to British life. But so long as histories of the Party, whether hostile or sympathetic, underestimate its cultural record, our understanding of its wider failures and successes is unlikely to be either adequate or very useful. There are four ways in which this case may be put.

Firstly, the Communist Party always took its cultural work very seriously indeed. It invested an enormous amount of energy in its cultural projects and placed great responsibilities on its 'cultural workers'. Only an organisation which placed such importance on culture could have spent most of the Cold War in open conflict with its own best artists. (Curiously, the Party paid rather more attention to the arts and to the encouragement of creativity during the High Stalinist years of the Cold War than it did during the ascendancy of *Marxism Today* in the 1980s, when culture more usually meant 'lifestyle'.) The arts were one of the ways in which communist ideas entered the mainstream of British life and through which the Party was able to identify itself as the defender of native, popular traditions and as the bearer of the new and, therefore, of the future. This was obviously the case in the 1930s and 1940s, when the Party attracted the avant-garde (Henry Moore), the fashionable (Stephen Spender) and the popular (Patrick Hamilton), when the communist jazz band leader Ben Frankel was writing dance music *and* film scores *and* chamber music. It was true in a more substantial sense during the Second World War, when communists in CEMA and ABCA found themselves at the head of the wartime 'cultural upsurge' which was articulated so powerfully in the Party's bestselling magazines, *Our Time* and *Seven*. Conversely, during the Cold War it was one of the ways in which the Party was seen to be locked in the past, hostile to every new cultural development (Bop, Sartre, Alban Berg, Graham Greene, Gershwin, Rock and Roll and even Picasso). The changing fortunes of communist artists are therefore a good measure of the Party's wider fortunes, its arguments about culture a coded history of wider strategy debates.

Secondly, the Communist Party created in practice a uniquely participatory artistic internal life which bore as little resemblance to the idea of the 'fighting unit in the Battle of Ideas' as it did to the usual caricatures of intellectuals seduced by Stalin. The Party's attempts to develop a native communist 'tradition' brought together professionals and amateurs in ways which, though sometimes high minded and patronising, were always accessible and educative (the classicist George Thomson once held open meetings at Marx House where comrades were invited to propose revisions to his *Marxism and Poetry*). What British newspaper but the *Daily Worker* ever celebrated Shakespeare's birthday by reproducing the full text of Gaunt's speech from *Richard II* (mischievously suggesting that it was 'Shakespeare's comment on the Marshall Plan')? What British newspaper but the *Daily Worker* ever had a playwright (Sean O' Casey) on its editorial board? For most of its life the paper carried a full page of book reviews each week (out of only six pages) as well as weekly columns surveying new cinema, jazz, theatre, music, art, records, dance, radio and later TV. It occasionally ran serialised stories (one ran for 21 weeks in 1949) and frequently carried comical, topical verse; the satirical poet 'Krasny' made an appearance as early as February 1930. The *Daily Worker*, and before that the *Sunday Worker*, regularly ran educational debates on issues of cultural history, part of a sustained, long-term project to introduce working-class readers to the 'best' of their cultural heritage. Much of the autobiographies of working-class Party leaders like Tom Bell and T.A. Jackson were essentially annotated reading lists of the books which made them communists. Party members were routinely encouraged to read, write, sing, speak, act, even to make films. During an otherwise unedifying debate in the *Daily Worker* in 1952 on the role of 'cultural workers', one

Party member confessed that although his borough committee had granted his request for a four-month 'sabbatical' from Party activity in order to finish a novel, he had been unable to do so; it was only when he resumed his responsibilities in the Party and in the Ex-Servicemen's Movement for Peace that he was able to regain the impulse to write. Writing in particular was a natural reflex among several generations of self-educating working-class communists. Imprisoned in 1916 for opposing the war, Bob Stewart put the experience to good use in a book of *Prison Rhymes*; when the Welsh poet T.E. Nicholas was gaoled in 1940 (under Defence Regulation 18B) he too wrote a book about the experience – a collection of prison sonnets *in Welsh*; taken prisoner in North Africa in 1942, a young barber called Dan Billany spent the rest of the war in an Italian prison camp, where he wrote *The Cage*, one of the great prison camp novels. Harry Pollitt used to review children's fiction in the *Daily Worker*, Willie Gallacher once published a book of satirical verse and Palme Dutt wrote a play about Dimitrov. The first Party meeting I attended in Middlesborough was devoted to a discussion of *Nineteen Eighty-Four*; Teesside communists played an important part in founding a local community-writing festival (now in its tenth year); one of the branch's last acts was to organise a poetry reading in support of the local campaign against the Gulf War.

Thirdly, although the Party's celebration of native, radical, democratic cultural traditions was inspired by the Soviet example, its cultural successes were much more than the sum of the Soviet cultural models it was expected to follow. With the exception of some musicians (the distinguished pianist Geraldine Peppin once described the Party Musicians Group as 'dead from the cock up') the cultural work of the Party was probably less damaged by international events than most other aspects of the Party's work.

Finally, this was an organisation entirely at ease with ideas of criticism and cultural debate. Despite the best efforts of King Street, the Communist Party never resolved its attitude to culture and the arts. There was always room for fierce controversy and argument; on one occasion an article by T.A. Jackson defending 'bourgeois culture' generated over a hundred letters to the *Daily Worker* in three days. In 1956 the paper had to interrupt a long-running controversy about Burns' Night to make space for readers' letters about the 25th Congress and the revelations about Stalin. Accounts of the Communist Party which underestimate its cultural life inevitably reduce the autodidact culture of this instinctively argumentative organisation to a stage army under orders from Moscow or King Street.

Moreover, not all King Street's cultural thinking was conducted in Moscow's military metaphors. 'Why do we want political power? What is it for?' asked John Gollan at that 1953 conference on 'Culture as a Weapon in the Fight for Socialism'. After ritually denouncing 'Western values' and genuflecting to supposed cultural freedoms in the Soviet Union, Gollan reminded Party members present that they were concerned about 'society and social systems' not for their own sake, but because they were committed to the cultural 'flowering' of the individual, recalling the Chartist slogan, 'political power is our means, social happiness our end.' That evening there was of course a concert. Bruce Turner played his clarinet in a scratch calypso band, Ewan MacColl and A.L. Lloyd sang miners', weavers' and seamen's ballads as well as songs by John Ireland and Vaughan Williams; there was a performance of scenes from Shaw's *Widowers' Houses*, a display of Scottish sword dancing, and singing and dancing by comrades from India, West Africa and the West Indies.

If the British Communist Party never made up its mind whether culture was a weapon in the struggle or the ultimate aim of that struggle, at least it asked important questions about the relationship between culture and politics, between art and society, enjoyment and thinking. In the context of British politics – particularly the philistinism, economism and electoralism of the British left – this was no small achievement. They may even be questions still worth asking.

Andy Croft
Middlesbrough
May 1997

1

H. Gustav Klaus

James Barke: A Great-Hearted Writer, a Hater of Oppression, a True Scot

'Well, Jimmy,' said MacBride, when the housekeeper had admitted Cain, 'and what brings you up my way tonight?'

'I want to return these books of yours, dominie.'

'Let me see what you've got.

'*Hymn to Lenin – Up the Noran Water – Grey Granite – The End of the High Bridge – Butcher's Broom*. That's a bundle of books. I was wondering where most of my stuff had gone. And what about the *Hymn to Lenin?*'

'Hymn to my backside! Rubbish, dominie: bad thinking, bad poetry. Wandering in the world of half-digested ideas like a sick duck wandering about in a mist – of course it impresses they reviewing sods that haven't enough ideas to get lost among. *Up the Noran Water*'s more like the thing. That lass has the glimmering o' poetry in her. Gin she gets a trauchle of weans round her skirt there's no saying where she might end.'

'You've got them weighed up, Jimmy. What about our Scots novelists?'

'That's no' so easy. Take Gibbon, now, with his *Sunset Song* – he wrote that out of the stuff of his youth, seen through eyes that thought they knew better – the same as Barke with *The World His Pillow*. But in *Cloud Howe* he's a' to hell thegither. He kens nothing about it but thinks that he does – and it convinces the folk that ken nothing either. It's the style that carries the thing along. But analyse it, dominie, and what do you get? Fantasy, dominie, and wild stuff at that.'

'Oh, but surely, Jimmy, well observed types?'

'Aye, here and there ... and he's a grand bawdy touch that's a pleasure to meet. But damnt man, dominie, he's not at the heart of Segget as he was o' Kinraddie. But this Gibbon childe's a randy, no doubt – if he only knew it kin to Burns – the best we've gotten since Burns's time. *Grey*

Granite's the stuff, though it's just clashed thegither. Its importance cannot be overstressed.'

'What about your *House with the Green Shutters* now?'

'I'm no' deserting George Douglas Brown – a fine lad George as far as he went. A bit swatch of Bakunin might have put him right.'

'And what about Barke – does he need Bakunin?'

'Man, dominie, Barke has it in his power – if he'll bide his time and gather his weapons – to blow the whole jing-bang to blazes. He's ta'en on the now with this Hielan' stuff: debunking the Gael with a show of success: showing they're human like every god-damn son of the human race – no' a special race of superior swine. That's what's wrong with this lad Gunn. He thinks the Highlander's something bi-ornar, so he's going bi-ornar as a result himself – clean away from the times of the present. That phrase o' Barke's sums that up – backward-looking, backward-longing. Damnt, let's get forward to the job on hand. The world's in a mess and needs redding up – it'll never be redd by a handful of Gaels, however willing – Barke shows that in *The Wild MacRaes*. But what Gunn and Gibbon and Barke need to learn is that the capitalist slave state will need to be blown to a bag of dithyrags proper!'

'So you don't like Gunn?'

'I wouldn't say that – he's got integrity and, by God, he's got art. That book of his is one of the greatest that's ever been written in the English tongue. The art of Gunn, the purpose of Barke, the fantastic of Gibbon: God! what a combination that would make.'

This is a striking, if unconventional, account of Scottish writing in the 1930s. Few readers outside Scotland will have heard of James Barke today. Fewer still would share the assumption that he was the equal of Neil Gunn and Lewis Grassic Gibbon. But this is clearly how Barke secretly hoped to be regarded by posterity – the passage was of course written by Barke himself[1] – and for a time this was how his writing was received, at least in some quarters.

Born James Bark – the 'e' was added later – in the Borders parish of Ladhope near Galashiels in 1906, the author worked for most of his life as a clerk in a Glasgow shipyard-cum-engineering firm. He published five novels and an early autobiography within the space of seven years, and followed this up with a highly controversial six-volume fictionalised life of Robert Burns and Jean Armour.[2] His other, indeed his first, love was the theatre. Barke had half a dozen plays performed (and one published),[3] he chaired Glasgow Unity Theatre during its first year (1941–42) and wrote a bagpipe march for the Scottish Ambulance Unit in Spain.[4] As so many writers of his generation he had become politicised in the early 1930s. He crossed the Rubicon some time in late 1932 or 1933 by joining the Communist Party in whose ranks he remained until his death in 1958. And it was from fellow communists and socialists that he received his greatest encouragement. He was befriended by Lewis Grassic Gibbon (to whom he dedicated *The End of the High Bridge*). Johnnie Campbell called *Major Operation* 'one of the greatest novels of working-class struggle yet written in any English-speaking country'; Ethel Mannin considered it 'one of the most stimulating pieces of revolutionary writing I ever hope to read, or ever have read'. A younger working-class writer, Robert Bonnar, later praised him as Scotland's 'greatest living novelist'. Even George Blake – in many ways an antipodean figure in Scottish letters – saw him as 'one of the innovators of the 1930s', one of 'first rate importance' to the development of the novel in Scotland.[5]

If Barke's work seems now too uneven to bear the comparison with Gunn and Grassic Gibbon, the best of his novels – *The Wild MacRaes, Major Operation* and *The Land of the Leal* – may at least remind us why, after Gibbon's death in 1935, great hopes were laid upon Barke as his natural successor. Both authors had their roots in the land, both considered themselves revolutionaries, both were prolific writers, churning out at least one novel a year. However, just as Gibbon's career was cut tragically short by death at the age of 33, at the same age James Barke stopped writing novels about contemporary life and devoted himself wholly to his study of Burns. Perhaps the burden of expectation was too great. Full-time work, a growing family to support and his own failing health cannot have helped. Or perhaps it was because of his growing sense that 'the events of our generation are on too vast a scale to come within the organisational scope' of the contemporary novel, a difficulty he admitted after he had just finished *The Land of the Leal* in 1938:

> [W]e cannot throw down our pens in despair and endeavour to console ourselves with the knowledge that, in a more leisured age, when the historic discords have been resolved, the future Tolstoy will then (and only then) be in a position to complete the sequel to *War and Peace*.
>
> In the meantime we must do our work as best we may ... And if honesty compels us to face the major political and economic issues of our generation then we confront an obligation which we must discharge, not as politicians or economists (far less as propagandists of a political party), but as artists conscious of our traditions, grateful for our heritage and imbued with a deep sense of the responsibility we share for that grand total of all art and human endeavour – civilisation.[6]

Large words indeed, but then James Barke's were large novels (the only one in print today, *The Land of the Leal*, has been called the longest Scottish novel since Scott).[7] And no one can say that James Barke did not try to bring the massive 'historic discords' of his time into fiction – national and international, rural and urban, industrial and political.

The Land

In his first published novel, *The World His Pillow* (1933), we find the protagonist, modelled on the youthful author, musing about the state of his nation:

> What a weak, poor land was this Scotland lying away to the north ... And yet how he loved it. A flowerpotful of Balcregggan was dearer to him than all the broad rolling acres of England. The main street of Glenaraig was more significant than Tottenham Court Road: MacRae's barn worth all the St Paul's and Westminsters ever built. All sentimental heresy no doubt. Well, he didn't care a sup of broth whether it was or not. London did not appeal to him ... he would rather be walking through the larches over to Banmoran than walking down the Strand even if it was fifty times the Strand. Ah, but he was forgetting that there were no longer larches on the road to Banmoran. Perhaps that office in Whitehall had been responsible for that. Perhaps London did matter after all. What was he thinking about? Of course, London mattered – mattered supremely. Wasn't London the real effective centre of Scotland? Hadn't Westminster and Throgmorton Street, and the Old Lady of Threadneedle Street executive powers? Hadn't they one hand on Auld Scotia's throat and the other in her sporran? (pp. 318–19)[8]

In choosing, contrary to his own background, a Highland scene for *The World His Pillow*, *The Wild MacRaes* (1934) and *The End of the High Bridge* (1935) Barke at once rode on a literary tide and progressively tried to stem and subvert it. He was well aware of writing in the shadow of Fionn MaColla's *The Albanach* (1932) and Neil Gunn's early fiction, *The Lost Glen* (1932), for example. But while susceptible to their blend of myth and realism, he was critical of the ideological implications underpinning their work. If they displayed indignation about Highland decline, if they resented, in now recognisably nostalgic terms, the invasion of the modern into the glen, if they celebrated the threatened or extinct community's strong vitality or moral superiority, Barke was out to 'debunk the Gael' and to demonstrate that all attempts to revive Gaelic culture were misplaced and ill-fated.

In *The World His Pillow*, which is a *Bildungsroman* with the artist left out (except for the occasional appearance of the piper), this stance is least apparent. This has as much to do with the uncertainty of direction of the novel's overall design as with the self-absorption of the protagonist, who has a tendency to blame every conceivable evil in the world, but especially the city, for what is in great measure his own malaise. His is an unchannelled directionless rebellion. It might even be argued that the novel reiterates the solutions offered by *The Albanach* and *The Lost Glen*, where the central hero is saved from despair by a return to his Highland village. It is not a question of imitation, for Barke's first novel was awaiting publication, if not actually in the press, when MacColla's and Gunn's works came out. It is rather a kindred impulse, an angry rejection, an abhorred shying away from the consequences of mass urban society. But where Barke differs from his immediate predecessors is in constructing the dichotomy in terms of country and city, rural and urban life rather than in the specific Scottish configuration of Highland and Lowland, Celtic and Anglo-Gael identity.

> The first tree was about to go over. The men had withdrawn the saw and were hammering a couple of wedges into the slit. Presently there was a warning crack. The great fir wavered, hung for a moment at a perilous angle, then with a sickening splintering and crashing, smashed itself down into the undergrowth. The arms it fell on snapped and splintered, burying themselves into the soft leaves and pine needles under the weight of the body. In its descent, the branches of a neighbouring tree had come in the way: they had been torn off like twigs. The lumbermen laughed: the officer smiled.
>
> Duncan had watched the scene with a growing sense of pain and horror. It was worse than watching a pig being stuck. At least a pig squealed and struggled for life. But how patiently a tree submitted to murder. If the trees could scream, thought Duncan, even God in heaven would be driven mad.
>
> As the tree fell, Duncan felt himself tremble at the knees. He felt sick.
> (p. 179)

The adolescent Duncan is watching a group of lumbermen felling trees for trench-building in the First World War. The scene is important, for it goes some way towards making sense of an otherwise improbable and unsatisfactory ending of the novel. Having tasted education, love and politics in the city and found all wanting, having lost faith in his remaining gospel, the 'Great God Shaw', a disillusioned Duncan returns to the Highlands to work in an afforestation project – and to bed his head on the pillow of a local girl, also a 'returned native'.

It is only the author's sensitive and introspective characters who have an antenna for the 'desecration' (the chapter title) of the land. Here is George Anderson, early on in *Major Operation* (1936), contemplating the effects of mass intrusion into nature: 'All very well for city lads and lassies to come out into the country for a breath of fresh air. But they needed discipline, education in the way to behave in the countryside. Burn all litter. Don't break down young trees. Preserve amenities.' (p. 109) The passage reveals his middle-class blinkers. His respect for nature is qualified in that he would prefer to reserve it for people like himself ('The workers were beginning to swarm everywhere like a plague of locusts devouring all green things.'

p. 109), but class-tainted though it is, it is nevertheless genuine and reflects a preoccupation dear to Barke's own heart.

In planting such views in the middle-class representative of the book Barke may have shielded himself, for the author's sympathies for felled trees had not endeared him to some quarters of the left. A reviewer of *The World His Pillow* had sneered in the *Glasgow Socialist Star*: 'Think of it – depopulating the forests of wood. Trees – mushrooms and cobwebs – fungus in a beer cellar – shed a tear for them and you have a soul!'[9] Such criticism did not let Barke rest. In his 'Chapter in Autobiography', *The Green Hills Far Away* (1940), he returned to the incident:

> I am well aware that my reactions to the felling of the Tullialan Forest will appear the most sentimental drivelling to many worthy people whose penny in the slot reactions to their environment is one of the sad things about humanity ... But the useless massacre of the trees did more to open my eyes to the savage anarchy of modern society and the overwhelming ghastliness of modern war than any theoretical formulations. (p. 268)

He goes on to concede that, had he known the Glasgow slums at this stage of his life, he would have hacked down the trees himself, if the timber could have helped to rehouse the slum dwellers decently. But then with renewed conviction: 'A tree takes a long time to grow. But it can beautify the earth for a hundred years. No man has the right to cut them down wantonly or selfishly, or without taking steps to replace their loss.' (p. 269)

The 'green' Barke who speaks here, the author who bothers about the 'larches on the road to Banmoran' and the fir trees in Tullialan, was, of course, born and bred in the country, and more especially to a life lived close to nature. He had grown up on an estate in Fife, the son of agricultural workers who were made redundant after the First World War and who were thus compelled to migrate to the city. But not every 'true son of the soil'[10] felt so deeply about the havoc wreaked upon the environment. Nor were there many people on the left in the 1930s who voiced such views or had any patience with them. Ecological considerations were not part of the socialist agenda of the period. Unemployment, the rise of Fascism and the threat of war appeared far more pressing problems, not 'the green hill far away, / Beyond a city wall'.[11] But in Barke's work they grow naturally out of one of his central concerns, which is a recreation of the lost world of the Scottish farmworkers and crofters, of their dislocation and disorientation in the city – always Glasgow – to which they are driven.

The Wild MacRaes, a much more concentrated, at times even gripping, novel, engages directly with the dream in some Scottish Nationalist quarters to breathe new life into the deserted glens:

Scotland was two nations: North and South: Highland and Lowland. The Lowlands had probably been destroyed by industrialism. Too late now for a revival of the Doric; and ploughing with a pair of horses was already an anachronism. But not too late in the Highlands for a revival of the Gaelic and the old essential Highland tradition: the clan system communalised in the light of the age. Not too late if you got the folk back on the land ... The pride of being self-supporting, and yet working with your fellow men towards a common end. Kill the slave mentality. Against the lairds. Against the parasitical bloodsuckers and sporting bloodhounds. (p. 128)

Thus the vision of Mary MacKinnon inspired by de Valera's ideal of a rural, self-sufficient Ireland, its back turned on the world.

The action is built around a dispute over some sheep between the new Laird, an English gentleman-officer eager to assert his authority, and the MacRaes, an old established crofter family. What starts as a quarrel turns into a feud, a major defiance of the machinery of law and finally into open rebellion. Things come to a head with the attempted land raid. As a realistic story with the crofters setting out, like the Diggers of old, equipped with pick and shovel to stake out their claims, the incident looks wildly anachronistic. But as a symbolic challenge to a feudal system of property law that has survived all other changes, and is enduring to this year of Grace 1998,[12] it is a powerful act. The MacRaes go down fighting in the uneven battle that unfolds. These proud, principled, independent-minded, heroically struggling people have all Barke's sympathies. But history, as he shows, has simply ridden over them.

In a perceptive review of the novel Lewis Grassic Gibbon drew a comparison between the crofters' struggles and the militancy of the factory proletariat:

[T]he wild MacRaes themselves – four sons of a gamekeeper – are heroic figures of myth, and not the less real for that. They centre and epitomise the struggle of the classes that is waged just as bitterly in the remote glen as in the nearby factory ... Their countryside ... seems on the verge of rising to their leadership in a miniature peasant rebellion ... There is this glimpse of a possibility, then it fades, as in real life it would fade. The weakness of even heroic peasants without a definitive creed or code of revolt destroys them; one by one they are lopped down, farcical or tragic in their fall.[13]

The passage sheds light on Gibbon's own conception, as put into practice in *A Scots Quair*, the last volume of which was in the making, of a continuity of the struggle for independence and dignity across generations and human spaces. But it also contains an interesting echo from the opening of Marx's *The Eighteenth Brumaire* with its distinction between the tragic dimension of a 'world-historical' event and its latter-day farcical 'second edition' on a miniature scale: after all, the story takes place in the 1920s.

In *The End of the High Bridge* we encounter another English landlord, this time of the 'absentee' type, another sly factor who engineers a gamekeeper's downfall, and another shooting incident. The Western Highlands, too, are by now familiar territory. But where there was a longing for the natural beauty associated with the vanished world of childhood in *The World His Pillow*, or compassion for the crofters in *The Wild MacRaes*, there is now only bitter resentment against the love- and pleasure-denying role of Presbyterianism. The novel is a study of an ordinary man pushed to the extremes of vanity and self-righteousness as a result of his having been raised to the eldership of the kirk. The *idée fixe* that he is one of God's chosen few totally unbalances John MacLeod. He alienates his wife and daughter, disowns his mistress, loses his home and livelihood, succumbs to drink and ends his days tramping the road in the company of a tinker – all the time deliriously persuading himself that these are just trials and tribulations on the path to God. But there are limits to the capacity for suffering of even an individual of MacLeod's iron constitution and determination. When it dawns on him, in a rare moment of lucidity, that instead of reaching the light he is facing 'darkness and utter void' he commits suicide. The somewhat melodramatic story inexorably moves to its bleak end, determinism being an ingredient of all Barke's fiction.

MacLeod's religious mania may be exceptional, but bigotry, narrow-mindedness and hypocrisy are shown to be an integral part of the fabric of Highland life. None of the other church elders commends himself to the reader. Humanity shines in the a-religious characters, who without exception leave the place.

The End of the High Bridge marks the end of Barke's infatuation with the 'Hielan stuff', as he put it in the opening passage, and his art only gained from the subsequent shift of interest to the city. When he returned to the country in *The Land of the Leal* (1939), he painted with advantage a much wider geographical, social and historical canvas. This last 'contemporary' novel, rightly considered as his *chef d'oeuvre*, does in fact start in the middle of the nineteenth century. It is a family saga based on the hard lives of his own ancestors, who had toiled in the Rhinns of Galloway, and in the next generation were carried first to the Borders, then to West Fife, before being absorbed by Clydeside. As these successive stages indicate, the migration of the family serves as a paradigm for the movement from agricultural to industrial labour, from farm to tenement, country to city. The episodic structure of the narrative allows for an immensely rich display of historical detail (the arrival of tea among the Galloway farmhands) and a memorable incident (the Herculean labour of unloading a limeboat in a violent winter storm). Thanks also to a baffling array of subordinate characters the author can strike a fair balance between tyrannical and lenient farmers, corrupt and benevolent ministers, sadistic and humane schoolmasters, mere quacks and able doctors, malicious and enlightened gentlemen. Victorian child labour in the fields of Galloway, the reader learns from a harrowing description, was as grim as the drudgery in the cotton mills of Glasgow. Yet beneath all the harshness there is also an elegiac note, a mourning for the seemingly traceless passing of a way of life that had produced some fine specimens of humanity. This sadness should not be confused with nostalgia. As David Ramsay, one of the two central characters from the middle generation foregrounded in the novel, acknowledges when in old age he revisits his native place: 'There was no way back to that life.' (p. 518) The only way forward was to the city – Glasgow.

The City

The first thing to note is that the depiction of the city in Barke's fiction is far from uniform. In *The World His Pillow* we get the combination of crowdedness, squalor, claustrophobia and meanness that we have come to associate with the Glasgow novel and which is, of course, a general characteristic of urban naturalistic fiction. Here are Duncan's first impressions of Glasgow gathered from the window of the train that carries the 17-year-old country lad, recently orphaned, into the city:

> [W]hen the grey tenements gradually began to close in, and he caught a glimpse of a big green tramcar, he began to shift about in his empty compartment uneasily, first to one side and then to the other. This was suffocating. He was being trapped. This was not the terrible inferno he had hoped for, even when he dreaded the thought. This was piled-up poverty, meanness and vulgarity. But heavens! what an endless pile. How many people lived in these tenements? Thousands and thousands and thousands of ants! Oh, but not bright and clean like ants. No: not ants. God forbid he should put such a slur on that intelligent and industrious insect. What then? Lice! Ah! he had got it. Lice! Swarming, filthy, biting lice. Nothing on the grand scale about lice. Lice live and breed in filth. And whether the lice made the filth, or the filth made the lice, it was sufficient for the moment that they were lice. And with that discovery he was switched into the rumbling darkness of Queen Street tunnel. Yes: a very proper entrance to the City of Lice. (p. 226)

City of 'Lice' instead of 'Light', though enlightenment will be sought and to some extent enjoyed there. Ostensibly the inner voice of Duncan, it is effectively the authorial voice which takes over at a certain point (endowed with a greater knowledge than Duncan can possess), recalling the author's own shock of arrival, which, if anything, must have been alleviated by the company of the family.

To the above are added the experience of disease and death (his partner Constanze dies from consumption), of unemployment and deprivation, of aimlessness and futility, as we follow Duncan's vagaries of adventures in 'this Capital of Drudges'. Nor is such a perception of the city restricted to Glasgow. The visit to London will lead him to conclude that this 'was just an immense interminable Glasgow ... dirt for dirt and meanness for meanness it was just Glasgow all over again'. (p. 318)

In none of Barke's subsequent novels is the outlook quite so bleak, quite so unrelentingly depressing. But this is also a result of the chosen perspective. We see the world through the narrow eyes of the central figure. That the intellectual maelstrom into which Duncan is whirled fails to provide a clear sense of direction, that an aesthetic experience (a Shaw play, a Beethoven concert) is only transiently invigorating, that the Labour Movement appears to be in a state of torpor has much to do with his own inner self, the constant shift from restlessness to lethargy, from exhilaration to doubt, his proneness to 'whining and snivelling'. Occasionally, as in this last instance, the narrative voice observes Duncan from a distance, but as a rule it is too close to Duncan's consciousness to allow for detachment and objectivity. Perhaps the novel is best seen as a study of the confusion and indecision with which a generation of working- and lower middle-class writers coming of age in the late 1920s and early 1930s had to come to terms.

Since no such personal involvement obtrudes on *The End of the High Bridge*, Glasgow can here function as an anchor of hope for those who are chained to an unbearable family situation or a dead-end job. For young Keith Cameron in particular Glasgow 'was a dream. The dream of a new life: a new world. A world of men and machines and endless exciting activity. A dream that was the more bitter and the more real because the lad that dreamed it did so while he racked his guts on the oars of an old ferry-boat – the relic of a dying and decayed existence'. (p. 113) Anna, who has become estranged from her husband because of his sudden bigotry and infidelity, harbours fewer illusions, but for her too the letter from her sister in Glasgow 'holds out promise of good things'. However, the city is never explored in this novel, we do not follow the fortunes of the departed Hebrideans, only the accelerating decline and fall of John MacLeod. This may be the reason why Glasgow's status as an antidote to the narrow-minded life on the Isle of Skye is never thrown into doubt.

The picture of Glasgow in *The Land of the Leal* is large enough to hold both attitudes simultaneously. The last section, 'Within the City Walls', opens with the description of a horrible industrial accident and then proceeds to an extended characterisation of Glasgow:

The cruelty and brutality of a city of endless streets. A city with a heart of stone and a frame of steel and iron; of ugliness and unfriendliness; of noise and clamour and dirt and garbage; an alien people streaming endlessly, unsympathetic, harsh-voiced. There was nothing soft in the city. Even in the parks the beauty of a leafy bough was imprisoned behind the iron bars of fence and paling. (p. 467)

Literally a crippling place, shockingly inhospitable, callously indifferent, it appears ultimately as a cage.[14] It is then fitting that David Ramsay should end his working days shut away in the gatehouse of a shipyard: 'There would come a day when ... the gate-box with his desk, an American stove and his weighbridge would become as intolerable as any prison cell.' (p. 555) And his death in a car accident finally epitomises the destructive force of the city. But this is, once again, to view Glasgow from a particular angle, from the perspective of a man, or rather a couple, who have spent two-thirds of their working lives in the country, as dairy workers and cheesemakers, byre-man and gardener, and who are thus plunged too late into an urban industrial environment to be able to adapt. It is not the whole story, not even with regard to David. Long before the Ramsays reach the end of their peregrinations they enjoyed 'A Breath of City Air' (as one chapter announces) during a stopover on their way from Galloway to the Borders. And though they had been warned of Glasgow as 'a place of robbers and thieves' and the tenement where they spend the night 'was dirty and smelled foully' and though to Jean it appears 'worse nor jail' (p. 233), David is alert to something smouldering beneath the degradation. Glasgow to him is not

all stinking wi' poverty and starvation. There's money and plenty in Glasgow. There's enough for a'body in Glasgow – and it's the men and women o' Glasgow that'll lead Scotland yet. Men and women continue to flock in frae the country looking for work and then one day there'll be no farmers then to single them out and starve them into submitting to their wills. For these men will be without masters entirely. And they'll band together in their thousands and take a bloody vengeance on the whores and whoresons o' wealth and privilege. It'll maybe no' in your day nor mine ... but the day will come. (pp. 244–45)

This is not awkwardly imposed on the text. The young David is a man of 'visions ... dreams ... ambitions', like his father something of a rebel, drawing inspiration both artistically – he is a great violinist – and politically from Rabbie Burns. His personal tragedy is that when the opportunity arises, during the General Strike, the rebel no less than the musical side in him is dead, killed by overwork and constant worry about how to earn a livelihood for the family, suppressed also by his wife's no-nonsense practical-mindedness, so that the man who sparked off a work stoppage in the fields of Fife before the First World War has become a blackleg by 1926, whose sole concern is the well-being of his family. Consequently even for the aged David there is something 'worse than all the manifold effects of the city', namely unemployment. Its consequences may be more dire in the city by its sheer mass appearance, but it is not in itself an urban phenomenon. Hence we find Andrew, the politically minded of the two sons, railing not against the city but against the capitalist system. Nor does his brother Tom, who studies for the pulpit, hanker after the land.

Still, when all is said and done the city never becomes a true *Heimat* for the Ramsays in the way that their previous abodes in the country have been. At the end of the novel Nancy has emigrated to North America, Tom obtains a manse in the country, Andrew dies in the Spanish Civil War, Jean is lost in dreams in which memories of the past and the biblical Land of the Leal mingle. Even so the ambivalence remains, for Tom, after his own political awakening, considers applying for a ministry in Glasgow and Andrew has joined the International Brigades so as to prevent Fascist bombs from being dropped on Glasgow and in that hope has fathered a child before leaving.

It is also important to note what Barke has chosen not to dwell upon in any detail in this depiction of working-class life in Glasgow, namely alcoholism, betting, violence, disease, the stock in trade, that is, of slum-life representation. The author is, of course, aware of their presence and indicates them in minor characters such as Anne MacClumpha. The reader cannot ignore that hunger, destitution, want, filth and stink are as much part of the picture as unemployment, the struggle for survival and the political fight. But they are not allowed to occupy the centre stage because Barke is at pains to present an alternative picture to the tableau of *misérabilisme* that had emerged by the mid-1930s. Barke writes as much against Edwin Muir's hatred of industralism in *Poor Tom* (1932) as against George Blake's bleak pessimism in *The Shipbuilders* (1935). He is countering the gang warfare image of Glasgow delivered by Alexander McArthur's *No Mean City* (1935) and the savage portrayal of the City's slum-dwellers as 'sub-humans as definitely as the Morlocks of Wells' in Lewis Grassic Gibbon's Glasgow chapter in *The Scottish Scene* (1934);[15] and in so doing he revises his own earlier descent into the 'inferno' of Glasgow.

All this is already recognisable in *Major Operation* where we find direct allusions to McArthur's sensationalist exploit ('Now you, Mr No-mean-citizen-of-no mean city') and where the symmetric structure recalls Blake's novel.[16] Jock MacKelvie, leader of a squad of tough shipyard workers, will tolerate no 'razor slashers, wife beaters, incestmongers, adulterers, drunkards, blackmailers, gangsters' (p. 41) among them.

The title of this novel may have been derived from poem 25 of C. Day Lewis's *The Magnetic Mountain* (1933), which ends with the urgent lines:

It is now or never, the hour of the knife,
The break with the past, the major operation.[17]

Major Operation is not, like *The World His Pillow*, *The Land of the Leal* or even *The End of the High Bridge*, a novel of mobility, whether educational, geographical or upwardly social. We are in the city from start to finish, we are dealing with adult lives. What movement there is is on the one hand the pulsating rhythm of the city rendered in a new style, on the other the common drift into the depression of a middle- and a working-class existence. In alternating chapters, with full use of cinematographic flashes from one milieu to the other, the novel contrasts the 'Two Worlds' (the subtitle of Book I) by singling out the fortunes of George Anderson, a coal merchant, and his opposite number, the communist Jock MacKelvie, whose paths coincidentally cross – seven years later – in a hospital ward. The novel's political theme is this middle-class/working-class encounter and its outcome, which is nothing less than a symbolic enactment of the Popular Front. For Anderson is won over to the workers' cause, after prolonged intellectual bombardment, by the not only physically but also mentally Big Jock.

Such a major operation on the mind of a character, if it is to be credible, cannot be performed in a day. The novel thus has a longer time span than other fictional treatments of modern city life (by Joyce, Woolf, Huxley or, for that matter, Sommerfield and Griffin).[18] But Barke clearly has his eye on modernist writing techniques, appropriating them for his own political purposes and turning them sometimes to comic effect. Here we have Anderson, still in business, though already sensing the impact of the economic crisis, waiting for a tram, his mind wandering and jumping:

Moderates mediocre. Labour Party just as bad though. Need a dictator: Mussolini. Not Hitler. Ignorant, dangerous type Hitler. Shoots pals. Caesar Borgia was it? Hun not dead yet. Prussianism: new disguise, Jews rotten. Still, old Sam a Jew: not bad fellow. Control finance. No Jews in Ireland? And yet ... what about that story of Jews cornering candles at Dublin Eucharistic Congress? Deserved to get away with it. Clever people. Think about business in their sleep. (pp. 126–27)

This staccato version of stream of consciousness is intended to provide an insight into the 'jig-sawed: scattered' mind process of the middle-class representative, where 'everything was chaos' as a 'result of months of worry'.

The method of at once enlisting and subverting a style that had become associated with subjectivity and self-analysis can also be seen at work in the following passage where we hear not one but a cacophony of voices belonging to a multitude of consciousnesses. Andy Croft has called this rambling and, in fact, much longer section 'a crazy picture, slapstick and satiric, allusive, inclusive and nonsensical, the life of the city caught in snapshots, snatches of conversation and thought: James Joyce writing about Glasgow with a Communist Party card in his pocket'.[19] Underlying all the playfulness there is, then, a serious political intention. To render the 'myriad impressions'[20] of street life is one thing only, the exposure of a collective state of mind the real purpose: most of the voices heard and the ideologies behind them are manifestly middle-class (in the depiction of MacKelvie's world, by contrast, the narrative reverts to 'a controlled naturalistic prose').[21] A march of the unemployed accompanied by flutes and drums is approaching:

In Xanadu did Kubla Khan –

Kubla Khan? I've got you, mister. In the 3.30? I can take you on, sir, up to twenty quid. Pay out in the lavatory of Tim O'Rafferty's bar at six o'clock. James MacMaster, sir, a God-fearing bookie's runner at your service. Kubla Khan is a good thing.

What about Red Biddy?

Don't touch it, sir. Been a Jake drinker in my day. Meth – lavender water – green paint. Pain in the guts now. Think of the money spent on drink that might bring back a fortune – a double coming up once or twice a week ...

Politics, thy name is acrimony. Let's have – music!

Sit, Jessica! Let the sound of music creep in our ears. Your name isn't Jessica by any chance?

Getting fresh, are you? My name's Sarah. Sarah Cannan. Call a flute band music?

Sorry, can't give you henry hall and His band. But don't despise the flute, dear lady. Orpheus and his lute – which, as you were doubtless told at school, is just the polite name for flute. It is the little rift within the flute ... Afraid it's the flutes that are causing the rift, however. Suppose you'd rather hear a Mae West story? Ah, Mae West! Sex! Taboo! Wonder what Mrs Bloom would have thought about Mae West? Or Mae West about Marion Bloom? Mummmh! Bulged right out in his face! Seven miles! Guess I've nothing on you, dearie.

Labour on the bench and a smutty story round the corner: under the trees. Music down the street. Hold the mirror up to nature and you get sex – sex and politics (moonlight is extra, but always in request) ...

Well we don't mind a little sex, sir, providing it's treated in a light, aphrodisiacal manner and provided there's a high moral tone prevailing throughout. Nothing the public likes better in fact. But – no politics! No, siree. Keep politics out of literature. (p. 122)

The Party

For the first time Barke had steered clear of the Highlands. He had addressed the question of how to represent urban reality under the impact of the economic crisis, and in confronting and giving embodiment to the concept of the Popular Front he had courageously treated a directly political subject. No less daringly, he had engaged with the experimental narrative techniques developed in the 1920s without committing himself to them, in fact ironising and challenging them. In short, he had set an example to socialist novelists. Small wonder that he pinned high hopes on *Major Operation*, and the critical response from the left-wing press seemed to endorse this optimism. Aitken Ferguson in the *Labour Monthly* heaped praises on the book: 'The description of the tremendous Hunger March in Glasgow, the absolutely steel-sharp etching of these unemployed demonstrations, is something that will live ... Here are no Carlylean Great Men, Gods of Destiny, flinging their Jovian thunderbolts far and wide, but ordinary men, caught up in the clutch of one of History's mutation periods, each reacting in his own way ... The book marks the entrance, definitely into the front-rank of literature, of a new force.' Jack Lindsay in *Left Review* considered Anderson's development 'finely realised; the sensation of Glasgow life turbulently conveyed; the characterisation, particularly of the patients in the ward, excellent ... and the symbolism of the relation of the individual collapse to the general bourgeois crisis effectively conveyed'. It was left to C. Day Lewis, at that time a fellow communist, to find more to indict than to praise ('crude rhapsodising, tedious moralising, and a spate of comments in the Transatlantic manner').[22]

With the reviews of Ferguson, Lindsay and Campbell in his pocket Barke proposed to John Strachey that the novel be adopted as a Left Book Club choice.[23] Great was his disappointment when he learnt that Gollancz would not hear of fiction. Nevertheless his reputation as a novelist to be reckoned with now seemed assured.

But how had he first found his way to socialism? Although his autobiography breaks off with the family's departure for Glasgow in 1918, some milestones on Barke's political trajectory may be reconstructed.

> All the buildings in Glasgow are grey
> With cruelty and meanness of spirit.
> But once in a while one greyer than the rest
>   A song shall merit
> Since a miracle of true courage is seen
> For a moment its walls between.

This is the first stanza of Hugh MacDiarmid's poem 'John MacLean (1879–1923)'.[24] The 'meanness', the 'cruelty', the 'greyness', the city 'walls' are, as we have seen, all evoked in Barke's novels. But so is the ray of hope, the unexampled courage, the miraculous spirit. In both *The World His Pillow* and *The Land of the Leal* there are fleeting images of 'the greatest Socialist agitator o'them all', his 'pitiably hoarse' voice and 'immense violence of gesture to drive home his vituperation'.[25] The year of MacLean's death was also the year in which according to one obituary Barke chaired his first Labour Party meeting. He was 17, attending Glasgow University's extramural classes on English Literature and writing his first sketches on top of his shipyard job.[26]

Next there came first the excitement, then the agony over the General Strike. Unconditional surrender, sell-out, betrayal. However differently latter-day historians may have evaluated the real power balance in May 1926, the shock went deep into the souls of hundreds of thousands, perhaps millions of dedicated militants. And so it must have been for Barke, if his fictional treatment of the event is anything to go by. Duncan quits the ILP and drops out of politics, so frustrated is he. Jock MacKelvie at the beginning of *Major Operation*, some time in the late 1920s, declares: 'The General Strike finished me and it's finished the labour movement.' (p. 66) Andrew Gibson has nothing but contempt and abuse for the TUC leadership after the calling-off of the strike: 'The bottom was finally out of Andrew's world,' his dream that socialism would be achieved in his day shattered.

But it is also true that all three eventually take heart again (Duncan only temporarily so), even if the mechanisms of their return to the political arena are not properly explored. Up to about 1932 the ILP appears to have been Barke's political home. In an undated letter to James Maxton,[27] written in the false hope of obtaining a preface to *The World His Pillow*, he calls himself 'an independent L. P. socialist' who is also 'an out-and-out Maxtonian'. And in the novel 'Duncan rallied to this frail, gaunt champion of the underdog. Not a statesman, not a scholar, not even a politician. Greater than all these. The Supreme Agitator. The Voice of the Poor was the voice of Maxton'. (p. 271) That, one feels, was at one time Barke's own idol. But it did not last. When he mailed a copy of the book to Palme Dutt, the editor of the *Labour Monthly*, he expressed his admiration for the way in which the chief theoretician of the Communist Party had effected 'a final irrefutable and masterly dismembering of a Great Man'. Once again the letter is undated, but *The World His Pillow* was published in March 1933 so that it is safe to assume that Barke had meanwhile shifted to a communist position – despite the ILP's own break with the Labour Party in 1932 and the fact that a fair number of pro-communist ILPers remained in its ranks until 1935.

These volatile sympathies may be attributed to a malleable mind in search of an all-embracing and unassailable creed, but there is also something disingenuous about it all. Now the aspiring author will solicit the help of George Blake, a director of Faber, in placing his first novel, then he will suspect the older man of getting a hack to do a demolition job on it. At one moment (1932) he will write an admiring letter to Middleton Murry, who, it is true, was just going through his own highly idiosyncratic communist phase, at the next instance he will decry Murry's dangerous influence on young writers. Not until Barke reached the haven of communism does this vacillation appear to have come to a standstill.

The 'moment' was, of course, the Class against Class policy of the Comintern and its affiliated parties. Perhaps this helps to explain some of the impatient outbursts, the uncompromising statements, which will reach well into the first years of the united front line, the 'sledgehammer' method of argument, as Barke himself referred to it in one letter.[28] A sharp, merciless, class-confrontational tone pervades his work from the mid-1930s: 'The role of the Labour Party,' we read in *Major Operation*, 'is class collaboration, reformism and defeatism.'(p. 223) The hectoring method of ruthless exposure, so typical of the Third Period rhetoric and understandable in the aftermath of Ramsay MacDonald's defection to the National Government, is built into the conception of *Major Operation*, which not only contains a devastating portrait of a corrupt local Labour politician (Bailie Pink) but proposes – on a second and this time socially symbolical level – an operation on such a major scale as to equal revolution; and not a mere defence of democracy through a Popular Front strategy.[29] The *Glasgow Herald* reviewer sensed this when he observed: 'Mr Barke's spirit will never, one feels, rest, nor will his sword rest in his hand, till we have built a Leningrad in Scotland's dull and dismal land.'[30]

This explains why Barke, in his assessment of Lewis Grassic Gibbon for *Left Review*, seizes on the representation of the class war: 'The participation in the strike blows sky-high the last of his [Ewan Tavendale's] illusions, blows sky-high the role of the Labour and Trade Union officials ... Herein lies the chief strength of *Grey Granite*. Here the confrontation of the classes is exposed. The open antagonism of the workers and the ruling class is laid bare.'[31]

The relationship between Barke and Gibbon had begun in December 1932 when the former wrote expressing his admiration for *Sunset Song*, the first volume of *The Scots Quair* trilogy. The exchange of letters, opinions and criticisms of each other's work, always forthright but with mutual respect, would go on uninterruptedly until Gibbon's death. The somewhat older, already (since 1930) established novelist would do his best to encourage his junior colleague, even pushing his work – some reservations about Barke's plot construction and longwindedness notwithstanding. He reviewed both *The World His Pillow* and *The Wild MacRaes* in *The Free Man*, published from Edinburgh, to Barke's grunting ('What the dockers' hook are you doing in this dead codfishmongery anyway?'). He planned to give *The End of the High Bridge* a notice in *Left Review*.

But it was really give and take. In his essay 'Literary Lights' from 1934, which is a survey of the contemporary *Scottish Scene*, Gibbon relies fully on Barke's judgement of the Gaelic writers of Scotland, quoting the assessment of this 'remarkable Anglo-Gael' over two pages. He had solicited this overview *expressis verbis*. Barke thanked him with the dedication of *The End of the High Bridge*. And only ten days before his death Gibbon tried to coax Barke into the pages of *Left Review* ('It's run by the communists [faintly disguised] as a sort of general Left production ... it's already a damned good medium and will get you known from the Maldives to Moscow').

In this interchange Barke would strike a dogmatic note at times ('either you stand by the working class and its heroic vanguard the Communist Party or you take your stand [directly, indirectly or benevolently neutral – it doesn't matter which] with Fascism'), but Gibbon was never deserted by his cheerfulness. He parried his correspondent's digs at diffusionism by sniping at 'historical Confusionists'.

Class first, nation second, is also the keynote of Barke's contribution to the special Scotland issue of *Left Review* in 1936. He readily concedes the appeal of the Nationalist platform to 'the professional class, university students and the so-called Scottish "intelligentsia" ... Sad to relate, however, the average Scot remained cruelly indifferent to all this Nationalist ballyhooing'.[32] For the Clydeside working class, he argues, it makes little difference whether the capital is in English or Scottish hands. This he had already demonstrated in *The Wild MacRaes* where the real antagonist of the crofters is not the landowning English gentleman-officer but his factor, a Scot, whose machinations triumph in due time and make him the Laird.

The upshot of all this is not to suggest that Barke slavishly followed the party line on all matters, merely that too rigid an application of class analysis does at times hamstring his representation of character. On the other hand, he was, as his initially cited preface to *The Land of the Leal* demonstrates, only too aware of the danger of propagandising. 'It is easy to criticise Barke's achievement,' Jack Mitchell wrote in a seminal essay on the Scottish working-class novel, 'but one should keep in mind two things. One: this man wrote his books in the evenings after a full day at the shipyard; two, he was a courageous pioneer who was not afraid to go out alone, but in fact made it his duty to do so.'[33] Neither of which is exactly true. Barke did not follow a proletarian trade, but worked in a shipyard office. He did not lay single-handed the foundation of the socialist novel in Scotland, but was actively encouraged by, and followed in the footsteps of, Lewis Grassic Gibbon. And both of them had in turn been preceded, in the 1920s, by the first Welsh, James C., then as famous as the second Welsh, Irvine, in the 1990s.[34]

But Barke was beyond question a writer of talent and stamina. He loved controversy, and to embrace communism was a controversial act, which made him for 25 years a dissident figure in Scottish letters. He displayed a sensitiveness to environmental issues which was quite rare in his time. He brought a critical perspective to the sub-genre of the Highland novel, 'debunking' it in the process. In *The Land of the Leal* he erected a memorial to generations of agricultural workers. With *Major*

Operation he challenged the gangland image and slum-life representation of Glasgow. He engaged with modernist writing techniques, aiming to functionally reorientate them. On the strength of his self-conscious, self-ironical writing illustrated in the opening quotation he might even be regarded as a forerunner of postmodernism. All in all this was no mean effort by no mean writer.

To the end James Barke remained steadfast in his interests, loyalties and convictions. Despite protests from the Burns Clubs he carried on his revision of the picture of Scotland's national bard. Conscious of his country's patrimony he never contemplated leaving his native land, as so many other writers had done before him. Nor did he walk out of the Communist Party in the aftermath of 1956 when other intellectuals and writers departed *en masse*. Interestingly, he found himself joined in the Party's thinned out ranks, for the last year of his life, by his compatriot Hugh MacDiarmid, who re-entered in a spirit of defiance and contrariety at a moment when it could not have been more unfashionable. When Barke died in March 1958, the graveside orations were delivered by 'Hugh MacDiarmid, Scotland's greatest living poet, and Willie Gallacher, Scotland's greatest living Marxist'.[35]

Notes

1   James Barke, 'Caledonian Comedy' (c. 1935), typescript of unpublished novel in the James Barke papers (italicisation of the book titles by me). I wish to thank the staff of the Mitchell Library, Glasgow, and especially Hamish Whyte for giving me access to this material and for their unfailing help more generally. The subtitle of my essay is taken from a profile of the author by Sydney Goodsir Smith, 'James Barke', *Saltire Review*, vol. III, no. 15 (Summer 1958), p. 15.

2   *The Wind that Shakes the Barley* (1946), *The Song in the Thorn Tree* (1947), *The Wonders of All the Gay World* (1949), *The Crest of a Broken Wave* (1953), *The Well of the Silent Harp* (1954) and *Bonnie Jean* (1958), all published by Collins, London. Another fruit of this absorbing interest in the bard was an edition of the *Complete Poems and Songs of Robert Burns* (London: HarperCollins, 1955).

3   *Glengarach* (1926), *Major Operation* (1941), *The Night of the Big Blitz* (1944), *When the Boys Come Home* (1945), *Her Name Was Barbara Allan* (1946) and *Domino* (1947). Dates indicate first performance. *Major Operation*, based on the novel of that title, was published by Collins in 1943. The plays of the forties were put on by Glasgow Unity Theatre.

4   See his essay 'Tunes the Pipers Play', *The Scottish Field* (January 1938), pp. 22–3.

5   J. R. Campbell, 'Two Worlds in the Second City', *Daily Worker*, 18 September 1936; Ethel Mannin, 'The Human Drama: Life in the East Ends of London and Glasgow', *The New Leader*, 23 October 1936; Robert Bonnar, 'James Barke – a True Son of the Soil' in *Essays in Honour of William Gallacher* (Berlin: Humboldt-Universität, 1966), p. 185; George Blake, *Annals of Scotland 1895–1955* (London: BBC, 1956), pp. 33–4.

6   Prefatory 'Note' to *The Land of the Leal* (London: Collins, 1939).

7   Canongate Classics no. 6 (Edinburgh, 1987); Harold Brighouse, 'Long and Shorter Novels', *Manchester Guardian*, 9 May 1939.

8   All references are to the first edition as indicated on the first mention of each novel; place of publication: London (Collins). Reprints such as those by Cedric Chivers in the 1970s are usually facsimiles.

9   Quoted in *The Green Hills Far Away* (London: Collins, 1940), p. 268.

10   See the title of Robert Bonnar's tribute to the author (quoted in note 5).

11   It is interesting that Lewis Grassic Gibbon should also refer to this hymn in his short story 'Greenden'. This was included in *The Scottish Scene* (1934), the miscellany written jointly with Hugh MacDiarmid.

12   See Andy Wightman, *Who Owns Scotland Now?* (Edinburgh: Mainstream, 1996).

13   Lewis Grassic Gibbon, 'New Novels: Mr Barke and Others', *The Free Man*, 24 February 1934; quoted from William K. Malcolm, *A Blasphemer and Reformer: A Study of James Leslie Mitchell / Lewis Grassic Gibbon* (Aberdeen: Aberdeen University Press, 1984), p. 132.

14   On the cage in 1930s' writing more generally see Valentine Cunningham, *British Writers of the Thirties* (Oxford: OUP, 1988), pp. 83–9.

15   McArthur was helped by the journalist H. Kingsley Long. Gibbon's essay 'Glasgow' first appeared in *The Scottish Scene* (see note 11); it is here quoted from the author's collection of short prose, *A Scots Hairst*, ed. Ian S. Munro (London: Hutchinson, 1967), p. 84.

16   For a comparison between the two novels, see Manfred Malzahn, 'Coming to Terms with Industrial Scotland: Two "Proletarian" Novels of the 1930s', and Christopher Whyte, 'Imagining the City: The Glasgow Novel', both in Joachim Schwend and Horst W. Drescher eds, *Studies in Scottish Fiction: Twentieth Century* (Frankfurt: Peter Lang, 1990), pp. 193–205, 317–33.

17   *The Complete Poems of C. Day Lewis* (London: Sinclair-Stevenson, 1992), p. 162. Barke has a predilection for the use of quotations as titles. *The Land of the Leal* probably goes back to Caroline Oliphant's poem 'The Land o' the Leal', first published anonymously in Robert Archibald Smith's *The Scottish Minstrel* (Edinburgh: Purdie, 1821–24), vol. III. See also note 11.

18   I am thinking here of two socialist novels, John Sommerfield's *May Day*, published in the same year as *Major Operation*, and Frank Griffin's *October Day* (1939), both set in London.

19   Andy Croft, *Red Letter Days* (London: Lawrence & Wishart, 1990), p. 277.

20   The term is Virginia Woolf's from her famous essay 'Modern Fiction' in *The Common Reader* (London: Hogarth Press, 1925), p. 189. In fact, a miniature sketch of the very scene elaborated by Barke can already be found in *Mrs. Dalloway*: 'The noise was tremendous; and suddenly there were trumpets (the unemployed) blaring, rattling about in the uproar; military music; as if people were marching.' (Harmondsworth: Penguin, 1964, pp. 152–53).

21   Ramón López Ortega, 'The Language of the Working-Class Novel of the 1930s' in H. Gustav Klaus ed., *The Socialist Novel in Britain* (Brighton: Harvester Press, 1982), p. 130.

22   Aitken Ferguson, 'A Marchers' Novel', *Labour Monthly*, vol. 18, no.10 (October 1936), p. 644; Jack Lindsay, 'Man in Society', *Left Review*, vol. II, no. 15 (December 1936), p. 838; C. Day Lewis, 'New Fiction: Tales of Two Cities', *Daily Telegraph*, 18 September 1936.

       Lindsay's lack of sustained conviction regarding Barke's fiction may, however, be gauged from the fact that he did not deem him worth a mention in his retrospective look at the 1930s, *After the Thirties: The Novel in Britain, and Its Future* (London: Lawrence & Wishart, 1956), whereas he refers to Mulk Raj Anand, Ralph Bates, Alec Brown, Arthur Calder-Marshall, Lewis Grassic Gibbon, James Hanley, Lewis Jones, Peadar O'Donnell, Naomi Mitchison, Montagu Slater and Sylvia Townsend Warner.

23   Undated letter (c. December 1936) in the James Barke papers.

24 Published in his collection *Stony Limits and Other Poems* (1934); here quoted from T. S. Law and Thurso Berwick eds, *Homage to John MacLean* (Edinburgh University Student Publications Board, 1979), p. 8.

25 *The Land of the Leal*, p. 476; *The World His Pillow*, p. 249.

26 Obituary, 'A Scot Who Loved His Burns', *The Scottish Co-Operator*, 29 March 1958.

27 All the letters referred to are in the James Barke papers.

28 Letter to J. S. Collis, 18 January 1934.

29 See H. Gustav Klaus, *The Literature of Labour* (Brighton: Harvester Press, 1985), pp. 121–25.

30 'New Novels: Affair of Honour', *Glasgow Herald*, 17 September 1936.

31 James Barke, 'Lewis Grassic Gibbon', *Left Review*, vol. II, no. 5 (February 1936), p. 224.

32 James Barke, 'The Scottish National Question', *Left Review*, vol. II, no. 14 (November 1936), pp. 739–40.

33 Jack Mitchell, 'The Struggle for the Working-Class Novel in Scotland 1900–1939', *Zeitschrift für Anglistik und Amerikanistik*, XXI (1973), p. 413.

34 See my article 'James C. Welsh: Major Miner Novelist', *Scottish Literary Journal*, vol. XIII, no. 2 (1986).

35 Bonnar, 'James Barke', p. 185.

2

Robert Radford

To Disable the Enemy: the Graphic Art of the Three Jameses

These artists do not go in for any 'distortion for distortion's sake'...(as do so many bourgeois caricaturists) but they disfigure, wound and mortally disable the enemy, this being their artistic contribution to the revolutionary remoulding of the world.[1]

This judgement by Alfred Durus (alias Kenemy) which appeared in *International Literature* in 1936 undoubtedly captures the level of anger and determination and the strategic intentions of the three British artists, James Boswell, James Fitton and James Holland, collectively, and apparently unresentfully, known from early days as 'The Three Jameses'. Their work was being exhibited at the Museum of Modern Western Art (the renamed Pushkin Museum) in Moscow which reflected the international recognition of the signal effect these artists had made as regular illustrators for *Left Review*. Durus's review, which later goes on to regret their failure to portray the heroic militancy of the working class, also indicates the state of scrupulous critique imposed on the practice of visual artists who were either members of or close to the Communist Party during the 1930s. The exhibition also included the cartoons of James Friell who had recently begun to work regularly for the *Daily Worker*.

Something of that down-to-earth anger and frustration with the political actualities of the time, the class animosity and the distorting effects of the dominant media, which was undoubtedly shared by the Three Jameses, is still apparent in a recent interview with Friell:

I stayed seething at all these bloody Baldwins, and platitudes over the radio ... the fatuous newsreels and I just wanted to hit out at them. I saw the Hunger Marchers on the streets, and on the cinema screens there were the Bright Young Things, pushing prams down Mayfair to some fancy dress party, or the wealthy at grouse shoots or Baldwin and Chamberlain invoking the national family 'all in it together' ... I don't know why there wasn't a bloody revolution.[2]

Friell was born in 1912, the son of a music hall performer who encountered long periods of unemployment; at 14 he started working as a solicitor's office boy but soon discovered that he could earn considerably more (about £4 per week) from freelance cartoon drawing for various Scottish newspapers. Aided by a scholarship, he took a year's course in commercial art at Glasgow School of Art before moving to London where he continued to find work with various newspapers. He found an outlet for his radical views when he agreed to join the staff of the *Daily Worker* in 1936, adopting the pen name of 'Gabriel'.

Friell's upbringing was indelibly marked by poverty and parental unemployment in Glasgow, a city famous for its culture of political radicalism; during the 1930s his professional ambition was centred exclusively on the production of the political cartoon, whereas the case of Boswell, Fitton and Holland is historically indicative of a new tendency for intellectuals and cultural workers to be increasingly attracted to the Communist Party as members or sympathisers during that period. They were of that generation of young male and female artists who had grown up and struggled through their training and initial careers in the 1920s and who had responded to the economic and political crisis at the start of the new decade by acting in a way which was totally unprecedented for artists in Britain – that is collectively – and formed the Artists' International (AI).

There are of course numerous instances in the past when artists collaborated in order to foster particular artistic programmes or formed professional societies to share the costs and practicalities of exhibiting, but this was the first occasion on which artists united to pursue a set of policies which were defined primarily in terms of their social responsibility. Furthermore, the Three Jameses are of interest in that they soon developed into highly effective graphic designers in the field of commercial advertising, yet at the same time maintained rather ambivalent attitudes towards this commercial work in comparison with their aspirations to be 'free' artists, working within the culture and value system of fine arts. A further element must be added to this framework of conditioning influences in order to appreciate the complex of artistic debates which this generation encountered and which is the growing salience of modernism in British art and design in the 1930s. The extent to which these frequently competing forces of individualism and collectivity, populism and elitism, tradition and modernity, the public duty and the private fulfilment could be ever reconciled or were destined to remain a frustrating dilemma for these artist-designers is also part of the project for this chapter.

James Boswell

James Boswell was born in 1906 in a small town in New Zealand; his father was a schoolmaster and amateur painter. When he was eleven the family moved to Auckland and James's artistic potential was noted and encouraged by a local artist who had worked in London prior to the First World War. It was as a result of his persuasion that Boswell came to London in 1925 to study at the Royal College of Art. No doubt he had set great store by this opportunity to take up a professional training in Europe but he was, in the event, to be sadly disappointed: 'You can have no idea how provincial and awful London was in the 1920s, painting was dreary, academic and rubbishy.[3] Boswell and the principal of the college, William Rothenstein, did not see eye to eye and at the end of his first year he was asked to leave on the basis of the quality of his work. He then encountered a fellow New Zealander, Fred Porter, a friend of Sickert, who had lived and worked in Paris before the war, developing a fauvist, painterly manner. Boswell had at last encountered a 'modern' artist who introduced him to the qualities of *belle peinture*, very different from the dry and dutifully tonal painting practised in England at the time. Porter was also a significant mentor on account of his political commitment; he was a radical socialist and had resisted enlistment into war service.

Boswell was readmitted to the Royal College, gained a diploma and a scholarship but was again dismissed since he preferred to spend his time in his own studio. The long-lasting friendship with James Holland who was a fellow student started at that time. His move towards radical politics was further signalled and encouraged by his meeting with Montagu Slater in 1929 and soon after with Edgell Rickword. He had been scraping together a career as a painter and lithographer, supported financially by occasional teaching, which he despised, but by 1932 his disillusionment with the level of promise that such a way of living offered in the face of the economic depression led him towards a new path. He joined the Communist Party and, for the next ten years, focused his artistic energy into two directions: as a graphic designer and as a political artist. His reaction was far from unusual and a comparable predicament is recorded by William Coldstream at a similar stage in his career:

> The 1930 slump affected us all considerably. Through making money much harder to come by, it caused an immense change in our general outlook. One painter I knew lost all his money and had to become a traveller in vacuum cleaners. Everyone began to be very interested in economics and then in politics. Two very talented painters who had been at the Slade with me, gave up painting altogether, one to work for the ILP, the other for the Communist Party. It was no longer the thing to be an artist delighting in isolation.[4]

Despite Boswell's disparaging appraisal of the qualities of work encouraged at the Royal College, there is no doubt that the thorough, general training in professional skills equipped its graduates to move into what was then termed 'commercial art' and the assumption was widely, if reluctantly, accepted that young artists should take on such work as advertising or book jacket design to support their private ambitions as 'fine artists' in their own time. This might even require keeping office hours every day in the studio of an advertising agency. Boswell was very successful in this field and in 1936 became art director of the publicity department of the Asiatic (later Shell) Petroleum Company.

James Fitton

James Fitton was the oldest of 'the three', born in 1899 in Oldham. His background was authentically working class and his early training followed a more traditional path of entry into the 'trade' of commercial art. At the age of 14 he was apprenticed to a calico printer and started his art training at evening classes at Manchester School of Art. There he benefited from the structured drawing course taught by Adolph Valette who aimed to pass on by example the techniques that he had himself learned as a studio assistant of Degas. A fellow student and friend of Fitton was L.S. Lowry who introduced him to Manchester's vibrant theatre and music hall life.

Fitton's father was a committed socialist and played a major role in labour organisations in Lancashire; Keir Hardie and Emmeline Pankhurst were amongst the speakers at the Fabian Society meetings that he organised. In 1920 he was appointed to be the national organiser of the Amalgamated Engineering Union which had its headquarters in South London. Shortly afterwards, Fitton moved to join the family and worked as a freelance, commercial artist. The attitudes of disdain and ridicule directed towards the privileged class which was to typify his caricatures for *Left Review* originated in a significant chance experience at this time.

A family acquaintance, a member of the first Labour government, John Robert Clynes, was appointed to the office of Lord Privy Seal and Leader of the Commons, a post which entitled him to accommodation in Downing Street and Fitton became a regular guest at social functions in the presence of the social and political establishment of the day. In 1925 he developed his accomplishment in lithography by attending evening classes at the Central School of Arts and Crafts. He was also determined to establish a reputation as a painter and was by the end of the decade exhibiting at the Royal Academy and the New English Art Club. By 1930 the course of his professional engagement during the decade ahead was confirmed with his appointment as director of the advertising agency, C.

Vernons, and by his submission of cartoons, under the name of 'Alpha', to the *Daily Worker*.

James Holland

James Holland was born in 1905, the son of a craftsman blacksmith at Chatham dockyard, and his fascination with the environment of shipping on the Thames first exercised his talents in drawing at school. He won the President's prize of the Royal Drawing Society and later followed courses at the Rochester School of Art before admission to the Royal College of Art, where he was a fellow student, not only of Boswell, but also of that important generation of artists such as Henry Moore, Eric Ravilious, Edward Bawden, Enid Marx and others who went on to accomodate British art with the aesthetics of European Modernism in the 1930s in the fields of both art and design. He came out of the Royal College, hoping, like others, to succeed as a painter and became a member of the London Group, which encouraged a modest, Bloomsburyesque Modernism, and of the New English Art Club, which had long ceased to be 'new'. Like Boswell and Fitton, however, he discovered that the only means of financial survival through art was to be found in advertising design, notably for Shell; their publicity director, Jack Beddington, was well known for his policy of employing contemporary artists, thereby associating the product with modernity of design. In 1936 Holland added further testimony to the sense of the new era of economic reality experienced by artists as a result of the slump:

> Economic crisis killed the active but undiscriminating patronage that the younger English artists had enjoyed since the war. About eight years ago these artists were faced with the choice of a cut-throat competition for what crumbs of patronage remained, continuing to paint until overtaken by starvation, giving up art, or using their abilities to discredit a system that makes art and culture dependent on the caprices of the money markets. The last has always seemed to me the only realistic course.[5]

The AIA

This matrix of historical and biographical factors helps to explain the presence of Boswell, Fitton and Holland among a small group gathered in the studio of a fellow artist-designer, Misha Black, in Earlham Street, Covent Garden, London, in the autumn of 1933. In an atmosphere of bohemian, candlelit conspiracy, they were setting out the initial aims of the Artists' International. Their first manifesto statement appeared in 1934 in the first issue of the *Artists' International Bulletin*. It proclaimed:

> The International Unity of Artists against Imperialist War on the Soviet Union, Fascism and colonial oppression. It is intended to further these ends by the following practical measures:
>
> 1. The uniting of all artists in Britain sympathetic to these aims, into working units, ready to execute posters, illustrations, cartoons, book jackets, banners, tableaux, stage decorations, etc.
> 2. The spreading of propaganda by means of exhibitions, the press, lectures and meetings.
> 3. The maintaining of contacts with similar groups already existing in 16 countries.

The statement then goes on to record in more detail how this programme was being currently put into practice:

> We have instituted fortnightly discussions on Communism and Art from all angles. We are working closely with the Marx Library and the Workers' School, we have taken part in strikes and elections, producing mimeographed newspapers on the spot, backed up by cartoons and posters. This will give us the direct experience we need of contact with the masses.
>
> We have made contact with revolutionary art groups abroad and plan international exhibits.
>
> Among our activities have been posters done for the Marxist Club of London University, preliminary work for an animated film cartoon for the Workers' Film Movement, drawings and illustrations for the first number of 'New Challenge', our new workers' sports paper; a puppet show to be shown in the streets, etc. We are also decorating halls for revolutionary meetings and other activities.[6]

This cascade of agitprop activity indicates not only the dominant presence in the founding group of Communist Party members but also the widespread attraction that the Soviet Union held for this generation of artists. Several of the early members of the AI, notably Cliff Rowe, Pearl Binder and Peggy Angus, had already visited Russia and they were able to report how, in contrast to the depressing circumstances for finding work in Britain, artists were highly valued there and the opportunities, particularly for graphic artists, seemed boundless.

The years 1933 and 1934 marked a period of major expansion of the communist cultural project in London. Marx House was inaugurated (through a donation by Clive Branson, the colleague mentioned by Coldstream who had joined the Communist Party) and a library and education centre for the movement were set up; in February 1934 The

Writers' International was founded and in April they published the journal, *Viewpoint*, with a claim to stand for 'militant Communism and for individualism and metaphysics in the arts'; in October it became *Left Review*. There was evidently a close working alliance between the artists' and the writers' groups and it was not surprising that Montagu Slater, one of its founding editors, asked Boswell to become the magazine's art editor. In fact the job was shared between 'The Three Jameses' and although a number of other artists, such as Pearl Binder and Pinchos (an East End garment worker), contributed from time to time, the mainstay of cartoons and illustrations over the four years following its publication was supplied by the trio.

Fitton took over from Archibold Standish Hartrick a lithography class at the Central School, which he later admitted was run largely for the benefit of his fellow AI artists, including Edward Ardizzone and Lynton Lamb. The aim was to develop their skills in this medium which, with the example of artists such as Steinlen and Forain, held out such promise as a vehicle for direct and inexpensive popular communication.

By 1935 a new policy had been adopted by the AI in line with the current blossoming of Popular Front strategies among left-wing organisations internationally. The most evident symbol of this change was its reformulated name, the Artists' International Association, and a new rallying cry: 'The AIA stands for Unity of Artists against Fascism and War and the Suppression of Culture.' The aim of attracting membership from a much broader range of the profession proved highly successful and it quickly increased to reach ultimately a high point of around a thousand. Contributors to its large-scale exhibitions in 1935, 1937 and 1939 included the majority of leading figures among exhibiting artists from academic, mainstream and modernist circles. In the first of these shows, for example, Eric Gill, Duncan Grant, Lucien Pissarro, Laura Knight, Augustus John, Barbara Hepworth, Henry Moore, Ben Nicholson, John Piper and Ethel Walker were among the many who were prepared to exhibit together under the slogan of 'Artists against Fascism and War'. Although Communist Party members maintained an influential presence at the heart of the organisation, they represented a relatively small percentage – probably below 20 per cent of the total body.

Left Review

Many commentators, recalling the impact that *Left Review* made during the 1930s, readily attest to the enduring impact of its visual imagery, rather than to any outstanding quality of its writing. Along with this recollection, there is often a tendency to merge the work of the three artists into a collective stereotype, yet such an impression is misconceived: their drawings differ quite distinctly not only in terms of style and technique but also in mode and function. Boswell's recurrent target is the class enemy whose caricature appears in the very first issue in October 1934. In 'You gotta have blue blood', the male is attired in riding breeches, which, over the years have obviously wrought a serious effect on the shape of his legs; the narrow sloping shoulders of his riding jacket are a sign of a poor capacity for physical work and the diminutive bowler hat implies that there is little of importance underneath it. The overall impression is that, once the clothing is removed, there is little of any humanity left. His female companions are equally the product of the couturier's expensive craft and their faces display nothing beyond an enduring distaste for the world around them. The frequent point of critique emanating from conventional Socialist Realist commentators on the work of the 'Three Jameses' rested on the view that an attack on identifiable class and political enemies through the weapon of ridicule was a valid practice but not a sufficient one. What was needed in addition to this, it was argued, were exhortatory images of heroic struggle and resistance. The fact that they could not find effective historical examples to indicate the achievement of this idea in terms of the tradition of popular graphic art, other than a vague invocation of the names of Goya or Daumier, should have alerted such critics to the illogicality of their demands. The political function of caricature is threefold: it involves the insult suffered by the targeted subject, the expressive anger of the artist and the conspiratorial amusement of the public. Its force has a profound but specific psychological origin; as Gombrich and Kriss have pointed out:

> ... such fun is connected with magic. To copy a person, to mimic his behaviour, means to annihilate his individuality. The very word, 'in-dividual' means inseparable. If we succeed in singling out and imitating a man's expression or way of walking, we have destroyed this individuality. It is as if we declared to our laughing fellow-creatures: 'Look, here is his whole secret, you need not be afraid nor even impressed; it is all a hollow sham.'[7]

Nevertheless, Boswell did undertake topics for which satirical derision would not be appropriate as the dominant tone. In the October 1935 issue of *Left Review* he deals with the Italian invasion of Abyssinia in a format which could be seen as a response to Socialist Realist criticism, by attempting to combine both the exhortatory and the caricatural mode within the one image: the massively built industrial worker, in cap and braces, restrains in his giant hands the absurd, ugly and diminutive figure of Mussolini, in the manner of a parent holding back a small child in the middle of a tantrum. It is notable that a different drawing technique is employed in the representation of the two figures to support the two different modes of signification.

As Arnold Rattenbury has pointed out, the presiding subject for Boswell's attacks was 'the violence of that motive called Profit'.[8] In 'Empire Builders' (fig. 1) for example, from 1935, his disdainful pen itemises the physiognomy of the capitalist class. Hair is worn close-cropped, slicked down or absent altogether, moustaches are permitted, especially inasmuch as they resemble that of Hitler, the nostrils tend to be as equally prominent as the eyes which betray no light of emotion or character but simply a steely determination to carve up the territory on the map in front of them. It is in articulating this range of subject matters that Boswell's typical manner of sharp, hard-edged profiles and stippled and scratched surfaces most recall the example of George Grosz. The transposition of such figures from 1920s' Berlin to the eating houses and offices of the City of London is no doubt entirely purposeful in insisting that the attitudes and behaviour of the capitalist class unite its members more recognisably than any incidental difference of nationality. Grosz's work was exhibited in London in 1934 at the Mayor Gallery, but Boswell was also widely acquainted with the work of cartoonists and caricaturists from the recent past, notably in the radical European tradition, and was a collector of such publications as *Simplicissimus* and *L'assiette au beurre*.[9]

Boswell's cartoon on the subject of the Surrealist exhibition of 1936 reveals something of the current debates involving AIA members about the justification of competing ideologies and styles of Modernism in respect of their claims of political efficacy.[10] Surrealism was late arriving in Britain and could claim very little support or understanding among artists, let alone the general public, prior to the New Burlington Galleries exhibition. But this event was crucial and led to the formation of a British Surrealist group and the inclusion of a number of significant English Modernists like Henry Moore, Paul Nash and Graham Sutherland in the exhibition. Its opening coincided with the first shots fired in the Spanish Civil War and the tone of the rhetoric surrounding the show was necessarily militant. André Breton's catalogue preface set out to justify in rigorously analytic terms how the demand by Marxist theory for 'realism' from revolutionary painters had been absolutely curtailed by photography and therefore the only valid function left to the painter was 'the necessity of expressing internal perception visually'. Herbert Read contributed an introduction equally affirming the radical potentiality of Surrealist practice:

Do not judge this movement kindly. It is not just another amusing stunt. It is defiant, the desperate act of men too profoundly convinced of the rottenness of our civilisation to want to save a shred of its respectability.

The problem for Boswell and for most Communist Party members was that it *was* seen by the general public precisely as 'just another amusing stunt'. Such incidents as the attempted lecture given by Salvador Dalí in

Figure 1 James Boswell, Empire Builders, 1935

a diving suit predictably caught the attention of the press and the exhibition was undoubtedly a great, fashionable success. Thus it was that Boswell contemptuously collaged the above quotation from Read over a representative body of the befurred, privileged classes who appeared to be totally immune to the supposed revolutionary aggression of the work on display.

Boswell's imagery was widely employed for a range of left-wing publications besides *Left Review*. The immediacy of hurried sketch pad notations is reproduced in the illustrations to his report on the Cable Street demonstrations, published in *The Eye* (the house journal of Lawrence & Wishart) in autumn 1936; a report in which he reveals his rarely published skills for evocative journalism. He also contributed frequently to the *Daily Worker* where, operating in the normal procedure of any professional designer for publicity, he adopted a style appropriate to the expectations of the particular consumer. His illustrations, sometimes in a rough-hewn woodcut technique, with a nod perhaps towards Masereel, made more of an obvious accommodation with a definition of realism than the manner of his caricature drawing.

He also adopted the working name 'Buchan' (Buchanan was one of his Christian names), when working for the Party newspaper. It has been said that this was to avoid the threat to his employment with Shell that this work, if openly acknowledged, might pose but this raises the question of how it was that his aggressive attacks on Capital in *Left Review* should be exempted from this concern. The answer is perhaps that the distinction between the two journals reflects precisely that point of bifurcation between the broad public consensus around anti-Fascism, which characterised the atmosphere of the Popular Front, and the public suspicion of the programme of authentic revolutionary commitment associated with the Communist Party.

James Holland's intentions for his cartoons and illustration are set out in his statement accompanying the Moscow exhibition of 'English Revolutionary Graphic Artists' of 1936. It seeks to make connections with the ideological call for Realism and at the same time to re-establish a continuity with the national popular art traditions associated with Hogarth, Gilray and Rowlandson:

> With the cartoons that have appeared in *Left Review*, we believe we have broken away from the middle-class and infantile code of 'Good Taste' that has reduced English cartooning to emasculated illustration or religious hysteria.
>
> With my own work I want to show something of the real life of this country, which goes on in its city suburbs, industrial towns, factories, shipyards, dockyards, shops, offices. This unfashionable material has only been used when falsified by a spurious romanticism. The English

tradition of realism has been lost for more than a century. I want to show the chaotic state of life under an inadequate and decaying social structure.[11]

His imagery for *Left Review* generally calls on more pictorial modes than that of his colleagues, exploiting more of the tonal qualities of lithography. This is revealed in 'The Sailor's Return', of March 1935 (fig.2). At the risk of earning the criticism of 'miserablism' frequently raised by Party propaganda theorists, this presumably unemployed sailor (with just a hint of Socialist Realist bodily proportions) ruminates on his fate, enclosed by the foreboding shadows and forms of his backyard. Another pictorial technique which Holland employed was to counterpose ironically text and image, for example, when he overlays a scene of an oppressive industrial cityscape with the jaunty, music hall refrain, 'With a ladder and some glasses you could see to Hackney marshes if it wasn't for the houses in between.' The same method is employed to make a comment on the Royal Jubilee celebrations of 1935. The general view of the left was that this was a pretty transparent attempt by the National Government to whip up some diversionary patriotism in celebration of a less than glorious period of reign. To illustrate this Holland depicts a horse-drawn refuse cart loaded with the torn remnants of bunting and loyal slogans, under an ironically patriotic verse.

In 1937 Holland was prominent among a group of AIA members who travelled to Paris to decorate the Peace Pavilion which was an unofficial addition to the site of the International Exposition. He reproduced a couple of images from his Paris sketchbook (August 1937) which capture the amused excitement of his engagement with the highly politicised French construction workers during the heady days of the *Front Populaire*. In 'Comment on Guernica' they haul down the German flag, and in 'Midday meeting' they engage in a debate on whether to take a one day strike against War and Fascism.

James Fitton was perhaps the readiest of the three to vary the modes of design for his cartoons. In 'A new use for perambulators' in November 1934 (fig.3), he collages two newspaper cuttings, arranged in the diagonal compositional form employed in contemporary publicity design but ultimately deriving from Synthetic Cubism, the one torn from the stock prices page and the other reporting on the declining birth rate in London. Over this he draws in a soft outline a simple motif of a young couple busking with the song 'Land of Hope and Glory' and using their pram to support a gramophone. There is a decorative lightness to the work which perhaps he felt needed to be restrained since it is no longer present in another piece which prominently employs collaged news items, 'The Bishop of London's Balance Sheet'. The scrawny-necked figure of the cleric wears a newspaper cutting in the form of a sandwich board, which invokes the reader's sympathy for the level of his £10,000 a year income (at a time

Figure 2 James Holland, The Sailor's Return,
Left Review, March 1935

Figure 3 James Fitton, A new use for perambulators, 1934

when £250 would have been a reasonable yearly sum for an industrial worker). Fitton could also attempt a more Grosz-like grimness of line when caricaturing the denizens of the jury box in 'Twelve Good Men and True', June 1935, or in the gluttonous restaurant scene of 'For Charity', though even here Fitton's decorative, rococo delight – just as with Rowlandson – cannot be totally suppressed. Again, working in a different mode, he devised telling ink and body colour caricature portraits of Churchill and of J. L. Garvin, the editor of what was then the right-wing *Observer*.

Radical Politics and Modernism

Edward Wadman in an article entitled 'Left Wing Layout', for *Typography*, in 1937, wrote about the noticeable tendency for leading young designers of the day, like Fitton, Holland and Boswell, to be associated with left-wing politics and went on to point out the good effect to which radical publishers like Lawrence & Wishart and Victor Gollancz and the Left Book Club were exploiting Modernist layout design:

> Latter-day capitalism has called into being an enormous machine of commercial propaganda, which is manned very largely by clever young men who are socialists. You will find them in newspapers, in cinemas, in advertising, in broadcasting. They are interesting and dangerous, these young creative people of the Left, because theirs is not the simple agitation of the have-nots. They are highly paid and comparatively free, but their daily work gives them exceptional opportunities for seeing the wasteful and trivial uses to which our economic system puts the vast powers of the modern world. When such men turn from their bread and butter to the sphere of popular propaganda the results are decidedly significant and may one day be decisive.[12]

One of the works illustrated in this article is the pamphlet that Fitton designed in 1936 for the Alpha Press, *It's Up To Us*, (cover design), priced at 6d., which had a 50,000 print run. Its theme was an appeal towards the cause of peace through international policies based on the League of Nations, reminding its readers of the human and economic loss of the First World War, and it firmly argued that the causes of current European rearmament were endemic to capitalism. What is still notable today is the adventurous use of Modernist typography and layout which would appear to have been derived from the example of Russian Constructivist designers of the late 1920s such as Gustav Klutsis and the Stenberg brothers, even though such tendencies were regarded as suspiciously 'leftist' by the Soviet regime in the mid-1930s. Fitton's achievement was to arrive at a set of design solutions in which text and image operated on equal and indivisible terms. Short quotations from economists and historians such as Maynard Keynes and R. P. Dutt were interspersed with newspaper reports and statistics from government agencies and the political message was neatly but forcefully demonstrated. Each page was treated differently, maintaining a vigorous visual engagement with the viewer/reader through the techniques of photomontage, caricature, graphic display of statistical information, overprinting, constant change of typeface and a layout determined by a dynamic, if not to say hectic, composition. With much the same conviction as his Soviet, Constructivist predecessors, Fitton was clearly offering his solution to the challenge of reconciling the ideological predisposition towards Modernism, associated with his design practice, with the ideological demands of a politically engaged popular art. Indeed this potential solution held a wide appeal for this generation of artist-designers in the 1930s; it seemed to many that the most effective way to propagate Modernist aesthetic ideas through the population as a whole was to sidestep the necessarily elitist associations of painting, insuperably tied to the economic facts of the high cost of production of scarce objects, by direct access to the people through advertising design. There was an eminent precedent within Modernism for a rationale, based on social efficacy, which gave priority to design over art production which might be derived from the example, not only of Constructivism, but also from the Bauhaus. James Holland, reflecting on the period, confirms this view of the relationship between agitational material and commercial advertising:

> I think some of our collective successes came from the circumstances that many of us were employed in advertising ... and the techniques for selling soap or petrol to a not-very-interested public are not so different from those needed to put across a political and social message. We didn't prevent the war, but perhaps we served as the bell on the fire engine.[13]

Holland would have clearly distinguished this kind of activity from that of the artist and he was the prime initiator of a scheme which aimed to overcome the economic barrier which prevented a wider public access to the work of contemporary artists. The AIA Everyman Prints scheme was launched in 1939; it aimed to supply, in the field of the visual arts, the equivalent means of mass distribution to the paperback book or the gramophone record by publishing standard size, 23 x 35cms, offset lithograph prints which could be sold in department stores at the price of 1s 6d(7½p) coloured or 1s (5p) plain. They aimed at allowing the artist to treat subjects in the manner of topical and ephemeral journalism and, because its inauguration was overtaken by the outbreak of the Second World War, many of its 52 titles provided a valuable, documentary record of the initial responses to the new circumstances. Holland himself, in

'Country Town – the Militia', depicted an unflattering view of the pimply-faced raw recruits; in 'News-Reel, Tommy's welcome from pretty French miss', the upbeat tone of the cinema news propaganda is bitterly derided with an image of a despondent soldier suffering the embrace of a prostitute. Boswell's contribution was 'Candidates for Glory', 'Hunger Marchers in Hyde Park' and 'Gitte Business'.

The War and the Doubt

Evidently the multiple effects of the war imposed crucial changes in the working circumstances, the very experiences of life and the ideological perspectives of all three artists. Holland worked as exhibition designer for the Ministry of Information; Fitton designed informational and wartime propaganda material for the Ministries of Food and Information. Boswell saw active service in the Royal Army Medical Corps and his military experience produced, in his private sketchbooks, a record of bitter indictment against the officer caste which rivals Goya in its depictions of brutish stupidity and which, predictably, document a very different world view than that communicated by those artists who received official commissions from the War Artists Advisory Committee.[14] To a considerable extent, however, the three artists continued to collaborate in contributing powerful satirical material to magazines like *Our Time* and later *Lilliput* but by the end of the war, the ideological certainties of the 1930s were no longer so clear-cut. The war had been fought on the basis of a national unity of action against Fascism and opposition to the official, government policy was no longer automatically implicit for artists who had previously been sympathetic to the communist direction; for many the promises of the new social contract outlined by the Labour Party's Welfare State programme was a sufficiently radical outcome and for those who remained Communist Party members, the growing difficulties of coming to terms with pre-war Stalinist persecution and postwar expansionism were severely testing. Boswell himself appears to have parted company with the Party towards the end of the war. It is highly indicative then that Boswell's book, *The Artist's Dilemma*, published in 1947, casts such a despondent perspective on the issues of the relations between the artist and society which had previously been confronted with such eager determination to achieve solutions. In 1944 he had taken on the post of chairing the AIA but that body was now engaged in a fierce battle between 'radical' and 'conservative' factions of its membership, which would only increase in antagonism during the atmosphere of the Cold War and which eventually led to the abandonment of the political objectives in its constitution in 1953. Boswell resigned the chair after a year and, although he returned briefly to his job with Shell, he also resigned from it in the year of the publication of *The Artist's Dilemma*. The relatively uncritical tolerance of advertising maintained during the 1930s as a route via which a wide public might be initiated into an acquaintance with the aesthetics of Modernism could no longer be sustained:

> The case against commercial art is not simply that it is commercial. It quite frankly calls itself commercial and is concerned with buying and selling, no matter what deceptions artists or writers use to elevate it above this sordid level. Since buying and selling are ... a matter of mass-persuasion, and the instruments of persuasion are the most base of motives to convince the customer, there seems little hope of anything of any real value to emerge from this huckster's barking.[15]

Neither was he sanguine about the likelihood of art dealers departing from their customary and profitable practice of treating the sale of pictures as an exclusive, luxury trade despite the success that artists themselves had had in initiating travelling exhibitions (through AIA projects) to factory canteens, village halls and service messes during the war and winning a resounding appreciation for contemporary art. He acknowledges that this particular period of wartime unity of spirit and the social role it allotted to the artist was temporary and untypical and can find no specific form to give structure to any future aspirations for the social function of the artist:

> It remains for the years ahead to show how influential an agent of change he can be, in the changes that must be made if we are to avoid the final destruction a Third World War will bring. He possesses the ability to give concrete form to the desires and aspirations of men, and in ways which seem destined to be strange and too private for general understanding he works steadily at this task until men begin to see their own lives and hopes and sorrows mirrored in the personal imagery he has created.[16]

Boswell was to turn increasingly to abstract painting as his chosen mode of expression, being much influenced by the 1957 exhibition of American Abstract Art at the Tate Gallery in London.

It would seem that the memorable production of radical graphic art in Britain, both in political and artistic terms, which characterised the 1930s was the result of a certain set of circumstances. It required the uncomplicated – perhaps even naive – idealism and energy of a young generation eager to respond to the demands of their times; it required a tangible and fearful historical threat that the tide of Fascism sweeping across Europe represented, and it required a permissive and inclusive cultural and agitational policy within the ideological programmes of the parties of the left, represented by the Popular Front, to achieve these results. In the aftermath of the Second World War all those conditions had been transformed and the moment of history had passed.

Acknowledgements

I am very grateful for the guidance and information so willingly given by Paul Hogarth and Arnold Rattenbury.

Notes

1   Alfred Durus, 'English Revolutionary Graphic Artists', *International Literature*, 1936, pp. l09–10.
2   Quoted in Peter Mellini, 'Gabriel's Message', *History Today*, February 1990, pp. 46–52.
3   Quoted from an autobiographical fragment contained in the entry for Boswell in J. M. Bellamy and J. Saville, (eds), *Dictionary of Labour Biography*, vol. 3, (London: Macmillan, 1976).
4   William Coldstream, 'The Artist Speaks', in R. S. Lambert, (ed.), *Art in England*, (Harmondsworth: Penguin, 1938). Coldstream along with his Euston Road School colleagues were active members of the AIA. His own crisis of conscience on the question of trying to reconcile modernist aesthetic and socialist political ideology led to his decision to abandon painting for a time and working in the field of documentary film-making. The artist he mentions who 'gave up painting altogether ... for the Communist Party' was Clive Branson; in fact he returned to painting, with a realist style which owed much to the manner of untrained art.
5   Quoted in Durus, 'English Revolutionary Graphic Artists', p. 110.
6   Taken from the first AI Bulletin (of which I have no record of surviving copies) quoted in, Anon. 'Revolutionary Artists Organise', *International Literature*, vol. I no. 7, p. 151. 'New Challenge' in fact appeared as *Challenge*.
7   E. H. Gombrich and E. Kriss, *Caricature*, (Harmondsworth: Penguin, 1940), p. l5.
8   Arnold Rattenbury, catalogue essay, ex. cat. *James Boswell: Artist Against Fascism*, Manchester City Art Gallery, 1986, unpaginated.
9   Information supplied by Paul Hogarth.
10   A useful indication of some of the territory of debate is mapped out in Betty Rea (ed.), *5 on Revolutionary Art*, (London: Lawrence & Wishart, 1936), which has essays from Herbert Read, F. D. Klingender, Eric Gill, A. L. Lloyd and Alick West. These originated in talks organised by the AIA. Two specific debates were held between the Realists and the Surrealists: the first took place at the Conway Hall to coincide with the 1936 International Surrealist Exhibition, the second at the Group Theatre rooms in March 1938. The critical exchange was kept alive by the presence of Picasso's 'Guernica' on exhibition in London at the New Burlington Galleries in October 1938, in support of Spanish Relief funds.
11   Durus, 'English Revolutionary Graphic Artists', p. 110.
12   Howard Wadman, 'Left Wing Layout', *Typography*, Summer 1937, pp. 24–8.
13   Letter from James Holland to the author, following a visit to the exhibition, 'The Story of the Artists' International Association', in Oxford in 1983.
14   Some of Boswell's war sketchbooks were acquired by the Imperial War Museum. Richard Cork wrote an appreciation of them, reproduced in the exhibition catalogue, *James Boswell*, Nottingham University Art Gallery, 1976, pp. 22–5.
15   James Boswell, *The Artist's Dilemma*, (London: The Bodley Head, 1947), p. 39.
16   Boswell, *The Artist's Dilemma*, p. 57.

Sources

Primary Sources
Artists' International Association Bulletin, (News-sheet, Newsletter) 1934–72.
International Literature, 1934–36
Left Review, 1934–36.
Our Time, 1941–55.

Secondary Sources
Ex. cat. *James Boswell*, Nottingham University Art Gallery, 1976.
Ex. cat. *James Boswell: Artist Against Fascism*, Manchester City Art Gallery, 1986.
Ex. cat. *James Fitton R.A.*, Dulwich Picture Gallery, 1986.
Lynda Morris and Robert Radford, *The Story of the Artists' International Association, 1933–1953*, Oxford Museum of Modern Art, 1983.
Robert Radford, *Art for a Purpose: The Artists' International Association, 1933–1953*, Winchester: Winchester School of Art Press, 1987.

3

Mick Wallis

Heirs to the Pageant: Mass Spectacle and the Popular Front[1]

On Sunday 20 September 1936, 20,000 people marched from the Embankment via Hyde Park to Shoreditch in a demonstration organised by the London District Communist Party. The procession took 25 minutes to pass by. 'It was a blaze of colour,' reported Ted Bramley, London District secretary, Central Committee member and (later) LCC communist councillor: 'Hundreds of red flags and banners interspersed with 85 gaily-painted banners depicting great figures and great events from English history from Magna Carta to the present day ... Branch after branch marched past giving one the impression of never-ending battalions of Communists.'[2] Banners depicting the Peasants' Revolt, Thomas More, the New Model Army, Peterloo, Robert Owen, Feargus O'Connor, the Chartists, William Morris, the Tolpuddle Martyrs, Keir Hardie, Marx and Engels were loudly cheered, 'especially the banners revealing England's contribution to the international struggle.' But the loudest roar was reserved for the appearance of Communist Party leaders Harry Pollitt and Willie Gallacher. The Poplar Branch banner celebrated the *Jolly George* incident (when the young Pollitt had led the London dockers in their refusal to load a vessel loaded with arms for Poland against the infant Soviet Union). There were banners paying tribute to James Connolly and Padraic Pearse, the Invergordon Mutiny, the 1919 police strike, and a portrait of Felicia Browne, the English communist artist killed in the recent fighting in Spain. As the *Daily Worker* put it, the 'ghosts of England's fighters for freedom, ghosts of stalwarts, dead and gone, must have marched yesterday through London streets':[3]

> The London Communists have shown the 'Progressive Tradition' in England's story. In showing it they help the present generation to go

forward still further along the road of progress. They also show that the 'Historical Elbow Room' gained for the English proletariat in its historic mission, was one dearly bought by struggle on England's very own soil. Today, when Fascism threatens, when liberties, rights, freedom are being attacked; when the 'Elbow Room' is being curtailed and pinched in, then such a march of history as London staged can only serve to inspire and nerve the present generation to defend the things their fathers fought so splendidly for. *Man does not live by economics alone, and pageantry, colour and tradition are among the myriad streams that serve to nourish the great working-class movement.*[4]

In his report for *Inprecorr*, Bramley claimed the Hyde Park event as a new form of public manifestation for the Party:

> The Communist Party is learning to speak to the English workers in a language they understand. With new and varied methods of propaganda, based upon the knowledge of history and experience of the English workers ... (Communism) is revealing itself as the legitimate heir of generations of great English fighters for freedom and progress. It is preparing and will lead the people forward to a free and merrie England.[5]

Banners on the demonstration declared not only that 'The Communist Party fights for democracy and progress', but also that 'The Communist Party fights for peace and freedom and a merry England'.[6] The attempt to appropriate the notion of 'merrie England' for communism may appear quaintly comical from a present perspective. But it is best seen as a conscious and unironic attempt to contest the construction of Englishness at one of its potent sites of construction – the historical pageant.

Historical Elbow Room

Pageant-making was, by the mid-1930s, a familiar and relatively popular pastime, much used for example in the Co-operative Movement to link narratives of locality, history and class.[7] The TUC included a parade of historical floats in its centenary celebrations of the Tolpuddle Martyrs at Dorchester in 1934. The Actresses' Franchise League had presented pageants of great women both in the streets and on stage in the first decade of the century.[8] Elsewhere, pageants were used to celebrate civic pride (the pageants of Anderson and Genn in Liverpool, Wakefield, Ayrshire and Morecambe between 1926 and 1934) or commercial achievements (in 1930 the Liverpool Manchester Railway celebrated its centenary with a mass *Pageant of Transport* in Liverpool, again by Anderson and Genn).[9]

The political potential of this kind of spectacle for the Communist Party during the Popular Front was clearly considerable. In a period of mass communication, the Communist Party had only a small circulation newspaper, limited ability to make or show films and no access to radio; pageants were the nearest thing it had to a mass medium. Like choirs and amateur theatre, pageants were participatory affairs which brought together working-class amateurs and middle-class professionals, ordinary Party members and Party leaders, communists and non-communists. Moreover, pageants turned audiences into participants and identified those taking part as historical agents.

Historical pageants enacting a celebratory historical narrative offered themselves as one part of that affirmatory culture. Their scale allowed the Party to suggest that it was indeed mobilising the masses, demonstrating communist muscle at the same time as inviting the participation of non-communists. They could show the Party as a site of celebration, tradition and community. They were an opportunity to popularise the Party's claim that 'Communism is English', the natural heartbeat of the common people, the proper outcome of their long struggle.[10] And as mass-participatory events they lent themselves to the production of a sense that communism was not only English, but also everywhere.

By 'Englishing' communism, the Party aimed to recruit: 810 joined at Hyde Park. But the same rhetorical strategy was also clearly aimed at lessening resistance to the Party's affiliationist ambitions at this time: Bramley predicted that 'the entry of the Communist Party into the Labour Party will bring a new stream of rich red blood to the Labour Movement'.[11] Also important is the manner in which the 1936 pageant fetishised the Party leader in a 'naturalising' way: Pollitt appears as if 'by chance', enshrined within an historical narrative at once grand and personal.

The success of the Hyde Park event was soon followed by communist historical pageants in other parts of Britain. In July 1937 the Party's Lancashire District Committee held a grand *Pageant of English History* in Manchester. A handbill advertising the day was decorated with portraits of Simon de Montfort, Wat Tyler, Milton, Cromwell, Owen, Morris, Burns, O'Connor, Tom Mann, Keir Hardie, Cobbett, Fox, Shelley and Byron, linked with a sash, 'Pageant of ENGLISH HISTORY WITH BANNERS OF GREAT HISTORICAL EVENTS'. Between 1500 and 3000 people marched from Ardwick Green to Debdale Park, Gorton, bearing 'one hundred beautiful banners and dozens of red flags' portraying 'the struggle of Lancashire people' – Peterloo, Chartism, Crippled Children in the Mills, the Rochdale Pioneers. A team of artists specially assembled by Barbara Niven in Manchester and London had spent a number of weeks designing and painting the scenes. These and the banners of 18 Party branches formed a semi-circle round the platform in the park where Pollitt called for the spirit and sacrifice of the pioneers to safeguard the liberties achieved through generations of struggle. The rise of Fascism and the struggle in

Spain called both for a sharpening of the struggle and for the unity of all progressive forces. Veteran communist Eddie Frow remembered Pollitt being 'really inspired', giving 'one of his best speeches'. The *Guardian* noted the presence, on this 'Communist demonstration of an unusual kind', of 'a good many women and girls'.[12]

In Liverpool, on 19 September 1937, the Party held *The March of History*, 'a message to you from the Communist Party', at Shiel Park. The speakers included Tom Mann and Frank Bright.[13] The Empress Hall rally of the (CP-sponsored) Youth Pilgrimage for Peace and Democracy in February 1938 culminated in an unrehearsed pageant of two hundred young people.[14] In June 1938 the Party organised a *Centenary Pageant* in Manchester with a sports gala, dancing, keep fit, community singing, an exhibition and free crèche, with speeches by Pollitt and Mann,[15] as a counter to the official *Manchester Historical Pageant* (which studiously avoided any mention of Peterloo).[16]

At the end of 1938 the Party organised a series of imaginative recruiting rallies in London at which professional actors in the Party represented 'figures from the long procession of men [*sic*] who in this country have continually denounced oppression and demanded justice in Parliament' – Thomas More, Robert Phelps, Sheridan, Byron, Macaulay, O'Connor, Keir Hardie. The communist Willie Gallacher played himself:

> All through the centuries the British people have demanded freedom – freedom of speech, freedom of the press, freedom of assembly. Freedom, in fact, to make their voices heard against tyrants and to use their energies for the building of a better world. Directly responsible today for safeguarding the ideals expressed in those speeches and for extending the demands they made is the Communist Party...[17]

Throughout the spring of 1938 the *Daily Worker* called for extensive and united celebrations of May Day:

> 'Towards May First. Urge for United Platform.' One of the outstanding features of the 1937 May First was the participation of the peace movement, whose blue and white banners for the first time floated side by side with the red flags of labour ... This year a proposal is being discussed to represent by an effective use of colour and tableaux, the international struggle for peace.[18]

Resistance to the initiative came as might be expected from some quarters of the state: for instance, Dundee magistrates refused permission for two local Communist Party rallies that May, the second of which was to be a *Pageant of History*.[19] But the initiative also suffered from the memory of disputes between local Labour and Communist Parties over control of May Day in the sectarian years of Class Against Class.[20] In Manchester a

Communist proposal that a *Centenary Pageant* be incorporated into the official 1938 May Day celebrations at Caxton Hall came to nothing.[21]

The most successful event was in Glasgow, where the Communist Party was able to present a *Pageant of Scottish History* as part of the May Day parade organised by the Glasgow Trades Council and Burgh Labour Party. The event was filmed by Helen Biggar for her *Challenge to Fascism*, which shows a street parade including miners carrying their lamps, a bagpipe band (plus police escort), *Daily Workers* on sale, and floats from socialist Sunday schools, the Labour Party, ILP, Glasgow Unity and Kino. The leading banner in the communist section, 'Pageant of Scottish History/Heroes/Glories/Culture and Fight for Freedom/Civil-National-Religious' is followed by banners tracing the history of the Miners' Federation in Scotland or bearing the bust portraits of heroes of the Scots Labour Movement like Keir Hardie and Willie Gallacher (who also addressed the rally). As this kind of street pageant brought the past into the present, it also made the present a part of the history it was celebrating: one banner depicted people *themselves* demonstrating with banners, demanding 'Education for All', 'Work for the Jobless' and 'Religious Freedom'.[22]

If nothing else, this still relatively small-scale, local *al fresco* pageantry helped to enliven the traditional parades of the Labour Movement. For instance, at the Durham Miners' Gala in July 1939, the Newcastle Left Book Club Theatre Guild presented a *Pageant of the Militant North* as part of a 'special effort to revive the tradition of the Chartists and to bring the big issues of the present day before the miners'.[23] The already established indoor curtain-stage pageant was also included in this general initiative. In March 1939 the Women's Committee for Peace and Democracy held an 'inspiring pageant of womanhood', *British Women Through the Ages*, at St Pancras Town Hall.[24] In 1938, Ewan McColl made two indoor pageants at Manchester 'dealing with the Spanish people's struggle against Fascism' and experimenting with environmental theatre effects such as planting speaker-witnesses in the audience.[25]

A Pageant of Pageants

The pageant procession is one example of those ritual celebrations, as well as symbolic definitions and defences, of community and place found in most cultures at most times. From the middle of the nineteenth century, urban populations not only continued, but also rediscovered, refurbished and reinvented such seemingly immemorial customs as a counter to the alienations of capitalist culture.[26] The Popular Front was consciously appropriating a cultural form which, while apparently 'organic', was also to a large extent compensatory.

A particular example of such 'invention of tradition' is the May Day parade itself, a memorialising event which consolidated and re-presented the more informal expressions of working-class strength and solidarity.[27] The annual repetition of the event constitutes a sort of pageant, just as much as the procession itself supports an episodic structure of passing groups and banners.

While communist pageant procession may re-present struggle and manufacture the occasion for feelings of solidarity and strength, it is also importantly both a direct and symbolic articulation of public space. The Hyde Park march territorially challenged both the state and the Fascists that the state appeased. Mass actions can gain morale by being repetitions, rehearsed actions. Calls in the *Daily Worker* for numbers at the Albert Hall to oppose a Fascist meeting on 22 March 1936 celebrated the demonstration against the blackshirts by 150,000 in Hyde Park on 9 September 1934.[28]

While, as David Cannadine has demonstrated,[29] the crown were themselves busily reinventing 'traditional' pageant from the time of Victoria's waning popularity, and while the London Lord Mayor's show continued (refurbished) its centuries-long parade, it is with the advent of the 'Parkerian' pageant in 1905 that a new and rhetorically potent form emerged.

Louis Napoleon Parker, an ex-schoolmaster who worked for a while with Beerbohm Tree (significantly for instance on Shakespeare's pageantic *Henry 8* in 1910: pageant was an important element in late Victorian stage spectacle),[30] made a festival play in 1905 for the anniversary of his public school. The *Sherborne Pageant*, as it became known, was a mass folk play modelled on the German *Festspiel* involving 900 locals of all classes. It presented a series of historical scenes, involving typical and historical characters, to recount the history of school, bishopric and town. The performance was given in a single location to a seated audience, who were able to buy a Book of the Pageant which both furnished the script and scenario and acted as a memorial to the event.[31] The *Sherborne Pageant* was resolutely conservative: Parker set out to suspend class antagonism both in its organisation and in its narrative – which terminates at a safe chronological distance from 1905.

The *Sherborne Pageant* was widely emulated. Anderson and Genn's civic and commercial pageants are examples, but so are events such as the 1911 *Festival of Empire*, official propaganda for Coronation year,[32] or the 1924 *Pageant of British Empire*, which sought 'to light the torches of the future at the glowing heart of the past'.[33] In these and subsequent celebrations of state, a selective and heroic national history is enacted with significant spectacle on dates of either calendrical or occasional significance. Interestingly, community pageants in England and the USA were a stimulus to Kerzhentsev in his contribution to the development of Soviet spectacle.[34] According to the American Robert Withington, whose history of the English pageant itself takes on a pageant form – the historical examples parade across the page – the Parkerian pageant bore 'much the same relation to us that the chronicle-play bore to the Elizabethan audience'.[35] There was, therefore, by the 1930s a well-established model for the historical pageant, an episodic drama performed in mass before a mass audience. The first significant use of the form by the left in Britain appears to be the *Pageant of Labour*, which brought together Anderson and Genn and communist composer Alan Bush. Mounted by the London Trades Council's Central Women's Organisation Committee, with the express aim of attracting women and young people to the movement, the *Pageant of Labour* was performed at Crystal Palace in October 1934. Michael Tippett assisted Bush with the music. The pageant proceeds through a series of Whiggish-Labourist historical tableaux ('Capital Enslaves the Worker', 'Martyrdom of the Children', 'Consolation of Philanthropy and Religion', 'The Triumph of the Trades Unions') before the anti-climactic promise of a world in which the working class will gain 'more rewards for your industry' and 'a share in the making of the laws'.

Towards Tomorrow

The potential of historical pageant-making for the Communist Party in the Popular Front was clear. As well as taking history on to the streets with the processional pageant, the Communist Party was also involved from 1938 in a number of huge theatrical spectacles, mass historical dramas which were professionally scripted, scored, choreographed and staged and which were performed by hundreds or thousands of people. The four communists who were prime movers in mounting these mass pageants in the late 1930s were the composer Alan Bush, the director André van Gyseghem, and the writers Montagu Slater and Randall Swingler.

Bush had been a central mover in the London Labour Choral Union from 1924. From 1936 he wrote many songs with Randall Swingler for its successor the Workers Music Association and together they edited *The Left Song Book* for the Left Book Club.[36] Van Gyseghem had met Piscator and worked with Okhlopkov in Moscow, and had already directed two of Slater's plays for Left Theatre. In 1937 he staged a pageant for the South African government.[37] Slater's dramaturgy in the 1930s attempted a synthesis between formal experiment and a popular register.[38] Benjamin Britten worked on a pageant with Slater for the Co-operative Movement in 1937.[39]

If the historical pageants of Bush, Slater, Swingler and van Gyseghem were no less teleological than the *Pageant of Labour*, they reached rather different conclusions, even though only one of them was made directly under the aegis of the Communist Party. The first full-scale collaboration (Bush, Slater and van Gyseghem) was commissioned by the London, Watford and South Suburban Co-operative Societies to mark the 16th International Co-operative Day in 1938. *Towards Tomorrow* was a huge enterprise, involving 3000 performers and 6000 costumes; it was so large that they had to rehearse in London parks or at the Crystal Palace, with Alan Bush rehearsing three or four choirs at a time. *Towards Tomorrow* was performed before an audience of 78,000 at Wembley Stadium on 2 July 1938. As one performer later recalled, 'There was more people there than I've ever seen in my life, I think. We all walked round the stadium singing. I loved it. We were all in white and dressed up as peace.'[40]

Slater's script moves chronologically from Merrie England to the present, aligning Capital with war and dystopia, and Co-operative democracy with peace and utopia.[41] As the participants move around the arena, a Commentator reflects on the action below. A pastoral opening fills the arena with images of Merrie England, which is identified as 'partly the invention of storytellers', partly the deep folk memory 'of a little country where eight million men and women and children lived on a rich wheat-growing soil'. Sirens and harsh music herald the entry of two 20-foot effigies of Capital, assisted by factory overseers dressed as medieval torturers brandishing whips. They drive people off and erect machines; a factory chimney thrusts 40 feet into the air. The new system is challenged first by Hunt, then Paine and Cobbett. After Hunt's speech the crowd attacks the machines and the chimney bursts into flame. Mounted soldiers gallop on to quell the rioting. It is only after Robert Owen has spoken that order and symmetry return to the arena. Children stand in a grid, performing physical exercise and running relays along the lines, dressed in clean white tunics instead of pauper clothes. Despite the persistence of the overseers, the Rochdale Pioneers then mount the rostrum, 'men of all sorts', Chartists, Owenites, socialists, reformers, while a banner parade tells the story of the growth of the Co-operative Movement from 1844 to 1914.

Capital then 'chooses' war. The arena fills with soldiers, smoke and tanks. Costumed dancers with outstretched arms represent aeroplanes; ragged black vultures stooping and lurching across the arena follow them. A Chorus and Procession of Mourning Women follow:

> We are women and proclaim
> This is the accepted time.
> Nations, peoples, men and women,
> Children in the glow of morning
>
> Make a ring round the aggressor;
> Dispossess the dispossessor.
> Build the warm alliances
> Of humanity for Peace.

Reviewing the scale of the international Co-operative Movement (especially in the Soviet Union) and concluding that 'ONLY IN THAT UNITY IS THERE HOPE FOR MANKIND AND PEACE', the Commentator remarks that 'the war is over – but for how long?'

A procession of national costumes fills the arena. A ballet of 'young workers' flourishes red flags, faces to the sky and legs astride. The figures of Capital have been toppled and the arena is triumphantly full: a co-operative plenitude. Two decorated cars representing Peace and Democracy enter and their personifications climb the central rostrum. Its sections revolve in opposite directions. Flags unfurl and a flock of white pigeons is released as the President of the London Co-operative Society, R.G. Gosling, urges those present to pledge themselves to

> Renew the declaration of their unshakeable faith in the principles of democracy, freedom and peace; manifest their abhorrence of all interference with the rights and liberties of free peoples ... proclaim their conviction that the economic principles and social ideals which lie at the basis of their world movement constitute the best hope for the regeneration of society and the surest guarantee of universal peace ...

In the Finale of what the *Daily Worker* called 'the greatest pageant of co-operation that has ever been organised in Britain – or anywhere else'[42] performers and audience joined together in song:

> Workers all!
> Heed the call!
> You who toil and sweat and slave
> From the cradle to the grave!
> You who strive with hand and brain,
> You who live in fear and pain!
> > You who slumber!
> > Countless number!
> You in mines and fact'ry stalls,
> You within the sweatshop's walls,
> You in life's forgotten heap
> You who sell your souls for keep!
>
> Men awake! Heed the warning.
> Men awake! The day is dawning.
> Break the chains that keep you bound
> And trample to the ground
> The barricades that hem you round!
> Men, a time to spare. Awake.
> Can't you see, Life can be what you make it.
> Life that's new, Life that's free, if you take it.
> Put away yesterday, and its sorrow,
> Men unite, we must fight for a new tomorrow.
>
> Wake! Fates are drumming!
> Men awake! The time is coming![43]

The Pageant of South Wales

The second Slater and van Gyseghem collaboration was for the South Wales Miners Federation and the Labour Research Department in 1939. Performed on May Day, simultaneously in Pontypool, Abertillary and Ystradgynlais by a total of 6000 people, the *Pageant of South Wales* was designed to trace the history of working-class struggle in the valleys from the 1839 Newport Rising to the present day. LRD Secretary Bill Williams, prime mover of the event and himself a working-class South Walean, later reflected that pageantry was 'in their blood'. Although there was some resistance at first to what felt like the initiative of outsiders, the swift involvement of local organisations such as choirs helped construct a sense of ownership over the pageant.[44] Accepted after this false start as a legitimate expression of organic sentiments of solidarity and history, the pageant stimulated huge local interest, involving Federation lodges, chapel and church choirs and operatic societies.[45]

Slater had been in the coalfield in 1934 to document the stay-down strikes in *Stay Down Miner* (1936), subsequently dramatised as *New Way Wins* (1937). The pageant uses an epic portion of the play where Time (history) in the shape of a mine ('the critical Present where the workings narrow') gives way to Time as an illegitimate organiser of work in the mine (the coal owners were currently introducing 'speed-up' in the industry):

WOMAN: Time for man, not man for Time
              Time for man; time for man;
              Have you got new men (otherwise we are lost)
              And mines will feed on men as wars do.

              Have you got new men to fight this other time?
              New men, new men to overcome it, till
              Time, in the shape of a mine, is the creator
              Of an enriching life.

MAN: Yes, we have new men.
              The new man, here, now, braving novel death,
              Stands upright in the mine, and in that posture
              Shakes more than pit-props.[46]

The pageant is in two parts, the action interspersed with a great deal of hymn singing. Episode One deals entirely with the Newport Trial, the Commentator invoking the power of working-class solidarity. Slater makes use of and adapts courtroom ritual to other ends. The announcement and entry in turn of the accused becomes a ceremony of their appearance from the significant past, into the presence of the audience as witness and inheritor. And then *after* this roll-call, the Commentator announces the

Judges and Counsels, who are thereby made to stand before the audience, as if they themselves are to be judged.

Episode Two tells the story from 1839 to 1926 – child labour, pit deaths, the secret beginnings of trade unionism, Tonypandy, the Lock-out of 1926 and the General Strike. In the final section a mining family looks at the past, the present (unemployment, Depression) and future ('And South Wales will be one great thriving country. And there's only one lot of people can do it and that's us, here, now.'). After a fanfare, local International Brigaders marched on to the arena as the Spanish Republican Hymn was sung and one of them addressed the crowd:

> I am one of the little band that went out from South Wales to fight in the International Brigade in Spain. I am going to ask you to rise, all of you, and swear with me this oath of victory.
>
> In the name of Wales and its people, in the name of our high-wrought past, in the name of our traditions, in the name of all our battles in the fight for freedom, on this day 1st May 1939, we solemnly swear not to relax until freedom, and the prosperity that can only be brought by the power of the people, bring back the sunshine to our land. All those in favour shout 'Aye'.

As participants and audience shouted their answer, the bands struck up and everyone sang the Internationale. The presence of the International Brigaders was living proof of the narrative of continuing struggle which the pageant sought to express. Locally lived history was thus put in a genuine continuity with events on an international scale, the sturdy might and the protective strength of a community performed by the community to and for itself.

In a note for the memorial programme van Gyseghem comments:

> The British working class has a tradition it can be proud of, a tradition of fight after fight successfully fought and won for freedom. In attempting to revive the form of the pageant to express this tradition we are, I think, choosing the only form which can truthfully frame so large a canvas. It is a form which calls for the co-operation of all for the sake of all. It demands crowds and processions and fine, rousing music which stirs the memory and sets the heart pounding.[47]

Music and the People

The mass pageant *Music and the People*, performed at the Albert Hall on 1 April 1939, was the singular brainchild of Alan Bush. It was part of a Festival of Music for the People, designed not only to celebrate popular music-making and democratic cultural energy, but also to challenge the almost simultaneous London Music Festival (a high-culture and nationalist jamboree organised by Beecham and Owen Mase). The other festival events were a concert of folk songs at the Conway Hall and a concert at the Queen's Hall which saw the first performance of Britten's *Ballad of Heroes* (text by Auden and Randall Swingler) and a performance of Bush's First Piano Concerto (with words for the finale written by Swingler). Swingler also wrote the text for *Music and the People*, which was set to music by an impressive line-up of contemporary classical composers – Vaughan Williams, Arnold Cooke, Elizabeth Lutyens, Victor Yates, Edmund Rubbra, Erik Chisholm, Christian Darnton, Frederic Austin, Norman Demuth, Elizabeth Maconchy, Alan Rawsthorne and Bush himself. It was directed by Unity director John Allen, danced by the Woodcraft Folk and the Unity Theatre Dance Group, and sung by Paul Robeson and the combined voices of twelve Co-operative and Labour Movement choirs.

It was the height of the Popular Front; Alan Rawsthorne, Edward Clark and Parry Jones were on the festival committee, which hoped to raise money for Basque refugee children. And the pageant demonstrated the extensive reach of individual communists like Bush and Swingler in late 1930s London culture, as well as their ability to mobilise it to the advantage of the Communist Party's current historical narrative (and without ever mentioning the word 'communism').[48]

After a flourish on bass and drums, a Speaker comes to the centre of the arena and delivers a direct address in a roughly regular iambic tetrameter, regularly rhymed like a moral interlude:

> Good people all within this hall
> Gallery, circle, pit and stall
> Be welcome to our festival ...[49]

At the outset therefore the discourse of 'tradition' is established, as well as a conscious good humour:

> No mystic rite we shall unfold
> Initiate to a world remote
> Where none but Muses had the vote.

The traditional presenter-prologue makes the traditional promises about the ensuing action:

> Our world is life. Our theme is man,
> Whose music since the world began
> Like tributaried river runs
> Through villages and swarming towns
> And whose original springs arise
> Deep down in man's necessities.

Music arises, as does knowledge that leads to power, from the meeting of human need in history. It is the pageant's means of expression as well as the subject of the pageant. Music is one of the inspirations of the struggle against oppression and a way of sustaining the hopes invested in a particular struggle long after it has been defeated. Music therefore both acts as a metaphor for, and is theorised as the material carrier of, humanity's persistent urge to realise its true potential – all the People, all the Past and all Music mobilised against the Final Enemy and its friends.

The text asserts the materialist basis of culture and therefore of music. But it also entertains an idealistic register, based on an ontological utopianism, the idea of a now-lost but recoverable natural essence. This finds particular expression in Swingler's association of 'music' and 'heart'. People have always sought 'One rhythm and one harmony,/Such as the heart, which beats for good'. But while men compete for private gain,

> Life's tune is broken, drowned its song;
> The rhythm that makes the heart beat strong
> Is buried deep, though still it keeps
> But faintly beating while we sleep.

By discouraging a nostalgic register available from the dominant culture ('A merry scene you say? In this/The fifteenth century/These men are serfs. Their life is harsh/And none of them is free'), Swingler probably also encourages his audience away from an ontological utopianism based in chronology (that some time even further back was freedom) to one based on a synchronic model of cause and effect. In this model an already existing but *never* materialised state of perfection is prevented from realisation by the persistence of an opposing ('evil') agency. Within the classic Marxist grand narrative, the idea of primitive communism mediates between synchronic and chronological modes of ontological utopianism: human potential was not yet forestalled by class oppression, yet still remained at this stage a *potential*.

The pageant proceeds through a series of linked episodes of history illustrated by music and episodes in the development of music illustrated by historical events: Feudal England (peasant songs from 1350), the Massacre of the Innocents ('Herod the Cock'), the Peasant's Revolt ('The Cutty Wren'), 1649 ('Stand Up You Diggers Now'), 'Village Green to Concert Hall' (tunes used in *The Beggar's Opera*), 'Changing Europe' ('La Carmagnole'), 'Prisoners' ('Peat-Bog Soldiers' Song'), 'Slaves' ('Kneelin' Low'), 'The People Advance' (the Chartist song 'We're Low' – 'People of England' – the 1905 Russian funeral march) to the present. In the Finale, the Speaker reflects on the meaning of the pageant:

And having present struggles and despairs
Sharp in our minds, remember too
The past whose urgent influence prepares
The issues of today, and know that you
By today's action map the future's road ...
Never so needed was that single will
That unity of the people, to fulfil
The claim to freedom, and to ensure our peace ...
It is time we answered, as they answer now
In Spain, in China, in every tortured land ...
Let our song rise whose simple power
Can flood the boundaries that divide us still
And make our common hope, our single will.

This was followed by a procession of groups representing various songs and categories of song: Christian Hymn, Levellers' Song, 'Marseillaise', 'People of England', 'Bandiera Rossa', German Solidarity Song, Chinese Student Song, Spanish National Anthem, Negro Choir. Behind the group representing the Spanish Republican Anthem marched a hundred International Brigaders led by Fred Copeman (the last Commander of the British Battalion). Paul Robeson sang the Soviet song, 'The Land of Freedom'; and Copeman, the Dean of Canterbury and the veteran communist Tom Mann addressed the audience (as themselves) before everyone sang the American song 'Men Awake! The Day is Dawning'.

Heirs to the Charter

The last of the pre-war mass spectacles, *Heirs to the Charter*, was made by Slater, van Gyseghem and the indefatigable Bush for the London District Communist Party in 1939 as part of a recruitment drive. It was held in the ice-hockey arena of the Empress Hall at Earl's Court, on 22 July 1939, the venue also for a theatricalised memorial parade of International Brigaders directed by van Gyseghem that February and the Youth Pilgrimage pageant in January. *Heirs to the Charter* attracted over 9000 people, the 'largest gathering of comrades in the Party' to date. More than £2000 was raised in half an hour for the dependants of the International Brigaders and nearly a thousand new recruits made for the Party.[50]

Heirs to the Charter shared several rhetorical devices with the 1936 Hyde Park march. It both celebrated the centenary of Chartism and directly claimed it as the heritage of the Communist Party; and it situated the Party leader securely within, and as an apotheosis of, that narrative. Part One argues the need for independent democratic working-class organisation.[51] From a workhouse about to be set on fire, the audience are transported to a magistrate's court where an arrested Luddite dies from a bullet in his back and where a man tried for selling the *Poor Man's Guardian* argues for Combination; via the presentation of the People's Charter to a meeting of the Working Man's Association, and the call for a People's Convention by Feargus O'Connor, to a massed torchlight procession by Chartists. This culmination of the first phase of action subtly shifts the nature of the performance. Past events have been viewed in their particularity; to this is now added the direct and emotive presence of the People *en masse*. The procession manifests the here and now of communality, purposiveness, pleasure and celebration (it comprises members of the Party and of Co-operative Women's Guilds). It also occupies the same space as, and thereby symbolically displaces, a previous parade by Queen Victoria.

Actors from Unity Theatre played individual witnesses to events – the liberal Lord Egremont, two reactionary interlocutors (Lord and Lady Marney) and Cradle Rocker, a 'little man' who helps Egremont disabuse himself of his One Nation beliefs. Cradle Rocker is the humble seer. When Egremont comments that these are 'strange times', he answers: 'When the infant begins to walk it also thinks that it lives in strange times,' explaining that 'society, still in its infancy, is beginning to feel its way'. These witnesses introduce a layer of dialogically-managed commentary on the scenes, a further 14 of which bring the pageant up to 1848. Several interlock action and commentary, so the need for organisation is argued politically at the same time as it is illustrated historically.

The second phase of action starts with Bronterre O'Brien's call for direct action: a run on the banks, a boycott of excisable goods, exclusive trade with Chartists and a general strike. But just as the six points of the Charter and O'Brien's four 'ulterior measures' have been listed like a litany in the arena, so now too are the five reasons why the Convention comes to deem itself unable to lead the strike. Worse, the leaders are in the next moment arrested, tried and sentenced.

After this reversal, a short 100-word scene in which the Convention calls for organisation is swiftly followed by news of spontaneous mass action – strikes in the North. The action feels swift and it rises. The names of the towns are chanted from the gallery; the arena fills with people who murmur 'General Strike'; a sturdy speech is delivered from the Convention stage. But again there is reversal: the Riot Act is read and people fall under military fire.

Slater's script economically figures both class struggle and a struggle *forwards*, a pattern of advancement and check which now culminates in a special point of arrival. There is news of the rising in Poland and Dr Karl Marx comes from Belgium to speak from the Convention stage: 'The moment you carry the six points of the Charter, the road to liberty will be open to the whole world.' Egremont asks what communism is: Cradle Rocker tells him it is 'a word – and a good deal more than a word'. And finally, the close coupling of rise and fall becomes first benign and then heroic. The Convention secretary has to report that a stiff letter has been sent demanding that Marx write the Manifesto soon or return valuable papers. This sentimental humour transforms into epic audience involvement when the draft of the famous prefatory passage is read in full, authentic words which bring the enactment of an authentic history to its culmination. For the *Communist Manifesto* is not locked in 1848: when someone asks if there are any copies available, programme sellers in the here and now of the Empress Hall fill the arena with shouts of '*Communist Manifesto*, threepence!' The scene explodes heroically into the present.

In Part Two, action, commentary, procession and audience are all invested in the transformation of the pageant into rally. A Woman Chorus now acts as seer, gradually bringing a First World War Soldier spotlit opposite her to class consciousness. A Soviet voice calls from the darkness for peace by revolutionary means. The English working class is called upon, in the light of their Chartist past, and in emulation of the revolution in Petrograd, to liberate mankind from war. Soldiers left in the field to fight Bolshevism desert, there is disruption at home and the Woman sees 'it' coming 'nearer, still nearer'. There is great rhetorical power in that 'it' – another of those enigmatic formulations that she and the Cradle Rocker have made, utterances that are like the ghosts of sense. The text of the *Manifesto* preface read in the arena has mocked the idea of the 'spectre' of Communism as a 'nursery tale'. The text that the preface announces, the manifesto for action, is based on the events and analysis being rehearsed and again shared – made specially present and clarified – in the Empress Hall. Present struggle is a clarification of the past; past clarifies the present. And those clarifications are shared between *Manifesto* and pageant.

To bring the pageant to its climax, the Chorus figure of Woman and the Soldier held in place as her interlocutor now definitively enter the world of concrete action, to make room for the special presence of another. The Woman chats with a second, whose lodger, Harry Pollitt, has stuffed his mattress with illegal anti-interventionist pamphlets. The young Soviet Union appeals to the world after Poland invades. News comes in of Harry Pollitt, who has been sacked for refusing to work on barges sending arms to Poland to be used against the Soviet Union, and the Soldier is persuaded to help similarly block the *Neptune*. As Poplar declares itself resolute to block the *Jolly George* and awaits a speech by Harry Pollitt, Pollitt himself is introduced, here now in 1939, part of an heroic narrative in which he stands but also *for* which he stands, to address the assembled performers and audience. Full heroic presence is achieved for and by the Party leader.

Endings

With the outbreak of war, the occasion for pageant-making lessened greatly. But while the opportunity for mass involvement was reduced, the rhetorical rationale for historical pageants persisted with the development of the Popular Front into the People's War. Hence, Bush, Slater and van Gyseghem collaborated on *An Agreement of the Peoples*, a cross between Living Newspaper and military tattoo given at the Empress Stadium on 20 June 1942, as part of the Second Front campaign.[52] Similar politics imbue some curtain-stage Co-operative pageants such as *The Flame of Freedom* (1940) and *We, the Women* (1941) made under joint auspices with the Workers Music Association. Bush conducted for the former.[53]

However, the form of the popular pageant soon fell into residue after the war, within the Communist Party and in British culture at large. Slater and Bush's *Communist Manifesto Centenary Pageant*, done at the Albert Hall on 30 March 1948,[54] was to have been followed in 1949 by a memorialising of the 1649 English Revolution, but the latter initiative was cancelled.[55] The final manifestations sought to promote resistance to the Cold War, but were – not surprisingly, given the circumstances – largely inward-looking affairs. Slater and Bush's *Thirty Years: A Non-Costume Pageant of Communist Party History* done at the Empress Hall on 24 September 1950 begins with the Hands Off Russia campaigns and has the 'voice' of the *Manifesto* explain the progress of Capital through imperialism, slump and war, to arrive at Hiroshima and the question of hope. Within this narrative, *Towards Tomorrow* (1938) is invoked as one episode in a 'pageant' of struggle and celebration.[56] Swingler's *Truth on the March* for Harringay Arena on Sunday 18 February 1951 celebrated the twenty-first birthday of the *Daily Worker*. While it proclaimed that it had dispensed with the regular trappings of pageantry, it definitively retained the rhetorical features of the Popular Front productions – the manufacture of Soviet plenitudes, special presence and narrative apotheoses.[57]

The context of the Cold War rendered such rhetorical devices mechanical, left them exposed for what they were. While the evidence is that the mass pageants of the late 1930s achieved moments of 'organic' celebration and solidarity, that organicity was itself manufactured. Both performer and spectator were treated to a selective narrative characterised by a fetish for authentic words and episodes; the comforting embrace of scale and sentiment supported an emotional rather than rational attitude, a feeling of power and aspiration; that feeling was drawn-by the strong narrative drive and the subtle shiftings between scene, commentary and parade-to the sensations both of the special moment and of the special presence of particular persons. And these devices were not, of course, ideologically neutral. At the end of *Heirs to the Charter*, fetishised moment and specially invested person combine in the appearance of Harry Pollitt to address the rally. He appears, perhaps, as a 'man of destiny'. The week before, the British Union of Fascists had their own (national) rally in the same hall, replete with procession, techniques of scale, and the fetishisistic production of Moseley as leader.[58] In this vignette, the Communist Party might be seen not only standing directly counter to, but also mutually mirroring, the Fascists, a view which suits some facile critiques of Marxism and communism as fundamentally and necessarily totalitarian practices. Even leaving these aside, there remain important questions about the politics of cultural form, asked from a left perspective. These pageants hardly offer, for instance, Brechtian defamiliarisation.

For all that, close reading of the pageant texts and some traces of the experience of witnesses each suggest a 'rational', relatively detached enjoyment of the plenitudes and simplifications on offer, a sense that they will do for the purposes of the present celebration, but cannot be mistaken for a fully adequate analysis or political attitude. The declaration early in *Towards Tomorrow* that the story being told at that moment is part history and part fancy is a case in point.

A full evaluation of these events must take place as part of an evaluation of the politics of the Popular Front itself. Within that frame, it would be too simplistic to see these events merely as *ersatz* community, evacuated history or diluted politics. At the very least, they are instances of self-fashioned community and the powerful popularisation of a Marxist perspective – a class history and indeed dialectical thought.[59]

In the week of the pageant *Music and the People*, Bush's 'Concerto for Pianoforte and Orchestra' with Baritone Solo and Male Voice Chorus was given at the Queen's Hall. Swingler's text for it concludes:

> Art is no drug, nor yet oblivion's river.
> Music is the mind-changer, the life-giver,
> The future's design, the release of new endeavour.
>
> Come then, there can be no more sides than two;
> War and waste for the privileges of the few
> Or a share for all in all men make or do.
>
> Therefore, friends, who sit here waiting and fearing,
> Know that in this fight only is the assuring
> Of your fulfilment, abundant and enduring.
>
> Upon our heads is laid such destiny
> As none knowing can coldly cast away.
> Man's future is to be fought for in our day.

Notes

1   Versions of this material have appeared in Mick Wallis, 'Pageantry and the Popular Front: Ideological Production in the Thirties', *New Theatre Quarterly*, no.38 (May 1994) pp. 132–56; and 'The Popular Front Pageant: its Emergence and Decline', *New Theatre Quarterly*, no.41 (February 1995), pp. 17–32. Thanks to Andy Croft for additional references and for crucial help during illness.

2   *International Press Correspondence*, 26 September 1936 (vol. 16 no. 4). See also Bramley, 'Communism Grows from English Soil', *Daily Worker*, 14 September 1936. The London District Committee published a pamphlet to accompany the march, *The March of English History*.

3   *Daily Worker*, 21 September 1936.

4   *Daily Worker*, 23 September 1936. Emphasis added.

5   Bramley, *International Press Correspondence*.

6   *Daily Worker*, 21 September 1936.

7   For a brief review, see Bernadette Kirwan, 'Aspects of Radical Theatre in England in the 1930s', PhD Thesis, Loughborough University of Technology, 1989.

8   See Viv Gardner, *Sketches from the Actresses' Franchise League* (Nottingham: Nottingham Drama Texts, 1985).

9   For bibliographical references to these and other similar events see Wallis, 'Ideological Production' and 'Emergence and Decline'.

10   The same claim was made by other artistic means. For example, Jack Lindsay wrote a trilogy of novels tracing the English revolutionary tradition and retold that narrative in condensed form in his successful essay *England My England* (London: Fore Publications, 1939). The essay describes itself as 'a Pageant of the English People' and declares that 'Communism is English'. His long declamatory poem, 'Who are the English?' (*Left Review*, 1936), helped develop the mass declamation in Britain.

11   Bramley, *International Press Correspondence*.

12   *Guardian*, 12 July 1937; *Daily Worker*, 12 July 1937; Handbill at Working Class Movement Library, Salford; Personal communication, Eddie Frow.

13   Programme at Working Class Movement Library, Salford.

14   Photograph in *News Chronicle*, 20 February 1939.

15   Programme at Working Class Movement Library, Salford.

16   *Manchester Evening News*, 29 March 1938. Press cuttings and the pageant *Book of Music* and *Book of Words* at Manchester Local History Library.

17   'Voices of Freedom Speak from Parliament' *Daily Worker*, 17 December 1938.

18   *Daily Worker*, 12 March 1938, p. 5.

19   Ibid., p. 6.

20   For an example of Labour complaints, see *London News*, June 1928, p. 2.

21   The plans are reported in *Daily Worker*, 7 March 1938.

22   Helen Biggar, *Challenge to Fascism* (1938), National Film Archive. Biggar's work is celebrated and recovered in *Traces Left* (1983), Birmingham Film Workshop, director Alan Lovell.

23   *Daily Worker*, 18, 22, 24 July 1939.

24   *Daily Worker*, 7, 9 March 1939. Stepney women organised their own rally and pageant, *Century of Women*, at the Ladies' Tailors' Union Hall.

25   Interview with author, 20 August 1984.

26   See for example A.E. Green, 'Popular Drama and the Mummers' Play' in David Bradby, Louis James and Bernard Sharratt (eds), *Performance and Politics in Popular Drama* (Cambridge University Press, 1980) pp. 139–66.

27   Eric Hobsbawm, 'Mass-Producing Traditions in Europe, 1870–1914' in Eric Hobsbawm and Terence Ranger (eds), *The Invention of Tradition* (Cambridge University Press, 1983), pp. 263–307.

28   *Daily Worker*, 14 March 1936. And see *Daily Worker*, 11 September 1934.

29   David Cannadine, 'The Context, Performance, and Meaning of Ritual: the British Monarchy and the 'Invention of Tradition', c.1820–1977' in Hobsbawm and Ranger (eds), *Invention*.

30   Michael R. Booth, *Victorian Spectacular Theatre 1850–1910* (London: Routledge & Kegan Paul, 1981), pp. 131–33; 154.

31   See Louis Napoleon Parker, *Several of My Lives* (London: Chapman and Hall, 1928); Robert Withington, *English Pageantry: an Historical Outline*, vol. 2 (Harvard University Press, 1920).

32   Programme at Museum of London archive.

33   Programme at Labour Party Archive, London.

34   See Robert Leach, *Revolutionary Theatre* (London: Routledge, 1994), pp. 22–25; 42–50.

35   Withington, *English Pageantry*, p. 218.

36   See Ian Watson, 'Alan Bush and Left Music in the Thirties: an Introduction and an Interview', *Gulliver*, no. XXIX, German-English Yearbook (Berlin: Argument-Verlag, 1978); Hanlon and Waite in this volume.

37   André van Gyseghem, 'British Theatre in the Thirties' in John Clark, Margot Heinemann, David Margolies and Carole Snee (eds), *Culture and Crisis in Britain in the Thirties* (London: Lawrence & Wishart, 1979), pp. 209–18.

38   Steve Nicholson, 'Montagu Slater and the Theater of the Thirties' in Patrick J. Quinn (ed.), *Recharting the Thirties* (Selingsgrove, PA: Susquehanna University Press, 1996), pp. 201–20.

39   Correspondence, Benjamin Britten to Arnold Rattenbury.

40   Age Exchange Theatre Company, *Of Whole Heart Cometh Hope: Memories of the Co-operative Women's Guild* (London: Age Exchange, 1983)

41   Souvenir Programme at Co-op Union, Manchester. This account is also based on a film of the event made to propagandise the principles of co-operation (Co-operative Retail Services, South Eastern Section).

42   *Daily Worker*, 2 July 1938.

43   Quoted in *Daily Worker*, 2 July 1938.

44   Bill Williams, interviewed 18 December 1984. There had been initial resistance from within the LRD, too. For one thing, it was doubted that Williams's absence could be afforded; for another, some resistance to the populist turn still remained active.

45   Bill Williams, interview. Report by W.H. Williams to May-Day Sub-Committee of LRD (LRD Archive, London).

46   Programme-script/scenario at LRD Archive, London. Montagu Slater, *Stay Down Miner* (London: Martin Lawrence, 1936); *New Way Wins* (London: Lawrence & Wishart, 1937).

47   Programme-script/scenario.

48   See Alan Bush's preview of the pageant in *Left News*, February 1939.

49   The following account from the synopsis printed in the programme and a lacunose script-scenario. (Alan Bush, posthumous papers).

50   *Picture Post*, 5 August 1939. See also *Daily Worker*, 17 and 24 July 1939.

51   Programme and duplicated typescript at Communist Party Archive, London.

52   See Steve Nicholson, 'Theatrical Pageants in the Second World War' *Theatre Research International*, vol. 18, no. 3 (Autumn 1993) pp. 186–96.

53   Programmes at London Co-operative Retail Society and Communist Party Archives respectively.

54   Programme, script and score, Alan Bush posthumous papers.

55   History Group Committee Minutes, 10 April 1948 (Communist Party Archive).

56   Scenario and score, Alan Bush posthumous papers.

57   Duplicated typescript, Judith Williams private collection.

58   *Picture Post*, 29 July 1939.

59   Wallis, 'Ideological Production' suggests (p. 147) how *Music and the People* celebrates dialectical thinking. It also demonstrates the translation of a class-political model into one of the People versus the Exploiters. The narratives remain male-centred.

4

Richard Hanlon and Mike Waite

Notes from the Left: Communism and British Classical Music

Two Musical Moments

At the end of the Second World War, the *Daily Express* ran a competition for a piece of classical music to commemorate the allied victory. This most conservative of papers awarded its prize to a *Symphony of Liberation* by the young card-carrying communist, Bernard Stevens. Working memorable related melodic material through three short movements of contrasting mood, entitled *Enslavement*, *Resistance* and *Liberation*, the composition was readily accessible and received many performances over the next year or so. Though the point cannot be pushed too far, it would be reasonable to see this detail of postwar British cultural life as representing a culmination of related trends: the success of the broad anti-Fascist alliance in touching aspects of cultural life as well as politics in the narrow sense; the way in which this helped establish the importance of classical music in the cultural life of the nation as a whole; and an approach to the democratisation of culture which was centred on providing access to the established forms of 'highbrow' art for working-class people.

These trends had been nourished by left-wing activists and sympathisers in musical life since the 1930s. Like other intellectuals and artists, members of the musical community had been attracted in significant numbers to the left in general and to communist politics specifically in the context of the Fascist threat and the failures of capitalist economics.[1] Though predominantly middle-class, they had given much energy to encouraging 'workers' music', taking performances of 'the classics' into working-class areas and encouraging amateur choirs of working people which often sang pieces from the established mainstream repertoires as well as arrangements of traditional folk songs and 'songs of struggle' written especially for them.

The determined optimism of the workers' music activists of the 1930s, and the positive feelings that all those concerned to see left-wing ideas being expressed and received through music must have felt at Stevens' success, can be thrown into relief by considering another musical moment.

The only public performance of any of Alan Bush's four full-scale operas which took place in Britain during his lifetime was in 1974. *Wat Tyler* was no doubt an enjoyable and memorable event for those involved in its three-night run at Sadlers Wells. But the circumstances of its production only underlined the ways in which the hopes of the 1930s had faded and how 'progressive' approaches to musical culture had suffered marginalisation. The 1970s were no longer times in which anyone could seriously argue that 'the socialist movement is the only movement today capable of restoring to music a concrete social basis for its development and of utilising the power of music to the full'.[2]

The opera had been written a full 23 years earlier and had won a prize then in the Festival of Britain competition. This recognition of artistic merit did not guarantee a performance though, and Bush's treatment of the 1381 peasants' rebellion was evidently not seen as a profit-making box office attraction.[3] When the performance did come, it was heavily subsidised by funds raised tirelessly by members of the Workers Music Association (WMA), an organisation born back in the 'Popular Front' days of 1936.[4] The WMA had moved through many stages and moments in its life:[5] solid origins as an umbrella organisation bringing together musical societies from choral groups to full-scale orchestras; early hopeful plans to resource the entire labour movement through 'a new adventure which was to help the members of every British trade union and co-operative society solve their cultural perplexities and give a unifying spiritual fillip to progressive social forces';[6] proposing detailed policies for the nation's musical life to the 1945 Labour government;[7] promoting the revival of folk music from the 1950s onwards, including through developing the Topic record company which had been set up back in 1940;[8] and running successful summer schools for ordinary people wanting to improve their skills in singing, playing instruments, conducting or composing. But by the 1970s, the WMA had begun its decline into a small grouping of mainly elderly people whose main interest seemed to be the unnecessarily sycophantic championing of Bush and his music – a fan club for one neglected composer rather than an organisation which was capable of relating to, let alone resourcing and leading, any vibrant trends in contemporary music.[9]

The WMA's developing fate was part of a wider story, in which we see the musical styles achieved through the labours of Stevens, Bush and other left-wing composers of the 1930s and 1940s suffering a double marginalisation. Firstly, within the world of classical music, the style adopted by most British left composers had become discredited, was seen as old fashioned and could not compete with the Modernist schools rooted in serialism and atonality. Secondly, classical music as a whole in all its forms had become much less central to the nation's cultural life. During the 1930s and the war, the way in which the nation conceived of itself had involved images of musical life. Pictures of classical concerts being attended by hundreds of 'home front' workers and service personnel on leave in Blitz-hit London had been part of the way the British community imagined and united itself in wartime. Such impulses fed through into the postwar settlement, with its discourses about the need for the 'best' (i.e. 'highbrow') art to be as widely appreciated as possible, as part of bettering the cultural level of the nation.

The idea was that in the new postwar times, the arts were to be more than merely decorative. They were to be part of the search for new ideas and integral to progressive education.[10] But a variety of social and artistic tendencies moved reality away from this project. Classical music (as with other established 'art' forms) came fairly quickly to have again an elite or at least a 'middle-class' image, so that the public subsidies it continued to receive failed to be the motor by which it could be accessed and appreciated by the financially less well-off. Whatever the association set up in their name might have wanted, workers' musical tastes moved in the direction of the popular, the light, the apolitical and the fun.

Although the trend was disdained by those whose left-wing politics were defined by anti-Americanism and a contempt for commercialism, it was in fact an indication of the steadily increasing social significance of the preferences and consumption patterns of (young) working-class people that popular tastes came less and less to be sniffily dismissed as inferior. By the early to mid-1960s, the Beatles' latest single was a more significant British musical event than a new Britten opera or a symphony from a middle-aged composer, and the musical voices of anti-establishment protest were the teenage troubadours imitating Bob Dylan rather than the tenors and baritones standing at the back of stiffy old-fashioned choirs rehearsing stirring choruses in draughty trade union halls.

To trace the connections between these musical moments and to consider their wider contexts, this chapter looks at such issues as the attraction of left politics for a number of composers from the 1930s through to the 1950s; the connections and relationships between some of these composers' music and their politics; the ways in which these composers' careers were affected by their politics and by changing attitudes to the styles they had developed; and the broader connections between these developments and the place of 'classical' music in national life.

Attracted to the Left

A number of composers associated themselves with the left in the 1930s. In listing some of them it is not our suggestion that they can be seen as a 'group', either in terms of their musical activity or in terms of their political commitments. Even where individuals knew each other and were friends, approaches to composition were often very different, as were the motives behind a variety of forms of more or less intense forms of political engagement. And the fact that some of them were at some time members of or closely aligned with the communist movement cannot be the basis for seeing their music as 'communist' music. In most cases, political interests were far from the central concern in their artistic work, and the nature of their commitment and the length of time they were associated with organised left politics varied from individual to individual.

Before beginning to look at British composers who were attracted to the left in the 1930s, it is worth acknowledging the role played by a number of foreign refugees in shaping the context of concern about Fascism and commitment to progressive politics in which this attraction developed. The range of musicians and composers who spent at least a little time and in some cases many years in Britain, in most cases as a result of flight from European Fascism, included Hans Eisler and Ernst Meyer. The influence of such figures was often indirect rather than taking the form of the exiles tutoring or directing developments in Britain, and most composers mentioned here certainly developed their connections with the left in response to domestic concerns as well as international issues. Benjamin Britten formed an association with a number of workers' choirs and wrote pieces for a number of the most ambitious one-off events aimed at serving progressive causes through music. He also composed music for Montagu Slater's plays, *Easter 1916* and *Stay Down Miner*, in 1935 and 1936 respectively.

Michael Tippett had a more focused period of political activity, working with Bush in the early days of the WMA, having previously conducted pieces at such events as 'an immense Pageant of Labour at the Crystal Palace in 1934, to commemorate the centenary of the Tolpuddle Martyrs'.[11] Tippett became a member of the Communist Party of Great Britain (CPGB) for a short while in 1935, but his motives were complex and atypical. At that period he had adopted ultra-left politics and his intention in attending a few meetings of the Camden Town CPGB branch was a futile bid to win the comrades for Trotskyism.[12]

Elisabeth Lutyens, who was to become a follower of Schoenberg and Webern with a style that got her dubbed 'twelve tone Lizzie', had a much less intense involvement with the organised left. In the context of an early 1930s 'laced with stern realities, left-wing book clubs, and League-of-Nations minded happenings',[13] she too moved close to the CPGB and joined in the early 1940s, but seems never to have attended a Party meeting and has written that the only contacts she had with King Street were when headquarters once offered her a babysitter if she'd come to an event and when they suggested publicising her concerts in Party publications: 'two offers I declined'.[14]

Another exponent of serial technique and atonality had a more sustained and loyal involvement with Communist Party politics throughout his career. Humphrey Searle took lessons from John Ireland before studying abroad with the very different Anton Webern, whose music was largely unknown in Britain at the time. Searle's music, which was written for a range of forces and included mayor symphonies and operas as well as miniature pieces, enjoyed considerable critical acclaim, but never became very popular. His commitment to serialism and atonality not only made him a relatively 'difficult' composer for the general public, but also cut him off from the other prominent composers who stayed loyal to the Party. Nevertheless, Searle was prepared to justify his decision to follow his musical interests against the grain of popular taste and sometimes gave talks and lectures to Party members and left-wing audiences on twelve tone music and experimental techniques in composition.[15]

Another composer who joined the CPGB was Benjamin Frankel, a jazz violinist and composer of film music in the 1930s whose success in these fields provided the financial basis for him to devote time to becoming a very respected 'serious' composer after the war. His music, with its clarity and propulsive logic, draws on the lyricism of Mahler and the open spaces suggested by Sibelius and adapts serialism in an original and highly melodic way. The critic Hans Keller admired the way Frankel's symphonies – all composed after he left the Party, between 1958 and 1972 – could not be categorised as the product of a member of a school, and there have been regular attempts to promote these remarkable pieces. The main political memory of Frankel today is as the central figure in a 1955 slander hearing which received national news coverage as a result of his decision to turn renegade on former comrades and indulge in Cold War anti-communist rhetoric in order to discredit Lutyens' left-wing husband, Edward Clark, and those of Clark's witnesses who were CPGB members. One of these was Christian Darnton, one of the most enthusiastic communists among the composers we touch on here. Contemporaries have used the adjective 'religious' to describe the nature of his commitment to the cause and remember him putting himself into the front line at demonstrations where police charges were a possibility as well as lying on the ground in front of scab lorries taking food into the Savoy during the waiters' strike.

Edward Clark is worth focusing on in some detail. In the 1930s, Clark had helped organise and nurture some of the events and trends which illustrated the extent to which members of the classical music community were supportive of the left. One such event was the 1939 Festival Of Music of the People, which took as its slogan 'Art Made By The People And For The People, A Joy To The Maker And To The User'. The ubiquitous Alan Bush worked with Clark to present a huge pageant at the Albert Hall, called *Music and the People*. The event was a success in terms of numbers attending and certainly made a lasting impression on many who took part.

Henry Fair was then a member of the co-operative childrens' organisation the Woodcraft Folk, who were invited by the WMA to act as stewards for the event. 'This we were happy to do, and I well recall running up and down the stairs ushering in the hundreds of people ... The Woodcraft Folk were also asked to supply folk dancers, and to dance around the guillotine in a French Revolution scene'.[16]

It is useful to temper the rosy recollections of many participants by considering the contemporary judgement of Edward Dent, who felt that 'most of it seemed very amateurish and boring, with the usual graceful young men and lumpy not very young women bundling about over the arena in folk dances'.[17] Snide and sexist as this comment is, it nevertheless illustrates that the interplay between even the best classical music composers and left-wing politics never resulted in left-wing musical events becoming mainstream. As Alan Bush honestly judged, the 'left music movement' never stamped the mainstream musical scene with a 'left image' as was the case in the literary movement of the 1930s. 'Only in exceptional circumstances did the musical establishment take note of exceptional works. There was no general influence at all, I would say, on the musical establishment from left professional musicians – or amateur musicians for that matter.' To underline the sadly limited impact of British 'left music', Bush noted that 'it was only important in London. We had a lot of concerts and various other events, but they nearly all took place in London, and in the provincial towns I think that music didn't play a very big part in the thirties movement'.[18]

Perhaps the most significant composer who was very closely associated with organised communism for many years but stopped short of actually joining was Alan Rawsthorne. His career at this time is indicative of the wider attraction of the Party for classical musicians who were never members and shows how it was possible to be a full participant in left musical culture without signing up with King Street. All of Rawsthorne's restrained and concise music – from his chamber pieces to his concertos and three symphonies – communicates his humanism and contains very identifiable individual 'fingerprints'. His close friend, the pianist Gordon Green, has recorded of the mid-1930s that, 'like many liberal-minded persons of our age and generation, we saw the world as dividing into two camps represented in quintessence by communism and Fascism, and we believed that the former was the only power ideologically and materially strong enough to meet the menace of the latter ... neither Alan nor I could accept the discipline of CP membership. Alan set too much value on individual autonomy ... and my pacifist convictions were too deep rooted. We certainly recognised the great organising power of the CP and the fact that among its members and fellow travellers were many men of the highest intelligence, but at a much lower level of importance, we found the jargon and the ready made opinions of some of its less sophisticated members difficult to accept, and some embarrassment mingled with our admiration of these naive, though immensely dedicated followers.'[19]

Those Party figures listed above were not the first composers with significant reputations to join the CPGB. Back in 1925, Rutland Boughton had taken what was then an unusual step for a middle-class intellectual. Boughton's turn to communism was not his first attempt to develop a sustained engagement with an 'exotic' ideology. Sometimes referred to as a 'would-be English Wagner', he had been central to the 'first' Glastonbury Festivals in the years around the First World War. Some of his ambitious operas on Arthurian themes had been premiered there, including *The Immortal Hour*, which then enjoyed hundreds of metropolitan performances and was described by Edward Elgar as a work of genius.[20] Boughton's musical work for socialism can be traced back to this period – he had links with the *Clarion* paper as far back as 1911 and had assumed control of the Clarion Vocal Unions following the death of their founder Montague Blatchford. His increasingly ardent politics led to problems – the demise of the Glastonbury series can partly be blamed on such negative reactions as that of one of his chief financial backers who told Boughton bluntly that 'we are not going to have any communism here'.[21]

His links with the communist movement in the late 1920s included involvement in the earliest incarnation of the Workers Theatre Movement (WTM). Christina Walshe, Boughton's ex-mistress, was first secretary of the organisation, and Ruby Boughton took part as a singer in some of the early performances.[22] Like other presiding spirits of the WTM in its first period (1926–1928), Boughton was a kind of upper middle-class bohemian – 'a passionate advocate of Modernism in the arts and of "advanced" ways of living as well as of revolutionary socialism.' Boughton himself has been remembered by some of the real workers who did have contact with the WTM at this time as being 'very aristacratickle' and as being 'up to his neck in money and down to his ass in long hair'.[23]

This 'bohemianism' is perhaps what lay behind Boughton's difficulties in relating to the temperament of the leaders of the CPGB. His frustrations with the limited extent to which the Party made use of the talents he felt he had to offer and the career difficulties caused by his open adherence to revolutionary politics led him to resign in November 1929.[24] But his left-wing commitment was sustained, and he continued his activities with the London Labour Choral Union (LLCU), which he had formed together with the Labour Party stalwart Herbert Morrison in 1924 and quickly organised 15 choirs with around 500 members. When the LLCU became one of the organisations that came together to form the WMA in 1936, it was guided by Alan Bush who had succeeded Boughton as its musical adviser and conductor and was from the very beginning the most prominent figure in the WMA.[25]

Music and Politics: the Case of Alan Bush

It is generally agreed that Bush stands out as the British composer most explicitly and consistently concerned to apply left-wing political considerations to the shape of his art and to use his music for political ends. It therefore seems appropriate to look at his career and work in some detail here, though we would like to stress that Bush should not be seen as being a representative figure for any of the other composers we have mentioned above. Nor do we suggest by focusing on Bush that he is the most significant or accomplished figure, in *musical* terms, of those musicians discussed in this chapter.

Parts of the explanation for Bush's lifelong commitment to organised communism must be that his political socialisation took place in the 1920s, when a man of his background needed some determination to make the then unfashionable move to the left (he was from a wealthy family and always enjoyed a private income which meant there was little pressure on him to work for a living); that there were intensely personal experiences informing this determination (his eldest brother had been killed in Flanders in 1917); and that his interest in the relations between music and politics had been nourished by sustained personal contact with some of the most significant left-wing artistic figures of his day (when studying in Berlin in the late 1920s, and during visits to other European countries, he had spent time with Bertolt Brecht and Hans Eisler). He joined the CPGB in 1935 after a few years on the left wing of the Independent Labour Party and in the Labour Party itself, and from these early days worked hard to connect his political and musical passions.[26]

His politics came to be expressed more and more directly in his music as his career developed. Bush's early work was characterised by an individual and rigorous Modernism, best illustrated by the 1929 string quartet which most critics still consider his masterpiece. Bush insisted that the title of *Dialectic* should not be taken as suggesting that the piece attempts to illustrate Marxist thought in music, but simply as referring to the way in which a synthesis emerges from interplay between themes, in which material is 'argued out with a mastery of contrapuntal technique and concentration of musical thought unparalleled in English music of the period'.[27] Bush's music of the early and mid-1930s has been described as shaped by a unique method of composition, 'allied to serialism, but based on tonality ... many of the works up to the Piano Concerto of 1937 were written in the most advanced central European idioms of the day'.[28]

Though it does not mark a sudden, all-at-once turning point in Bush's music, the piano concerto clearly illustrates his increasing concern to shape his work explicitly around politics. It includes a choral ending, to a text by his regular collaborator Swingler, describing the orchestra as a model of the integrated society which socialism would bring, developing work, art and creativity. The concerto's premiere received such an enthusiastic response from the left-wing audience who had crowded into the BBC halls to hear it that the somewhat conservative conductor Adrian Boult cut short the applause and took the edge off the composer's triumph by moving straight into an unscheduled rendition of *God Save The King*.

Choosing texts with literal content is a straightforward way of expressing beliefs through music and Bush wrote many songs and larger works with explicit left-wing messages throughout his career.[29] He seems to have believed that making an explicit connection with his politics was necessary in order to avoid the fate suffered by works of earlier composers of a revolutionary disposition – Beethoven's symphonies, for example, were being misused in the 1930s in the service of German Fascism. Bush's operas all dealt with issues of oppression and resistance: *Men of Blackmoor* (1956) told a tale of Northumbrian miners in the early nineteenth century; *The Sugar Reapers* or *Guyana Johnny* (1964) was about the Guyanese peoples' fight against British imperialism; and *Joe Hill, The Man Who Never Died* (1967) told the story of the American trade union organiser and political songwriter who was framed on a murder charge and executed in 1915.

It needs to be acknowledged that Bush's fairly prolific output was fuelled by his politics and that although 'the plots of his operas and themes of his vocal work have often been criticised for reflecting his political views too directly and for lack of psychological subtlety ... the themes he has chosen to treat have been a powerful stimulus, and have given Bush a new sense of direction'.[30]

Bush also sought to shape his approaches to musical composition around his political beliefs. In a way which was particularly marked after the war, he began to relax, simplify and adapt his style in an attempt to reach a wide, non-specialist audience. In his *Nottingham Symphony* of 1949, for example, commissioned for the city's quincentenary celebrations by the local Co-operative Society, Bush set himself the task of 'completely eliminating confusing elements'. This project was linked to the views which had built up during the war that 'proper' music should not just be for the social elite, but should be widely accessible, and that it was part of the duty of an artist with talent to serve the nation through developing the extent to which ordinary people could enjoy 'culture' and be educated in its ways.[31]

Careers Crippled by Communism?

There is, though, a more negative set of reasons and consequences involved in the shift in Bush's style during the late 1940s. Essentially, he aimed to conform to the norms and expectations being imposed by Zhdanov and the cultural policemen of the Soviet Union. Russian composers of the status of Prokofiev and Shostakovich experienced such cultural Stalinism as oppressive and restrictive, and increasingly wrote their most stimulating and emotionally charged works for 'the bottom drawer', whilst finding ingenious ways to send out signals of dissent through the use of irony and pastiche in their public works.[32] Bush, on the other hand, freely chose Socialist Realism and voluntarily discarded the challenging experimental techniques which had made him such a distinctive young composer. In their place, he adopted a dogmatic commitment to producing 'national music', which drew from local tradition and based musical phrases on patterns of national speech, but also involved (at least in its Stalinist form) a reactionary opposition to Modernist techniques which were habitually denounced as the artificial inventions of 'cosmopolitans' (which was, of course, a code word for Jews). Thus, whilst Shostakovich was sticking his neck out in the Soviet Union with such musically and politically challenging works as the songs based on Jewish folk poetry, Bush was setting leftish doggerel to simple folk tunes in the context of a political culture which would have allowed him to explore the many interesting musical worlds which his earliest pieces had hinted at.

Broader considerations here may help to set the development of Bush's career in a wider context. It is worth stressing that interest in folk music has not always resulted in classical composers' work becoming less interesting or less experimental. Indeed, Bela Bartok's journey towards complex and polytonal music was fuelled by his analysis of supposedly 'archaic' Eastern European folk music.[33] Many other composers have also succeeded in integrating folk melody or techniques into their music so as to make it the *more* complex and challenging, ranging from the Greek Nikos Skalkottas to a wide variety of contemporary composers from former Soviet and East European countries, including Stefan Niculescu and Bronius Kutavicius. But Bush's shift towards folk style was patterned on an affirmation of what has been called English 'radical pastoral' – a nostalgic post-Romantic style centred on the work of Holst and Vaughan Williams who were the routine targets of the 'young champions of the Schoenbergian revolution'.

Thus the stylistic choice made by Bush related to an ongoing rivalry and interplay between experimental Modernism and the simple 'directness' and 'forthrightness' for which Vaughan Williams' work was celebrated by his followers.[34] In taking up and developing the 'radical pastoral' tradition in English music, Bush was no doubt conscious of the politics which had motivated its prime exponents. Inspired by William Morris, Holst had joined the Hammersmith Socialist Club late in 1895. Vaughan Williams often recalled (as here, in a letter to Boughton) how he and a few friends had 'read the Fabian tracts and, in opposition to the majority of undergraduates, become socialists' whilst at Cambridge in the 1890s.[35]

But it was primarily the political need or desire to follow Soviet cultural orthodoxy which motivated Bush. The hold which the Moscow line on music had on Bush can be sensed in a testy exchange during an interview he gave in the early 1960s. He offered a strong condemnation of 'formalism', judged a crime by Zhdanov for the way in which it prioritised experimentation with, and interest in, *form* over the communication of *content*, which communists were expected to know should be a positive content communicating the human effort to overcome problems and make a better world and so on. Asked whether he had ever himself been 'convicted' of formalism, Bush accepted that he had, 'and with justification. Mine was an unconscious formalism for I never practised formalism for its own sake. My music was always designed to express the feelings within me. But the education I had received had not clarified my mind on this point, and I became much influenced by Central European music of the twentieth century. Whilst I never actually wrote atonal music, I ceased to strive in any way after a national style. My music became eclectic and I was concentrating too much on the technical procedures. I lost my balance'.

The interviewer had done his research, and was able to challenge Bush on his denial of ever having flirted with atonality. Pressed on the matter of whether or not he had ever as a younger man used the twelve tone technique, a question to which Bush quickly realised they both knew the true answer, he retreated to the statement that 'it is a theory of Marxism that you should employ all the technical apparatus of the bourgeoisie against them', pointing out that he had only made use of the deviant and cosmopolitan techniques pioneered by Schoenberg in order to illustrate their decadent nature. In reading such exchanges, and in some of Bush's essays, one is reminded of the tone of confessions required in a Moscow show trial, even though the 1963 interview was being conducted in his 'compact and tidy' study, in which 'a large window affords a pleasant view into the garden of his suburban home' in leafy Hertfordshire.[36]

Zhdanovism was welcomed even more enthusiastically by the 70 year old Rutland Boughton, who had rejoined the Party in 1945 and had been an enthusiastic participant in the postwar World Peace Conferences. He wrote to Bush that 'the Russian CP criticism of composers is, as you can imagine, a great satisfaction to me. Having struggled ... under the implication of being a musical reactionary, it is good to see daybreak ahead'. Rather than toning down his delight at Zhdanovism in his public comments, Boughton's contribution to the Party press was *more* strident. He diagnosed Shostakovich, Prokofiev, Katchaturian and others as 'suffering from a musical disease' and being influenced by the Western poison associated, 'curiously enough', with the 'Russian White émigré Stravinsky' and with Schoenberg ... 'cacophony ... musical ugliness consequent on an emotional upset ... resulting from the love of discord for discord's sake ... a reactionary movement back towards the earliest musical noises made by savage tribes'.[37]

Whilst Boughton's feelings in the late 1940s can be seen as the emotional response of an old man who feels that his own artistic style and choices are at last being acknowledged and validated by the Russian authorities, some element of the explanation of Bush's voluntary adherence to the cultural requirements of the leaders of Soviet and East European communism must be the fact that he became something of an establishment composer behind 'the Iron Curtain'. Whilst suffering relative neglect in Britain, he was regularly performed and recorded in the Soviet Union and in other communist countries, particularly in the German Democratic Republic.[38] *Wat Tyler* was premiered there and Bush's other three operas were East German commissions. The contrast between the way his work was promoted and taken up in the East and his limited reputation and standing in his own country was often cited by his supporters as evidence of anti-communist and political discrimination.

In fact, the main reasons for the limited number of his British peformances and broadcasts were that his musical styles were increasingly unfashionable at the BBC and among concert programmers: other composers whose politics were uncontroversial but who also generated traditionalist classical works from folk material experienced a decline in popularity in the late 1950s and 1960s. At the same time, a number of composers with various degrees of left-wing affiliation whose experimental styles were coming into vogue experienced a boost to their career as Bush fell from that limited level of favour he had enjoyed.[39] In so far as blocks were put in Bush's way by figures in the British musical establishment, it seems that this may have been the result of jealousy and resentment at the way that his loyal Stalinism and personal links with figures in the East German establishment, rather than the quality of his music, led to him receiving European performances at a time when this was quite unusual for all but a very few other British composers.[40]

The one moment of clear-cut political discrimination which Bush did suffer was in 1940, when the BBC moved to ban his work as a consequence of his support for the communist-sponsored Peoples' Convention, an initiative which stopped well short of revolutionary defeatism, but was nevertheless widely perceived as likely to undermine the patriotism needed for the war effort against Hitler.[41] Even in this context, the direct ban was lifted when Vaughan Williams protested and threatened to sever connections with the BBC. Such a moment must be assessed against such facts as that Bush's long tenure as Professor of Composition at London's Royal Academy of Music (RAM) never became controversial. Notwithstanding the fact that Bush was always careful not to use his position to proselytise or to recruit students for the Party, it is clear that Bush's public and outspoken support for left causes could have focused Cold War 'McCarthyism' against him at RAM. That this never happened is evidence of the limits of anti-communist discrimination against him and more generally in relation to the musicians and composers who were associated with British communism.

The Frankel Affair Assessed

Although it is sometimes cited as evidence of Cold War hysteria in Britain, 'the Frankel affair' also shows the limited extent to which the careers of those composers who had joined or associated themselves with the Party were 'crippled by communism'. The background to this 'affair' in the complicated internal politics of the International Society for Contemporary Music (ISCM) and its British Section has been carefully detailed by Harries and Harries.[42] The essence of the matter is that Edward Clark, a member of the Society for 30 years, was being marginalised, and his arguments on how the ISCM should operate and the aesthetics it should promote were being regularly defeated. Benjamin Frankel, whose 'serious' compositions had earlier been enthusiastically promoted by Clark, was central to the group which Clark now saw as working against him. Things began to come to a head when Clark thumped Frankel during a 1953 meeting, had his honorary presidency of the ISCM revoked and then became convinced that Frankel was spreading what he saw as slander about him.

In June 1955, Clark brought forward a court case against Frankel. The divisions which seemed to lie behind the truth or falsity of the allegations and accusations were varied – radical versus middle ground music, the British section of the ISCM against the central organisation and, perhaps, Gentile against Jewish musicians. But the division that led to the case's prominence was that of communist stalwart against communist apostate. Clark and his key witnesses, the CPGB members and composers Christian Darnton and Bernard Stevens, argued that Frankel had been saying that Clark had been embezzling ISCM funds, which Clark insisted he had not. Frankel's defence was that he had certainly not made such statements, but should he have done so, the statements would have been true. This clever tack was developed by turning attention to the reliability and credibility of Clark's witnesses.

Frankel's argument was that the Communist Party wanted to harm him because he had left in 1952, with maximum publicity, in protest at show trials and executions in Prague. He suggested that Darnton and Stevens were lying at the behest of the Party, as all communists were supposedly prepared to do. And he made much use of the courtroom sensation that had been generated by Stevens' refusing to take the oath on the Bible. The jury decided that Frankel had not uttered the slander and Clark lost the case in a decision which implicitly rejected the testimony of Stevens and Darnton.

Although this outline description of the case might lead to a reading of it as communists being rubbished and disdained by the courts, there are other facts which need to be acknowledged. The jury softened the blow with a 'small print' statement that 'Mr Clark's reputation is not in doubt', thus separating the judgement as to whether Frankel had engaged in slander from the accusations about Clark's honesty, and the financial burden of the case was shared between the parties. Furthermore, even though Clark's legal representatives knew that the judge didn't like their client, his friends or their politics, they felt that 'McCarthyism never percolated the judiciary' and remembered that the judge warned the jury against being swayed by politics.[43]

Although political prejudices did play some part in the ups and downs of careers, the aftermath of the Frankel affair reinforces our key argument in relation to the composers we are considering in this chapter: that they were *not* a group of variously talented and inclined composers whose reputations and careers were all damaged because of anti-communism, but that their particular musical and career fortunes rose and fell as a result of the artistic and aesthetic choices made by themselves and by the sponsors of composed music in the wider context of the shift away from general attention which classical music experienced nationally. Whilst Frankel enjoyed some success in the 1950s, at a time when the forms of music Clark had supported were relatively neglected, in the 1960s he came to suspect that he had paid the price for the trial. By this time musical fashions were back in line with the Modernism Clark had championed, and his partner Lutyens' work was more prominent than that of Frankel ... although that did not stop her indulging in an ugly anti-Semitism that had become more focused and explicit around the time of the Frankel affair.

Between Cheltenham and Darmstadt: the Changing Locations of Classical Music

Whilst Lutyens (and the loyal Communist Party member Humphrey Searle) were able to benefit from the Modernist ascendancy of the 1960s, in which their handling of Webern's influence was more readily understood and accepted, many of the composers mentioned in this chapter were finding that their careers were closing with a *fading* of recognition and appreciation.

Such different figures as Stevens, Darnton, Rawsthorne and Boughton (who died in 1960 at the age of 82) found themselves classed together with 'the Cheltenham symphonists' who were increasingly disparaged as Modernism took hold. Indeed, the very term 'Cheltenham symphony' lost its simple purpose as a description of one of the many British works premiered at the decreasingly important annual festival held in the town and began to be used as a mildly insulting way of branding the products of composers whose traditionalism made them seem irrelevant to modern developments.

In the context of the more general fall from fashion of national style linked to melodic, tonal styles, the skills which many composers of the British left had applied to the integration of popular folk tunes into compositions with more or less literal programmatic content were judged worthless by musicians and listeners who were turning to such figures as Stockhausen, Boulez and Berio (and, it should be said, such outspoken leftists and communists as Henze, Nono and Xenakis) and the avant-garde traditions and experimental techniques they were developing from German, French and other mainland European bases.

Interesting debates and developments were still set to take place in the shifting and contested boundaries and spaces between traditionalism and Modernism. They deserve to be traced and explored in relation to the career of Cornelius Cardew, which began with composition in the most challenging abstract styles of the late 1950s, and then developed through to a fierce Maoist condemnation of his former mentor in the extraordinary 1974 tract, *Stockhausen Serves Imperialism*, in which he sets out the views that informed his 'mass music' turn to 'accessible' melodic folk styles. Cardew's most important achievements centred on the remarkable and influential work of the improvising group AMM and the London based Scratch Orchestra from the mid and the late 1960s. There are a number of interesting points of contact between Cardew's life and career and the main story we are drawing attention to here.

The composer was the nephew of the bandleader Phil Cardew, who had been a sponsor of the 1940 People's Convention and one of the communist figures in musical life whose career does seem to have been blighted by discrimination resulting from his politics. Perhaps these family connections help explain the particular resentment which was directed against Cardew when his art was not in line with communist preferences. He was the composer targeted in a document which the CP Music Group prepared in 1962 as a supplement to the *British Road To Socialism* programme. Considering 'modern trends in composition', they decided that 'the latest fashion – indeterminism – in particular is a policy of despair, an admission that life has become too much for us, and that we are incapable of controlling it, something no communist can agree to'.[44]

In spite of the contrasts between the different styles and theories he used and espoused at different points, the whole of Cardew's career can be read as a series of varied attempts to address goals which were consistently held: the democratisation of musical practice and the search for new languages which challenged orthodoxy in order to achieve 'connectedness' with musicians he knew and with wider audiences, both real and imagined.[45] Cardew's efforts to raise questions about the ways in which serious composed music was created, presented, appreciated and experienced, and to find innovative, even revolutionary, ways to make modern music accessible, throw into sharp contrast the failure to deal with these matters by the composers and classical musical figures most closely associated with the CPGB.[46] The limited awareness of questions of musical democracy and participation in the postwar WMA may be judged from the tone of awe struck in some anecdotes about Bush by his summer school followers in the association, where his willingness to pass the toast at the breakfast table, drink Barnsley bitter among school participants in the evening, and 'even' his preparedness to give up his single bedroom one year 'so that a talented young student who unfortunately suffered from insomnia could be made more comfortable' have repeatedly been cited as evidence of the unique and distinctive ability of the WMA to break down the barriers and mystifications around music-making.[47]

Even the most strenuous efforts of Bush and of the other composers who worked with the WMA in composing pieces which they could then support workers' choirs or amateur orchestras in performing stopped well short of disrupting or even questioning some of the established conventions about musical life. Their concerns in relation to accessibility of the arts merely generated campaigns to get local authorities to spend a little more money on concert halls and subsidies for local music societies. And their response to new trends, ideas and experiments was an increasingly defensive assertion of the value of the aesthetic choices they had made, all too often presented in the arrogant tones of those whose communism made them feel and sound certain about everything.[48] Bush and the critics who shared his views suffered an isolation which 'echoed that of (establishment) Soviet music in the world ... a grounding in a nineteenth century academic tradition and his existence in a national musical culture deeply entrenched in nostalgia and stylistic stasis saw him overtaken by events elsewhere'.[49]

Thus, as their increasing marginalisation within the world of classical music was compounded by the comprehensive sidelining of the classics in national culture generally, their responses became very negative, ranging from the resigned and disillusioned to the apoplectic. During the 1950s, the tone of much of their music lost its straightforward optimism and became more ironic as the hopes of the immediate postwar period were tempered by disappointment. There was an overlaying and introducing of dissonance into the responsible, high-minded moods which had characterised such works as Stevens' *Symphony of Liberation*.

Towards the end of the 1950s, folk music 'revived' (or was reinvented) in a movement which the WMA did much to support.[50] But the most vital energies in musical life were increasingly being found in pop music, a genre which left traditionalists disapproved of. Even though groups like the Beatles were from working-class backgrounds and their music drew from blues and folk traditions, those who had taken it on themselves to develop and voice the British communist line on music could not change tack and get on board with the new scene in order to relate to it in such a way as might have allowed them to contact and influence younger people (including many Young Communist Leaguers who were dancing to the Kinks and Manfred Mann in spite of Executive Committee misgivings).

In terms which suggested that the editors would have condemned the Beatles as enemies of the people if they had had the power to, the cyclostyled quarterly bulletin of the CP Music Group reported a discussion held late in 1964 to try to fathom why it was that young people liked the group. 'In spite of invitations having been sent out to Young Communist League branches, there was a marked absence of young people,' for some reason, and the old timers had to get on with it themselves. *Music and Life* noted the spluttering anger of an unnamed professor at RAM who was almost certainly Bush. Describing the screaming audience participation, he compares it to voodoo in British Guyana and concludes that we have reached a new low in mass culture. He thought that the Party in 1965 should do far more to propagate those (ideologically acceptable) forms of music which it had been shown 'do appeal to young people, such as the Ian Campbell Folk Group'.[51]

The divisions which were emerging around musical tastes in the 1960s pointed to the way that generational divisions were disrupting the work of those who sought to manage British communism and its values and connections to wider society.[52] Few of those children of the communists of the 1940s and 1950s who had an interest in playing music were interested in learning 'strict counterpoint in the Palestrina style' and applying such discipline to the development of a national style informing concert music for 'the workers' of the WMA's and CP Music Group's imagination.[53] Instead, coming out of and feeling part of the crowds of *real* working-class students and apprentices who made up their audiences, they could be found in bands like Pink Floyd (Roger Waters) and the Who (Pete Townsend), setting their controls for the heart of the sun and hoping to die before they got old.[54]

Coda

Somewhere between the 1930s and the 1970s, the strands which left-wing activists sought to weave together between classical music, popular taste and the organised Labour Movement had become irrevocably unravelled. The models of democratising culture and the means by which it was thought that musical culture could be used to resource left-wing parties and the wider Labour Movement had become unworkable long before the crisis of decline which the organised working class faced from the 1970s. Explicitly political music in this decade did not come from the traditions which we have looked at here – at least directly. From the Strawbs' hit *Part of the Union*, turned into a recruiting song by Jack Jones' TGWU even though the band had recorded it originally 'as a kind of joke', through to the Anti-Nazi League or *Morning Star* sponsored events featuring bands like the Clash, Essential Logic, Scritti Politti and the Slits, there was much evidence of music's ability to express anger and determination and to draw in audiences for left causes. But the points of contact between classical music and this potential were few and sporadic. Most of the composers mentioned here, including Britten, Tippett and even Stevens, were sadly listed by Bush in a 1966 article published in East Germany as long ago having 'moved away from' or 'having withdrawn from direct participation in the struggle of the working class'.[55] Very few younger composers came to replace them by taking up positions on the left. And even in these cases, the usually implicit political content of works expressed the personal choices and allegiances of individuals, rather than reflecting and pointing to systems of contact and interplay between the two increasingly marginal worlds of the organised left and the concert hall.

Acknowledgements

We would like to thank the staff responsible for the CPGB Archive at the National Museum of Labour History, Manchester; volunteers and workers at London's Marx Memorial Library (and particularly Mike Squires who read columns of Rutland Boughton's vitriol from the *Daily Worker* to us over the telephone); staff responsible for the Stocks Massey Music Library held at Lancashire County Council's library in Burnley; and to staff at the Henry Watson Music Library at Manchester Central Library. Thanks are also due to those participants who commented on our paper 'Alan Bush and the WMA' at the May 1996 Manchester conference on culture and the CPGB; and to Andy Croft and James Gibb who commented on earlier drafts of this chapter. Responsibility for factual accuracy (and inaccuracy) and for the judgements and arguments in this chapter lies, of course, entirely with ourselves.

Notes

1 Given that this chapter focuses on composers, it is as well to mention that other members of the musical community attracted to the left in the 1930s included such players, conductors and critics as Martin Lawrence, Geraldine and Mary Peppin, James Gibb and Tom Russell.

2 Alan Bush and Randall Swingler, assisted by members of the WMA and the Left Book Club Musicians Group, *The Left Song Book* (London: Gollancz/Left Book Club, 1938).

3 Bush's fate in not seeing his prizewinning opera performed was not so frustrating as the experience of Christian Darnton. His work, *Fantasy Fair*, for which Swingler had written the libretto, was not seen by all the judges before it was decided not to award a prize. He assumed that this was political discrimination and campaigned to persuade the Composers' Guild to take legal action against the Arts Council.

4 The July/August 1974 *WMA Bulletin* was given over to material celebrating the *Wat Tyler* production. The editors judged that 'the work involved both in fund raising and helping to make the production known in advance ... has had a revitalising effect on the WMA'.

5 Highlights of the early years are detailed in *Twenty One Years*, (London: WMA, 1957). Reissued, London: WMA, 1994.

6 Will Sahnow, in *Tribute to Alan Bush on his Fiftieth Birthday*, (London: WMA, 1951), p. 28.

7   WMA, *A Policy For Music in Post-war Britain*, (London: WMA, 1945), 24 pp. For an important example of similar thinking, see Jack Lindsay, *British Achievement in Art and Music*, (London: Pilot Press, 1945).

8   The folk music/roots record label's beginnings are traced by Ken Hunt in 'A Topic of Conversation', *Folk Roots*, no. 47, May 1987, p. 19 ff. Hunt notes that 'the WMA worked this potential silver mine, it would appear, less than assiduously for, rather than becoming a profitable source of income for the [Communist] Party, it became a financial liability, a burden to be jettisoned'. The WMA's history of its first *Twenty One Years* is clearer than Hunt about the first activities of 'the Topic Record Club', which was set up in 1940 and 'provided a record of the month to members at 1s 6d ... mostly recordings of popular workers songs and one or two interesting musical works by Soviet composers – hitherto unknown to this country but soon to become firm favourites in the wave of Anglo-Soviet friendship which swept the country in 1941 when the Soviet Union entered the war and such songs as *Steppe Cavalry* and *Sovietland* were broadcast and recorded', p. 5.

9   The 'cult of personality' which grew up around Bush is illustrated by the regular birthday tributes in special and expanded issues of the *WMA Bulletin*, the CP Music Group's quarterly *Music and Life*, pamphlets such as the *Tribute to Alan Bush on his Fiftieth Birthday*, (London: WMA, 1951), and by most contributions to the 'Alan Bush Special Supplement' of the *WMA Bulletin*, London, April, 1996.

10   This point was developed in a broadcast by Roderick Swainston, BBC Radio 3, October 1995.

11   Tippett, *Those Twentieth Century Blues; an autobiography*, (London: Hutchinson, 1991), p. 44.

12   There is an informative short note on 'Michael Tippett and the Trotskyist Movement' in Sam Bornstein and Al Richardson, *Against The Stream ; a history of the Trotskyist movement in Britain 1924–1938*, (London: Socialist Platform, 1986), p. 296.

13   Elizabeth Lutyens, *A Goldfish Bowl*, (London: Cassell, 1972), p. 74.

14   Lutyens, *A Goldfish Bowl*, p. 233. Lutyens' biographers have judged that 'she did not find the Party congenial', although she is unlikely to have confided whatever misgivings she had with her close relations, given that her 'gesture' in joining 'was not received well in a family whose politics were to be better represented, if in an extreme form' by her nephew Nicholas Ridley, the Thatcherite government minister of the 1980s. Meirion Harries and Susie Harries, *A Pilgrim Soul : the life and work of Elisabeth Lutyens*, (London: Michael Joseph, 1989), p. 100.

15   See, for example, references to a talk given by Searle in Marx House, London, as late as July 1962, in issues of the CP Music Group quarterly *Music and Life* in that year.

16   Letter to Mike Waite, 30 January 1996.

17   Cited in Harries and Harries, *A Pilgrim Soul*, p. 98.

18   Ian Watson, 'Alan Bush and Left Music in the Thirties', *Gulliver*, issue 4, Germany, 1978, pp. 85–86.

19   Gordon Green, 'Record of a Friendship', *The Composer*, London, 1971.

20   See Michael Hurd, *Rutland Boughton and the Glastonbury Festivals*, (Oxford: Clarendon Press, 1993). This book consistently underplays Boughton's long commitment to communist politics and seeks to explain it away when it has to be acknowledged.

21   Donald Brook, *Composers' Gallery : biographical sketches of contemporary composers*, (London: Rockliff, 1946), p. 32. There are detailed points on Boughton's pre-war career and its wider context in Chris Waters, *British Socialists and the Politics of Popular Culture 1884–1914*, (Manchester: Manchester University Press, 1990).

22   Raphael Samuel, 'Theatre and Socialism in Britain (1880–1935)' in Raphael Samuel, Ewan McColl and Stuart Cosgrove, *Theatres of the Left 1880–1935: workers' theatre movements in Britain and America*, (London: Routledge & Kegan Paul (History Workshop series), 1985), p. 34 and note on p. 97.

23   Samuel, 'Theatre and Socialism in Britain', p. 50.

24   Hurd, *Rutland Boughton*, p 197. Boughton continued to consider himself a communist, and rejoined the Party in 1945, resigning again in 1956.

25   Another of the organisations which came together into the WMA was the Workers' Music League, which was formed from members of the WTM in London by Joan Horrocks. She had earlier taken on the running of the music side of the WTM, 'issuing song sheets and song books'. Tom Thomas, 'A Propertyless Theatre for the Propertyless Class', in Samuel, MacColl and Cosgrove, *Theatres of the Left*, pp. 90 and 94.

26   Bush wrote an extremely interesting, well-written and often charming and moving autobiographical essay which is collected in the volume In My Eighth Decade and Other Essays, (London: Kahn and Averill, 1980).

27   Murray Schafer, *British Composers in Interview*, (London: Faber and Faber, 1963), p. 59, and Hugh Wood in Howard Hartog, ed., *European Music in the Twentieth Century*, (Harmondsworth: Penguin Books, 1957), p. 148.

28   Stanley Sadie, ed., *The New Grove Dictionary of Music and Musicians*, (London: Macmillan, 1980 edition), p. 502.

29   Notable amongst these are *Lidice* and *To the Men of England*. There are also a great many arrangements of international socialist songs and anthemic compositions such as *The Great Red Army*, *A Song of Friendship*, *Make Your Meaning Clear*, *Against the People's Enemies*, *Truth on the March* and *Till Right Is Done*. Members of the 'what if' school of history might like to reflect that if British communists had ever come to power, they would have most likely made such a piece into the national anthem.

30   Sadie, *The New Grove*, p. 503.

31   The WMA had spelled out such expectations. 'As we see it, the postwar problem is how to bring music – and the best music –to the ordinary people, how to stimulate their appreciation, and how to bring out their natural abilities for making music ... this implies a programme of action. Not necessarily direct political action. Not necessarily the manning of barricades or even the writing of Beveridge symphonies. But action as a musician nevertheless.' *A Policy for Music In Post War Britain*, (London: WMA, 1945), p. 3.

32   Prokofiev was never again to enjoy the satisfaction of living and working without the threatening shadow of totalitarian disapproval looming over him. He died on the very same day as Stalin. For a comment on the impact of Zhdanovism on Shostakovich, see Richard Hanlon, 'The Music Was Not To Blame', in *The Personal and the Political: Socialist History number 6*, (London: Pluto Press, 1994), pp. 40–41.

33   See an interesting discussion around this point in Michael Chanan, *Musica Practica; the Social Practice of Western Music from Gregorian Chant to Postmodernism*, (London: Verso, 1994), pp. 234–35.

34   See the chapter by Paul Harrington, 'Holst and Vaughan Williams : Radical Pastoral' in Christopher Norris, ed., *Music and the Politics of Culture*, (London: Lawrence & Wishart, 1989).

35   Harrington, 'Holst and Vaughan Williams', p. 108.

36   Schafer, *British Composers in Interview*, p. 58.

37   Rutland Boughton, 'Why They Criticise Their Soviet Composers', *Daily Worker*, 1 March 1948.

38   In his obituary of Bush for the *Guardian*, John Amis notes that 'behind the Iron Curtain, after the war', the composer 'was an honoured guest, treated as an equal by the leading Soviet composers', 3 November 1995.

39   Modernist composers with different forms of commitment to left politics coming into fashion at this time included the Italian Luigi Nono and the German Hans Werner Henze (living in self-imposed exile in Italy) as well as the British composer Maxwell Davies.

40   One example of a communist composer who failed to make a breakthrough in Eastern Europe and thus fell unhappily between two stools was Darnton. His frustrations in respect of his opera *Fantasy Fair*, mentioned above in note 3, were compounded when the Polish Ministry of Culture, who had promised him a production, lost interest after

they realised it contained 'jazz' elements. Darnton's exasperation can easily be imagined – he was being quite 'politically correct' and was using jazz to represent the 'decadent' West! This is an example of the double bind in which some communist composers found themselves in the Cold War – too 'political' for the West, too 'musical' for the East.

41   Other 'musical' supporters of the Convention movement included Boughton, Edward Dent, Frankel and Rawsthorne. For a careful discussion of communist politics in this period, see Kevin Morgan, *Against Fascism and War*, (Manchester: Manchester University Press, 1989), especially pp. 201–213.

42   Harries and Harries, *A Pilgrim Soul*. Our account of the slander trial here draws on its careful treatment in this book, to which readers are directed for fuller details.

43   Leslie (now Lord) Scarman, in Harries and Harries, *A Pilgrim Soul*, p. 178.

44   *Music and Life*, February 1962.

45   In an aside in an interesting recent book on one strand of development of 'the musical avant-garde', Georgina Born (sometime member of Henry Cow) has stated that the 'Scratch Orchestra, and AMM, emphasised changes in the social relations of music production and performance in their attempts at a new interactive, collective, and non-hierarchical group practice. The social dimension of music was seen as a crucible for experiments in collective and democratic social relations'. *Rationalizing Culture*, (Berkeley, LA and London: University of California Press, 1995), p. 58. Stimulating points on Cardew were made in a documentary by Sam Richards in the series 'Towards Musical Democracy', broadcast on BBC Radio 3 in February 1996.

46   In fairness we should note that Bernard Stevens grappled with these issues to some degree at a theoretical level in the late 1960s. By then he had left the Communist Party, though he remained a Marxist.

47   Joan Horrocks, in Ronald Stevenson, ed., *Time Remembered: Alan Bush: an 80th birthday symposium*, (Kidderminster: Bravura Publications, 1981), p. 86.

48   There were occasional arguments of 'the case for modern music' in the WMA and CP Music Group circles, as in Bill Sweeny's enthusiastic review of Stockhausen's *Gruppen* in *Music and Life*, February 1968. But the editors' bewildered questions about the music of Berio and Boulez are more typical.

49   Paul Stump, 'Quavering Ideals', *New Statesman and Society*, 15/29 December 1995, pp. 54–55.

50   See the chapter by Porter elsewhere in this book ; and Ewan MacColl, *Journeyman; an autobiography*, (London: Sidgwick and Jackson, 1990); and Dave Harker, *Fakesong; the manufacture of British 'folksong' from 1700 to the present day*, (Milton Keynes: OUP, 1985), especially chapter 11, on A. L. Lloyd; and Ian Watson, *Song and Democratic Culture in Britain*, (London: Croom Helm, 1983), especially chapter 10.

51   'The Good and Bad Of Pop Music', *Music and Life*, CP Music Group, January 1965. The reference to British Guyana fits with the fact that this was the period Bush was working on *The Sugar Reapers*.

52   For a wider discussion of generational conflicts in British communism in the 1960s, and their links to cultural politics, see Mike Waite, 'Sex'n'Drugs'n'Rock'n'Roll (and Communism) in the 1960s', in Geoff Andrews, Nina Fishman and Kevin Morgan, eds, *Opening the Books; essays on the social and cultural history of the British Communist Party*, (London: Pluto Press, 1995).

53   Bush's treatise on Palestrina was written in 1948 and remains a textbook in some musical colleges.

54   Andy Croft has pointed out to us a host of other children of communist musicians who have become more or less well-known pop stars, including UB40's Campbell brothers, Kirsty McColl and Chris Cutler (sometime member of Henry Cow and promoter of a wide range of remarkable new music).

55   'Musicians and the Working Class in Britain', in Humboldt Universität, *Essays in Honour of William Gallacher*, (Berlin: Humboldt Universität, 1966).

5

Maroula Joannou

Sylvia Townsend Warner in the 1930s[1]

At the end of Sylvia Townsend Warner's *Summer Will Show*, set in Paris amid the revolutionary turmoil of 1848, the protagonist is found reading a political tract which she has been distributing in the streets: 'A spectre is haunting Europe – the spectre of Communism. All the powers of old Europe have united in a holy alliance to exorcise this spectre.'[2] Like the cultured and privileged Sophia Willoughby in *Summer Will Show* Sylvia Townsend Warner – the only daughter of a master at Harrow public school – might at first appear an unlikely convert to the cause of communism. But Sylvia and her partner, Valentine Ackland, had been politicised by another spectre that was haunting European intellectuals in the 1930s, the spectre of Fascism: 'What influenced almost all the people of my generation more than anything was the Reichstag fire trial ... And that was very well reported in *The Times* and made me very interested in ordinary politics. And that of course made me immediately interested in the doings of the Black Shirts, and *that's* how I came to meet the people in *Left Review* and eventually to do some writing.'[3]

This chapter is concerned with Sylvia Townsend Warner as a representative of the seemingly limitless energy and indefatigable optimism that was characteristic of many communist intellectuals of the 1930s. The political commitment of Sylvia, and other writers of her generation who shared her vision of international justice, peace and freedom, has now become a historical memory, but was for many years an inspiration to socialists of a younger generation like myself. It is not my purpose here to establish what is axiomatic to many of Sylvia's readers, that she is among the most accomplished and versatile of early twentieth-century English writers, or to expand upon the explanations which have been advanced to show why her work has often failed to receive the recognition that its quality deserves. As Simon Watney has put it, Sylvia was 'intensely literary, a far leftist, an intellectual to her fingertips, a woman and a lesbian' and all this was 'hardly a combination likely to ensure her reputation in modern Britain'.[4] Instead, I want to discuss her as a figure who is crucial to an informed understanding of the left cultural history of the 1930s; as a woman whose writing brings into question the notion that Modernism was the alpha and omega of literary creativity and the idea that the 1930s was a disreputable, dishonest decade in English letters.[5] There is also another orthodoxy that I wish to challenge and that is the orthodoxy to be found in respected histories of the left in Britain which have consistently marginalised or excluded the achievements of women.[6] To this end, I shall note the importance of Sylvia's political activism; her close association with the path-breaking journal, *Left Review*; her work in support of the Spanish Republic; and the poems and novels that she wrote in the 1930s. There are a number of contexts in which Sylvia is essential to a revisionary reading of the 1930s. Among these are a new understanding of the significance of the left initiatives against rural poverty, the importance of gender and sexuality, and of the role of women in the Spanish Civil War, in which the well-known 'story of concerned male artists and writers has now to be supplemented by the story of engaged women writers and artists.'[7] Moreover, the contribution of lesbians, of whom Sylvia and Valentine are the best-known representatives, to the history of the Communist Party has yet to be properly acknowledged. For feminists today Sylvia remains important as a writer in whom feminist and socialist and lesbian consciousness are combined, and whose sense of obligation 'to do something for my sex'[8] can be consistently traced throughout her life and art.

Political Activity

Sylvia's life and work were the antithesis of everything held dear in the metropolitan literary circles from which she distanced herself by her flight into the depths of rural England early in the 1930s. From there she continued to write 'with deadly accuracy and wit of the chronic meanness of spirit of British society'[9] for much of the rest of her life. By the time she came to join the Communist Party in 1935 Sylvia was already a well-known novelist on the strength of *Mr. Fortune's Magot* (1927), *The True Heart* (1929) and the best-selling *Lolly Willowes* (1926), which she later came to dislike because of its lack of social relevance: 'It seems so poor a welcome for the General Strike – though I had begun it long ago in 1923/4.'[10] Such an established writer was an invaluable recruit to the influential group of Communist Party's literary intellectuals who at that time included Edgell Rickword, Ralph Fox, Randall Swingler, Alick West, Edward Upward, Montagu Slater, Christopher Caudwell and Cecil Day Lewis.

Sylvia excelled at speaking in public ('I have developed quite a talent for public speaking, and ornament the platforms of Wessex. I enjoy it very much, especially the applause').[11] She contributed to the *Daily Worker*, in which she wrote an appeal for a boycott of Japanese goods in protest against the Japanese aggression against China, and reviews of Storm Jameson's *No Time Like the Present* and Margaret Goldsmith's *Seven Women Against the World*.[12] She was involved in the launch of the Left Book Club's Writers and Readers' Group and addressed the Group's meetings at Bournemouth, Street and Portsmouth.[13] She lectured at the Left Book Club summer school in Welwyn in Hertfordshire in 1937 and reviewed Hilary Newitt's *Women Must Choose* for the LBC monthly paper, *Left News*.

Sylvia does not appear to have been on any national party committees in the 1930s, but she threw herself energetically into local political activities in Dorset where she worked for the Labour Party candidate in 1935. Her name appeared on a list of people opposed to the Jubilee celebrations in *Left Review*[14] and she organised an alternative party to the 'official' celebrations taking place in her village. Sylvia and Valentine were the key initiators of communist activity in the locality, organising an abortive women's protest against bad housing, a peace march through Bridport and a rally in Dorchester addressed by Vera Brittain and George Lansbury. Sylvia served as the secretary of the Dorset Peace Council and travelled further afield to do political work: to London to attend May Day rallies, to Wales in support of striking miners and to Brussels as a member of the British delegation to an international peace conference organised by the Communist Party in 1936. She called in to party headquarters on her return from the Spanish Civil War.

The Work for *Left Review*

Sylvia was closely involved with the hegemonic project associated with *Left Review*.[15] This was the journal of the British section of the Writers' International, later the Association of Writers for the Defence of Culture. As Margot Heinemann has argued, *Left Review* signified an important transitional moment in the cultural work of the left, helping to define 'the beginnings of a more open, historically-minded kind of Marxism – what we may now call "Gramscian"', while 'the very existence of *Left Review* was a sign that the British Communist Party was beginning to take cultural politics more seriously'.[16] The contributors to *Left Review* included many discontented Labour Party members who were openly in sympathy with the Communist Party's aim of establishing the broadest possible alliance against Fascism.

Left Review, which was edited for part of its history by a woman, Amabel Williams-Ellis, placed great emphasis upon recovering 'the democratic, popular traditions of English literature and history'.[17] The authors in whom it was especially interested included Milton, Bunyan, Owen, Morris,

Burns, Dickens, Swift, Langland, Shakespeare and Shaw. Among the 20 or so women who wrote for it were Valentine Ackland, Barbara Niven, Catherine Carswell, Pearl Binder, Storm Jameson, Vera Kay, Christina Stead, Joan Robinson, Willa Muir, Charlotte Haldane, Pamela Hansford Johnson, Nancy Cunard, Phyllis Bentley, Naomi Mitchison, Winifred Holtby and Philippa Polson. While *Left Review* was far from achieving gender balance among its contributors women featured more prominently in its pages than in comparable publications of the time.

In its short existence between 1934 and 1938 *Left Review* functioned as an important forum in which writing for the 'common people' was discussed. Warning of the dangers of literary conformity, Virginia Woolf suggested that there might be 'some force, influence, outer pressure which is strong enough to stamp itself upon a whole group of different writers so that all their writing has a certain common likeness'. The notion that the dead hand of authority weighed heavily on the committed writer of the 1930s has proved difficult to dispel.[18] However, Sylvia's adjudication of a *Left Review* writing competition in 1936 clearly intimates that there was no Party line to be followed. What was demanded of Party writers was freshness and originality: diversity of style and outlook were positively encouraged: 'When we can publish rich, vigorous and varied stories, this will be the finest propaganda for the working-class cause.'[19]Good writing was seldom overtly propagandist, workerist or narrowly prescriptive and Sylvia's criticism of the typical proletarian story was of the poverty of its stock responses. ('You are quite right, Bill. I am going to join the Communist Party, as it is the only party fighting back against the bosses' offensive.')[20]

The Democratisation of the Countryside

Sylvia featured prominently in the communist-led initiative to democratise the countryside of which the mass trespass on Kinder Scout in 1932 is the most famous example. The second issue of the *The Country Standard*, a campaigning paper which is still in existence, and which was established by the Communist Party in 1936 as a forum for the discussion of rural issues, contains a spirited contribution by Sylvia about the working conditions of agricultural labourers.[21] Although Sylvia admired the industrial achievements of the Soviet Union her vision of socialism owed much to the English socialist traditions, particularly to William Morris's *News from Nowhere* with its emphasis on the English countryside. Much of Sylvia's poetry is pastoral with recognisable echoes of John Clare and Thomas Hardy in its subject matter and diction. The heroine of her first novel, *Lolly Willowes* (1926), is a fugitive from urban conformity who rejoices in the sylvan and the pagan pleasures of her newly found freedom in the countryside, 'the weight of all her unhappy years behind her at last'.[22]

The subject of Sylvia's long narrative poem, *Opus 7* (1931).[23] 'a truthful pastoral in the jog-trot English couplet', is Rebecca Random, a gin-besotted but sturdily independent old woman who ekes out a living in the countryside by selling flowers.

The revolutionary rhetoric of the Internationale made much of the insurrectionary potential of the peasantry but in the 1930s the Communist Party prided itself on deriving its support from workers in the large industrial cities. Sylvia's public opposition to rural squalor was a salutory reminder to many socialists that poverty and deprivation were not exclusively urban phenomena. As Patrick Wright has observed, it was 'thanks to Sylvia and Valentine the Weld estate became a source of the British left's view of the misery of rural conditions'.[24]

Sylvia was strenuously opposed to any attempt to romanticise the English countryside ('English pastoral was a grim and melancholy thing').[25] For all the enjoyment that she derived from her cottage garden and the natural beauty by which she was surrounded, Sylvia perceived the countryside in terms of its social relationships rather than its picturesque qualities; she was always alert to the evils of tied cottages which were permitted to fall into disrepair and exploitative landlords whose way of life she despised. Her attempts, with Valentine, to transform a patch of rural England into a little Soviet included encouraging the village 'to run its own pleasures without any interference from the gentry'[26] and initiating a scheme to lend radical books. The short pieces about rural issues which Valentine wrote for *Left Review* were published by Lawrence & Wishart in book form as *Country Conditions* (1936).

Sylvia's curiosity about her neighbours was expressed in the minutely observed details of everyday life which she amassed. This kind of fact-finding was a popular activity in the 1930s, occupying amateur volunteers in the 'Mass Observation' project as well as professional writers like Orwell and Priestley. Her interests listed in an article written for *The Countryman* included 'the average amount of unpaid overtime filched from the labourer ... the average weekly mileage covered by the labourer's wife who fetches all her water from the well and carries all her slops to the ditch ... the average number of sleepers per bedroom and of rats per sleeper, and the speculation whether insufficient sleep is not quite as serious a defect in country hygiene as bad housing, impure water, and monotonous diet'.[27]

The Relationship with Valentine Ackland

Although much has been written about the Auden-Isherwood circle and the importance of homosocial bonding among male intellectuals on the left, little is known about lesbians in the Communist Party. Claire Harman has suggested that Sylvia's 'wholehearted enthusiasm for Communism' was determined by 'the way in which it underlined the sense of ostracism she and Valentine had been made to feel because they were lesbians'.[28] To Sylvia and her partner the Communist Party was a place of safety in which deeply held political convictions which were reviled elsewhere were reinforced and their sense of isolation diminished. Moreover, Sylvia had great respect for the Party's unique ability to bring together intellectuals and ordinary working people who would never otherwise have met on a basis of equality. For Sylvia and Valentine the Communist Party fulfilled some of the functions of a large extended family, recognising them as a couple and enabling them to work together for common objectives, judged, if they were judged at all, on the usefulness of the work they did in public and not their sexuality. Both have left particulars of their intimate relationship: Sylvia in the diaries which were published posthumously, and Valentine in her autobiographical fragment, *For Sylvia: an Honest Account*. This describes Valentine's relationships with men and women ('with women I was released and happy, and I gave happiness and pleasure; and I did not need any kind of help from drink, to make me feel competent and secure in making love').[29] A diary entry of Sylvia's records, 'our most completed night, and after our love I slept unstirring in her arms, still covered with her love, till we woke and ate whatever meal it is lovers eat at five in the morning'. She said, remembering Lady C, 'that Lawrence in heaven would be taken down a peg to see us, specimens of what he so violently disliked, loving according to all his precepts, and perhaps the only lovers that night really to observe them'.[30]

Their 40-year relationship, sustained until Valentine's death in 1969, with a brief separation in 1938, was for all intents and purposes a marriage. Sylvia thought of it as such from a very early stage – a diary entry in 1933 refers to their second 'anniversary'.[31] *For Sylvia: an Honest Account* is an agonised apologia for Valentine's history of drinking and other problems: 'But I know beyond any doubt that my whole being is rooted in Sylvia – and that out of my being, however base and bad it seems to be, this matchless faith and love has grown, which is the love she has for me and I have for her.'[32] This happy, if sometimes turbulent, partnership was maintained within the context of a political party in which outward respectability was required of all its leading cadres and homosexual activity of any kind was looked upon askance. This was a culture in which Sylvia appears to have been more comfortable than Valentine ('I suppose CP is at once too tight a pot and too draughty for her roots to settle in to their own comfort. She feels at once unused and misused').[33] Sylvia was probably as open as it was possible to be about the nature of her relationship with Valentine, bearing in mind the social stigma commonly attached to lesbian sexual practices and the danger of scandal in the small, conservative rural communities in which she and Valentine were both well known. Moreover, the homophobic attitudes of the day required circumspect behaviour of lesbian couples after the public furore which had caused Radclyffe Hall's lesbian novel, *The Well of Loneliness*, to be banned in 1928.

The Poetry

Whether a Dove or a Seagull (1934) is a collection of 109 poems, 55 of which are attributed to Valentine and 54 to Sylvia. Very few of the poems are given individual titles but a key at the back identifies each by the initials of the author.[34] The volume is described as 'an experiment in the presentation of poetry'[35] and the prefatory note explains that it is 'a protest against the frame of mind which judges a poem by looking to see who wrote it'.[36] The unusual mode of organisation reflects Sylvia's desire to link her own name as an established writer (with three published books of poetry behind her)[37] to that of her partner, an unknown poet who was twelve years younger. The poems are not marked by the revolutionary rhetoric of Sylvia's poems in *Left Review*, 'Some Make This Answer', ' Red Front' and ' In this Midwinter'.[38] A number deploy the idioms of the traditional ballad, fairy story or folk tale using deceptively simple diction and odd, rustic archaisms. Many are love poems, usually oblique, but sometimes, as in Valentine's ' the eyes of body, being blindfolded by night',[39] unexpectedly direct; poems in which the sexual identity of the love object is sometimes withheld or disguised by the use of a misleading pronoun (as Auden does in the most beautiful of all 1930s' love poems, 'Lay Your Sleeping Head, My Love'). Janet Montefiore has noted that this sleight of hand 'disrupts what could otherwise be thought of as purely female discourse'.[40] Claire Harman has justified her exclusion of all Sylvia's poems in *Whether a Dove or a Seagull* from her edited edition of *The Collected Poems*[41] on the grounds that their proper place is alongside Valentine's. The effect of this somewhat surprising editorial decision is to ensure that a body of poems which are clearly of importance to students of lesbian literature and history cannot be scrutinised by those readers who do not have access to the original edition which has long been out of print.

Support for Republican Spain

Sylvia and Valentine first went to Spain as medical auxiliaries in 1936; they were two of a total of some 200 women from the English-speaking countries whose stories are not well known, although the extent to which 'the great campaign to aid and support the Republic was a women's movement' has now been recognised.[42] As Jim Fyrth has put it, 'no other conflict in which their own countries were not directly involved has ever drawn so many women to give so much.' [43]

The scale of involvement of intellectuals who, with Edgell Rickword, believed that 'the continued existence of human cultural activity is dependent upon the Spanish people's successful defence of their freedom and political independence'[44] was remarkable. In Sylvia's words, writers were finally 'released from the old fear that by giving one's support as a representative of culture to a cause one had at heart one might be doing that cause more harm than good'.[45]

Sylvia and Valentine spoke on platforms at medical aid meetings, and organised local screenings of *The Defence of Madrid*, fundraising events and support for refugee Basque children. The campaign to reverse Britain's policy of non-intervention was spearheaded in Parliament by Ellen Wilkinson, who had visited Spain in a women's delegation led by the Duchess of Atholl: 'What they [the Spanish people – *my insertion*] could not understand was ... that non-intervention should be used by this country in such a way as to form the most effective weapon that General Franco had.'[46] Naomi Mitchison was also prominent in the campaign to allow the Spanish government to buy arms. Rosamond Lehmann, whose husband Wogan Phillips was wounded in Spain, appealed in the *New Statesman* for books for Spain ('the wounded in Spain are as likely as we are to find dull books dull and bad books bad')[47] and booked the Queen's Hall in London for what Virginia Woolf described as 'Rosamond's great meeting for writers to protest against Spain'.[48] Another *Left Review* writer, Charlotte Haldane, was secretary of the Dependants' Aid Committee which helped the families of International Brigaders.

Sylvia's anti-clericalism – Valentine was brought up as a Catholic and reverted to religion later in life – was confirmed on her visit to Barcelona: 'I have never seen churches so heavy and hulking and bullying, one can see at a glance that they have always been reactionary fortresses. I did not find a single person who resented their being gutted.'[49] 'Barcelona' is an eyewitness account of the July revolution with churches 'cleaned out exactly as sick-rooms are cleaned out after a pestilence. Everything that could preserve the contagion has been destroyed'.[50] In a similar vein, Valentine's poem, 'Instructions from England', criticises the selective vision of those who note 'churches burned and popes in pain' but not 'the men who die'.[51]

A visit to Valencia and Madrid as delegates to the Second Congress of the International Association of Writers for the Defence of Culture took place in July 1937. The journey was fraught with difficulties. Sylvia and Valentine were refused travel permits, 'as representatives of culture we were not included in the Foreign Office's *Weltanschauung*, cultural reasons are not among those reasons recognised as valid reasons for wishing to travel to Spain.'[52] Sylvia later contrasted the unco-operative attitudes of British officials to the smooth passage afforded Mr Semple, a businessman whose journey from Spain to Portugal is expedited by a supposedly neutral representative of the British government in a short story, 'With the

Nationalists'.[53] In 'Benicasim', published in *Left Review*, the town in which the 'risen-from-the-dead' (the republican wounded) are tended is the 'bright-painted landscape of Acheron'.[54] 'Waiting at Cerbere' (the border post on the French side) was published in Spender's *Poems for Spain* in 1939 and written in a similar lyrical vein to 'Benicasim':[55]

> And on the hillside
> That is the colour of peasant's bread
> Is the rectangular
> White village of the dead.
>
> No one stirs in those streets
> Out of those dark doorways no one comes.
> At the tavern of the Black Cross
> Only the cicada strums.
>
> And below, where the headland
> Strips into rock, the white mane
> Of foam like a quickened breath
> Rises and falls again;
>
> And above, the road
> Zigzagging tier on tier
> Above the terraced vineyards,
> Goes on to the frontier.

Valentine's enthusiastic account of the Congress in which 60 intellectuals, among whom were Neruda, Malraux, Hemingway and Ehrenburg, 'discussed the immediate problems of literature in the fight against Fascism and for the liberty of peoples' appeared in the *Daily Worker* in July 1937.[56] Sylvia too found the experience exhilarating: 'We learned to hear ourselves spoken of as *los intelectuales* without dreading words usually so dubious in good intent, without feeling the social embarrassment and defiant shrinking.'[57] These journeys implanted her lifelong love of the Spanish people and landscape ('I've never seen people who I admired more. I never again saw a country I loved as much as I loved Spain')[58] expressed in articles, poems and stories including 'El Heroe' and 'Journey to Barcelona' in *The Collected Poems* (1982)[59] and two short stories, ' A Red Carnation', and 'The Language of Flowers' in *A Garland of Straw* (1943). On her return Sylvia attempted to raise money from women writers to pay for a consignment of soap ('Women, for some reason, are supposed to be particularly concerned with soap; at any rate, we have a reputation for being practical').[60] She was a signatory for the Spanish government in Nancy Cunard's *Authors Take Sides on the Spanish War*: 'I am for the people of Spain, and for their Government, chosen by them and true to them. And I am against Fascism because Fascism is based upon mistrust of human potentialities. Its tyranny is an expression of envy, its terrorism is an expression of fear.'[61] In 1937 she became secretary of the Association of Writers for Intellectual Liberty.

The Second World War

The start of hostilities in 1939 saw Sylvia loyally defending the Communist Party's opposition to the 'imperialist' war. With Walter Greenwood, Patrick Hamilton, Rosamond Lehmann and Sean O' Casey she was a signatory to the People's Convention (a litmus test of the loyalty of Party members and of its fellow travellers). She spoke at an anti-Fascist conference in New York in 1939. A spirited article, 'The People Have No Generals', complaining about the civilian population's lack of preparation for war appeared in the first issue of the journal, *Our Time*,[62] in 1941. In a letter to Nancy Cunard about the conscription of single women into the war effort Sylvia complained that 'being kept by a husband is of national importance enough. But be femme sole, and self supporting, that hands you over, no more claim to consideration than a biscuit'.[63] She added 'the great civil war, Nancy, that will come and must come before the world can begin to grow up, will be fought on the terrain of man and woman, and we must storm and hold Cape Turk before we talk of social justice'.[64]

The Fiction

Sylvia Townsend Warner's claim to be a writer of distinction rests largely upon her fiction. Her seven novels are disparate in content and form. Two written in the 1930s, *Summer Will Show* (1936) and *After the Death of Don Juan* (1938),[65] are historical novels, a form of writing to which she was to return in *The Corner that Held Them* (1948). She had already shown an interest in historical fiction in several short stories including 'The Democrat's Daughter' (1935) which is concerned with the republican sympathies of a member of the aristocracy.[66] Both *Summer Will Show* and *After the Death of Don Juan* are novels set at historical moments of acute social upheaval and internecine conflict. Sylvia's understanding of the potential uses of the historical novel is similar to that of Georg Lukacs, whose seminal Marxist study, *The Historical Novel*, was written in 1937 but not translated into English until 1962.[67]

For Sylvia, as for Walter Scott, whose work Lukacs cites to exemplify the best in the traditions of the historical novel, historical crisis was never an abstraction. On the contrary, 'The split of the nation into warring parties always runs through the centre of the closest human relationships.

Parents and children, lover and beloved, old friends, etc. confront one another as opponents or the inevitabilty of this confrontation carries the collision deep into their personal lives.'[68] As John Coombes has observed, the revolution of 1848, which Sylvia chose as a setting for *Summer Will Show*, was of particular significance to left-wing intellectuals in the 1930s because supporters of the *Front Populaire* in France (a 'brief, problematic and ultimately fissiparous alliance of proletarian and liberal loyalties')[69] which had probably reached the height of its organised strength in 1936, sometimes claimed the earlier revolution as a historical antecedent.

In *Summer Will Show*, Sophia Willoughby, who is separated from her husband, Frederick, is inadvertently drawn into the revolutionary struggle through her husband's mistress, Minna. The enchanting Minna, who becomes Sophia's lover, is a member of a despised minority; a refugee who endured the terrors of the Jewish pogroms as a child – a reminder to the reader of the persecution of the Jews in Hitler's Germany – and has survived to tell the tale. When hostilities break out in the streets of Paris Minna is killed by Sophia's young black nephew, Caspar (the illegitimate son of her father's half-brother, a West Indian merchant), who, in a dramatic enactment of how contradictory subject positions are created by the accidents of history, has taken arms in support of the French government. As in *Mansfield Park*, the family fortunes are tainted by their association with the slave plantations in the Caribbean. As in *Lolly Willowes*, in which her nephew Titus is an uninvited visitor who disrupts Lolly's enjoyment of her rural idyll, the return of Caspar, who is shot by a newly empowered Sophia, is the unwanted reminder of family responsibilities from which women in pursuit of personal happiness cannot escape.

Summer Will Show was Sylvia's attempt to write a novel inspired by Marxist and feminist ideas, and critics have recently been attracted by its incisive critique of class and racial privilege and sexual propriety. Terry Castle has analysed *Summer Will Show* as an example of 'post-marital lesbian fiction', that is, a novel in which a woman-to-woman love affair decanonises 'the canonical structure of desire itself'.[70] Jane Marcus has observed that 'it is in *Summer Will Show* that Sylvia most fully confronts the question, "what is the role of the bourgeois (and female) intellectual in making the revolution?"'[71] This question was of immediate importance to Sylvia in the context of the Spanish Civil War and her membership of a party which at that time expected its members to work towards a revolution in Britain. Sylvia depicts the great transformations of history in eighteenth-century Spain and nineteenth-century France as the transformation of popular life. In *Summer Will Show* she illustrates how important historical changes affect everyday life and the effect of material and psychological change upon characters who react quickly, and sometimes violently, without always having a full understanding of the cause. As Barbara Brothers has pointed out, there is a similarity between the ending of the events of 1848 and the outcome of the Spanish Civil War, although Sylvia could not, of course, have been aware of this at the time she was writing.[72]

Sylvia Townsend Warner's writing reverberates with the strong dislike of all patriarchal structures including the 'stud-farm frame of mind which debases not only woman, but the entire race'.[73] Moreover, she attempted to situate her work resolutely within women's literary traditions. A lecture on the subject of 'Women as Writers', given to the Royal Society of Arts in 1959 (with Leonard Woolf in the chair) extends some of the arguments about women and writing in *A Room of One's Own*. Here Sylvia cited 'ease and appreciation in low company' and 'workaday democracy' as characteristics of the woman writer: 'A woman has to be most exceptionally secluded if she never goes to her own back door, is not on visiting terms with people poorer than herself.'[74] Jane Austen, the subject of a monograph which she wrote for the British Council in 1950,[75] was a strong influence on Sylvia's writing. Mr Alban, a Trotskyist with literary leanings, has a passion for Austen's novels in her short story, 'Persuasion'.[76]

What is immediately striking about *Summer Will Show* is the self-conscious imitation of different styles of women's writing; the opening chapters are reminiscent of Fanny Burney, Charlotte Brontë, George Eliot and Jane Austen. Sophia Willoughby, who possesses a fine house, a country estate in Dorset and servants who attend to her every whim, had been 'brought up in a world policed by oughts' (p. 290) and to regard the 'chiefest part of mankind as an inferior race, people to be addressed in a selected tone of voice and with a selected brand of language' (p. 286). The death of her two children from smallpox disrupts a cushioned existence that had hitherto remained undisturbed despite her husband's wandering eye ('how control a man by resolution or reason, when any pretty face or leaning bosom could deflect him?' (p. 78). A labourer on her estate reminds Sophia that the death of children thereabouts is common: 'There's the smallpox, and the typhus, and the cholera. There's the low fever, and quick consumption. And there's starvation. Plenty of things for children to die of' (p. 96). Sophia's 'ambition for seemliness and prosperity' (p. 80) is abandoned; she pursues her husband to Paris, intending to become pregnant by him once again, but instead falls in love with the wayward Minna and stumbles inadvertently on the Paris uprising of 1848. The issues of sexual and political revolution in *Summer Will Show* are seen to be inextricably linked and the one to be a prerequisite for the other. It is only after Sophia has obtained her sexual freedom and acknowledged the depth of her feeling for Minna that she desires to partake in the revolution. In an episode which makes strange the rivalry that is usually expected of women in relation to men, the hapless Frederick is surprised to find his mistress and his wife 'seated together on the pink sofa, knit into this fathomless intimacy, and turning from it to entertain him with an identical patient politeness' (p. 157). Moreover, 'neither woman absorbed in this extraordinary colloquy had expressed by word or sign the slightest consciousness that there was anything unusual about it' (ibid.).

Sophia leaves Frederick not just because her sympathies are with the revolution but 'because I saw a chance of being happy and took it' (p. 277). As Minna puts it, she has run away from domesticity and 'from sitting bored among the tyrants. From Sunday schools, and cold-hearted repectability, and hypocrisy and prison' (p. 217). But Frederick cuts off her income to signal his displeasure. As the character of Ingelbrecht (loosely modelled on Engels) points out, relationships of gender and class are analogous and mutinous workers and wives must expect to receive their proper punishment.

Like the other improbable liaisons in the novels that preceded *Summer Will Show* – between the eponymous heroine of *Lolly Willowes* and the devil, the missionary, Mr Fortune and his boy disciple, and the orphaned Victorian servant Suky Bond and her mentally retarded husband in *The True Heart* [77] – the liaison between Minna and Sophia dramatises Sylvia's conviction that joy and sadness are inseparable and unpredictable aspects of the human condition and that the will-o'-the-wisp of happiness must be pursued with a total disregard for convention, propriety, guilt and 'the impeding petticoat' of sexual decorum (p. 4). Thus Sophia muses:

> Behind every love or respect stood a monitorial reason, and one's emotions were the expression of a bargaining between demand and supply, a sort of political economy. At a stroke, Minna had freed her from all this. Unbeautiful and middle-aged, unprincipled and not intellectual, vain, unreposeful, and with a complexion that could look greasy, she offered her one flower, liberty. One could love her freely, unadmonished and unblackmailed by any merits of body or mind. (p. 291)

It is only a short step to Sophia's complete change of attitude to the working men who appear to feel none of the 'awkward hostility which she could not help feeling towards them. They were cordial, sincere, dispassionate; discovering that she was English they began to question her about the Chartists, the poor-law, the franchise, the Fenians, the amount of bacon eaten by English peasants, the experiments of the Co-operatives' (p. 241). By the end of the novel 'the decorum of class had gone, the probity of class had gone too ... Even the prudence of her class had shrivelled' (pp. 288–9).

Her next novel, *After the Death of Don Juan*, is a veiled response to the Spanish Civil War, 'a parable if you like the word, or an allegory or what you will, of the political chemistry of the Spanish War, with the Don Juan – more of Molière than of Mozart – developing as the Fascist of the piece.'[78] Sylvia, who had spent ten years co-editing the voluminous *Tudor*

Church Music, was an accomplished musicologist whose plans to study under Schoenberg in Vienna had been disrupted by the 1914 war. *After the Death of Don Juan*, a literary sequel to Mozart's opera *Don Giovanni*, provided an opportunity to combine her interests in literature and music in a novel ostensibly set in eighteenth-century Spain but redolent with modern meaning for any reader familiar with the lassitude, self-seeking and corruption that were to prove such a fertile breeding ground for Franco's Fascists in twentieth-century Spain. The novel begins after the death – or rather the disappearance – of the aristocratic philanderer, upon whose departure the infatuated Dona Ana, and the time-serving Don Ottavio, journey from Seville to Don Juan's remote castle at Tenorio Viejo in the provinces to inform Don Saturno of his son's fate. Scattered over the wide estates on the fatiguing journey small groups of peasants labour: 'No songs, no dances, no sounds of happy industry! How different from Italy!' (p. 15). The baroque settings of the castle are the backcloth against which the affectation of the grandees is satirised and the suffering of the tenants is enacted. For generations the descendants of Don Juan and his kind have oppressed the peasants whose forefathers were forced to hew the stone and build the castle with their own hands (p. 116): 'For the rich, quarrelling never so much among themselves, corrupting each other's wives, driving steel into each other's bellies, were as one in cheating the poor' (p. 98). Don Saturno devises well-intentioned schemes to educate the peasants. He reflects that 'in times to come his simple village will become a hive of revolutionaries'. Meanwhile, they have 'learned enough book-keeping to swindle the tax collector' (p. 54).

But liberal ideas for irrigating the land do not get very far: 'For prating of philanthropy and progress, Don Saturno paid no real attention to people, did not censure and chastise' (p. 155). This leaves a vacuum to be filled by the sacristan, Don Gil, who loves the sense of power and represents the control exerted by the Catholic Church over the people (ibid.). The villain lurking in the wings is naturally Don Juan himself who returns to his fiefdom 'immured in profligacy as in a cloister, a vocation as irrevocable as the vocation of a St John of the Cross fastened him to the card-table and the alcove' (pp. 193–4). Don Juan has no sentimental attachment to the past. The tenants are to be evicted from the land when the irrigation scheme makes this more profitable. A delegation is formed to express the peasants' anxieties in relation to water for their crops and troops are ordered into the village and instructed to shoot. The novel ends with the village on the brink of civil war.

After the Death of Don Juan is a remarkable evocation of the deep-rooted divisions in Spanish society and the stolid resignation and fatalism common to both the aristocrats and peasants in that most deeply troubled of countries. As one of the peasants reflects, 'if Tenorio Viejo were to become a paradise it would still be in Spain' (p. 109).

Two further novels were to come, *The Corner that Held Them* (1948) and *The Flint Anchor* (1954). Unlike many intellectuals who repudiated their communist convictions – most famously in the recantatory statements from Koestler, Spender, Richard Wright and others, *The God that Failed*[79] – Sylvia retained her radical politics long after her membership of the Communist Party lapsed in the 1950s – there appears to have been no formal resignation from the Party. But her pre-war reputation went into decline after 'the worm of McCarthyism had got into English critical fashion'[80] during the 1950s. In common with many of her contemporaries on the left she became a literary casualty of the Cold War. Asked why she had written no more novels after *The Flint Anchor* she replied, 'We had fought, we had retreated, we were betrayed, and now we were misrepresented.'[81]

Notes

1   My interest in Sylvia Townsend Warner began when I read Wendy Mulford's superb study, *This Narrow Place: Sylvia Townsend Warner and Valentine Ackland: Life, Letters and Politics, 1930–1951* (London: Pandora, 1988). I am indebted to Wendy Mulford for many insights into Sylvia's life and for the pleasure that her wonderful book has given me on each successive reading. I wish to thank the executors of Sylvia Townsend Warner's literary estate for permission to reprint the poem, 'Waiting at Cerbere', and Andy Croft and David Margolies for reading and commenting helpfully on this essay.

2   Sylvia Townsend Warner, *Summer Will Show* (London: Chatto and Windus, 1936) p. 406.

3   Val Warner and Michael Schmidt, 'Sylvia Townsend Warner in Conversation', *PN Review*, 23, vol. 8, no. 3. (1981), p. 35.

4   Simon Watney, 'Who is Sylvia? Townsend Warner: Love's Labours Lost', *The Village Voice* (23 January 1990), pp. 54–56, p. 56.

5   This misconception of the period has been discussed by Andy Croft in *Red Letter Days: British Fiction of the 1930s* (London: Lawrence & Wishart, 1990), pp. 15–29.

6   See, for example, Willie Thomson, *The Good Old Cause* (London: Pluto Press, 1982).

7   Valentine Cunningham (ed.), *Spanish Front: Writers on the Civil War* (Oxford: The Oxford University Press, 1986), p. xxxii.

8   Townsend Warner, *The Diaries*, 30 June 1930, p. 65.

9   Simon Watney, 'Who is Sylvia?', p. 56.

10   Quoted in Rattenbury, 'Plain Heart, Light Tether', *PN Review*, 23 (1981), p. 47.

11   Letter to Steven Clark dated 11 May 1938, in William Maxwell (ed.), *The Letters of Sylvia Townsend Warner* (London: Chatto and Windus, 1982) p. 51.

12   Sylvia Townsend Warner, 'Your Shopping and Murder', *Daily Worker*, 15 November 1938, p. 2, 4 December 1935, p. 7, 18 December, 1935, p. 7.

13   *Left News*, April 1938, September 1938, February 1939.

14   *Left Review*, May 1935, p. 91.

15   See David Margolies (ed.), *Writing the Revolution: Cultural Criticism from Left Review* (London: Pluto Press, 1997), for a recent discussion of the work of this periodical.

16   Margot Heinemann, 'Left Review, New Writing and the Broad Alliance Against Fascism', in Edward Timms and Peter Collier (eds), *Visions and Blueprints: Avant-Garde Culture and Radical Politics in Early Twentieth-Century Europe* (Manchester: Manchester University Press, 1988) p. 118.

17   Ibid., p. 123.

18 Virginia Woolf, 'The Leaning Tower', Leonard Woolf (ed.), *The Collected Essays of Virginia Woolf*, 4 vols (London: The Hogarth Press, 1966–7) p. 163.
19 Sylvia Townsend Warner, 'Competition in Criticism', *Left Review*, January 1936, p. 179.
20 Ibid., p. 178.
21 Sylvia Townsend Warner, 'Underpayment of Agricultural Workers: Black Figures from Blue Books', *The Country Standard*, April 1936, p. 5.
22 Sylvia Townsend Warner, *Lolly Willowes; or the Loving Huntsman* (London: Chatto and Windus, 1924) p. 149.
23 'The Way By Which I Have Come', p. 480.
24 Patrick Wright, *The Village That Died for England: The Strange Story of Tyneham* (London: Jonathan Cape, 1995) p. 140.
25 *The Dorset Chronicle*, quoted by Valentine Ackland, *Country Conditions* (London: Lawrence & Wishart, 1936) p. 69.
26 Valentine Ackland, letter to Julius Lipton, quoted in Mulford, *This Narrow Place*, pp. 61–62.
27 Sylvia Townsend Warner, 'The Way By Which I Have Come', *The Countryman*, vol. xix, no. 2, (July 1939) pp. 484–5.
28 Claire Harman, *Sylvia Townsend Warner: A Biography* (London: Chatto and Windus, 1989) p. 142.
29 Valentine Ackland, *For Sylvia: an Honest Account* (London: Chatto and Windus, 1985) p. 119.
30 *The Diaries*, 12 January 1931, p. 77.
31 Ibid., 2 January 1933, p. 94.
32 Ackland, *For Sylvia*, p. 132.
33 *The Diaries*, 2 November 1937, pp. 100–101.
34 Sylvia Townsend Warner and Valentine Ackland, *Whether a Dove or a Seagull: Poems by Sylvia Townsend Warner and Valentine Ackland* (London: Chatto and Windus, 1934) p. 152.
35 Ibid.
36 'Note to the Reader', *Whether a Dove or a Seagull*.
37 Sylvia Townsend Warner, *The Espalier* (London: Chatto and Windus, 1925), *Time Importuned* (London: Chatto and Windus, 1928), *Opus 7* (London: Chatto and Windus [The Dolphin Books], 1931).
38 *Left Review*, February 1936, p. 214, *Left Review*, April 1935, pp. 255–57, *Left Review*, January 1935, p. 101, *Left Review*, March 1938, p. 841.
39 Townsend Warner and Ackland, *Whether a Dove or a Seagull*, p. 43.
40 Janet Montefiore, *Feminism and Poetry: Language, Experience, Identity in Women's Writing* (London: Pandora, 1987) p. 178.
41 Claire Harman, preface to *The Collected Poems* (Manchester: The Carcanet Press, 1982) p. xx.
42 Jim Fyrth, Foreword to Jim Fyrth and Sally Alexander (eds), *Women's Voices from the Spanish Civil War* (London: Lawrence & Wishart, 1991) p. 34. For Spanish women's experience, see Shirley Mangini, *Memories of Resistance: Voices from the Spanish Civil War* (New Haven and London: The Yale University Press, 1995).
43 Fyrth and Alexander, *Women's Voices*, p. 34.
44 Edgell Rickword, ' In Defence of Culture: The Second Congress of the International Association of Writers, Madrid, July 1937', *Left Review*, August 1937, p. 381.
45 Sylvia Townsend Warner, 'What the Soldier Said', *Time and Tide* (August 1937) p. 1092.
46 Ellen Wilkinson quoted in Fyrth and Alexander, *Women's Voices from the Spanish Civil War*, p. 282.
47 Rosamond Lehmann, 'Books for Spain', *New Statesman*, 21 August 1937, p. 179.
48 Anne Olivier-Bell and Andrew McNellie (eds), *The Diary of Virginia Woolf* (5 vols) (Harmondsworth: Penguin, 1979–85), vol. 5, 1936–41, 1985, p. 142.

49   Letter to Elizabeth Wade White dated 14 December 1938, *The Letters*, p. 42.
50   Sylvia Townsend Warner, 'Barcelona', *Left Review*, December 1936, p. 816.
51   Valentine Ackland, 'Instructions from England' (1936), first published in Valentine Cunningham (ed.), *The Penguin Book of Spanish Civil War Verse* (Harmondsworth: Penguin, 1980) p. 372.
52   Townsend Warner, 'What the Soldier Said', p. 1092.
53   'Sylvia Townsend Warner, 'With the Nationalists', *A Garland of Straw* (London: Chatto and Windus) pp. 111–17.
54   *Left Review*, March 1938, p. 841.
55   Stephen Spender and John Lehmann (eds), *Poems for Spain* (London: The Hogarth Press, 1939), pp. 6–7.
56   Valentine Ackland, 'Writers in Madrid, *Daily Worker*, 21 July 1937, p. 7.
57   Townsend Warner, 'What the Soldier Said', p. 1092.
58   Warner and Schmidt, 'Sylvia Townsend Warner in Conversation', p. 35.
59   Townsend Warner, *The Collected Poems*, pp. 36–7, *A Garland of Straw*, pp. 34–43.
60   Letter to Naomi Mitchison dated 17 July 1937, *The Letters*, p. 46.
61   Quoted in Valentine Cunningham (ed.), *Spanish Front: Writers on the Civil War* (Oxford: The Oxford University Press, 1986) p. 228.
62   Sylvia Townsend Warner, 'The People Have No Generals', *Our Time*, vol. 1, no. 1, 1941, pp. 18–21.
63   Letter to Nancy Cunard, dated 28 April 1944, *The Letters*, p. 84.
64   Ibid.
65   Sylvia Townsend Warner, *After the Death of Don Juan* (London: Chatto and Windus, 1938).
66   Sylvia Townsend Warner, 'The Democrat's Daughter', *More Joy in Heaven* (London: The Cresset Press, 1935), pp. 82–3.
67   Georg Lukacs, *The Historical Novel* (London: The Merlin Press, 1962).
68   Ibid., p. 42.
69   John Coombes, *Writing from the Left: Socialism, Liberalism and the Popular Front* (London: Harvester Wheatsheaf, 1989), p. 106.
70   Terry Castle, 'Sylvia Townsend Warner and the Counterplot of Lesbian Fiction', *Textual Practice*, vol. 4, no. 2 (Summer 1990) p. 231.
71   Jane Marcus, 'Sylvia Townsend Warner (1893–1978)', in Bonnie Kime Scott (ed.), *The Gender of Modernism* (Bloomington: The University of Indiana Press, 1990), p. 543.
72   Barbara Brothers, 'Summer Will Show: The Historical Novel as Social Criticism', in Lorrayne Y. Baird-Lange and Thomas Copeland (eds), *Women in History, Literature and the Arts* (Youngstown: The Youngstown State University Press, 1989), pp. 262–74, p. 262.
73   Review of Hilary Newitt, 'Women Must Choose', *Left News*, April 1937, p. 326.
74   Sylvia Townsend Warner, 'Women as Writers', the Peter Le Neve Foster Lecture, *The Journal of the Royal Society of Arts*, vol. 7, no. 5034, May 1959, p. 384.
75   *Jane Austen*, British Council Writers Series (London: Longmans, Green, 1951).
76   Sylvia Townsend Warner, 'Persuasion', *A Garland of Straw: Twenty-Eight Stories* (London: Chatto and Windus, 1943), pp. 143–55.
77   Sylvia Townsend Warner, *Mr. Fortune's Magot* (London: Chatto and Windus, 1927), *The True Heart* (London: Chatto and Windus, 1929).
78   Letter to Nancy Cunard, dated 28 August 1945, *The Letters*, p. 51.
79   Richard Crossman, (ed.), *The God that Failed: Six Studies in Communism* (London: Hamish Hamilton, 1950).
80   Arnold Rattenbury, 'Plain Heart, Light Tether', *PN Review* 23, p. 47.
81   Ibid.

6

Hanna Behrend

An Intellectual Irrelevance? Marxist Literary Criticism in the 1930s

> There will be time to audit
> The accounts later, there will be sunlight later
> And the equation will come out at last.
> (Louis MacNeice)

The reputation of Marxist literary criticism in Britain has never been high. Unlike the contributions made by communists to other aspects of British cultural and intellectual life, Marxist literary criticism in Britain has always looked like an alien activity, sometimes comical, sometimes sinister, always intrusive. In such a highly individualised literary culture, ideologically naive and historically resistant to theory, the idea that Marxism might have anything to say at all about the world of the imagination has simply looked offensive, a crass and heavy-handed attempt at intellectual policing. 'Good novels,' noted George Orwell in the late 1930s, 'are not written by orthodoxy-sniffers, nor by people who are conscious-stricken about their own unorthodoxy.'[1]

Marxism was not of course the critical orthodoxy of literary London in the late 1930s, although it has suited some people since to pretend that it was. And thanks to a rather different kind of 'orthodoxy-sniffing' the short-lived school of Marxist literary criticism in this country almost disappeared from view in the years after the Second World War. As one literary historian confidently put it, 'The flirtation of the British intelligentsia with Marxism in the era of the Spanish Civil War was too transient, and too stubbornly English and moralistic, to create a genuine Marxist school of letters.' As communism became distinctly *un*fashionable, London publishers lost interest, other critics lost patience and Marxist literary critics began to fall out among themselves. For some anyway it had never amounted to much more than an eccentric, amateur, English mixture of populist, left-Leavisite Russophilia, damned as much by their debt to *Scrutiny* as by the influence of *The Short History of the CPSU (B)*. By the 1970s, when Marxist literary theory briefly regained some intellectual clout, at least within academic circles, the British Marxist critics of the 1930s and 1940s were, as Terry Eagleton put it, 'little more than an intellectual irrelevance.' Their work was characterised by 'vulgar Marxism, bourgeois empiricism and Romantic idealism', doomed to failure because they were 'insulated from much of Europe, intellectually isolated even within [their] own society, permeated by Stalinism and idealism, bereft of a "theory of superstructures"'.[2]

It is not hard to find evidence from the 1930s to substantiate this combination: 'LITERARY ENGLISH FROM CAXTON TO US IS AN ARTIFICIAL JARGON OF THE RULING CLASS: WRITTEN ENGLISH BEGINS WITH US' (Alec Brown); 'No book written at the present time can be "good" unless it is written from a Marxist or near-Marxist viewpoint' (Edward Upward); 'Capitalism has no further use for culture' (Rex Warner); 'The old world must die before the new socialist world of the future can begin to live. Let us help to kill and bury it before it buries us all in the ruins of its inevitable collapse' (Philip Henderson); 'Only revolutionary activity can make a revolutionary poet' (Cecil Day Lewis).[3]

This kind of criticism was a product of the prevailing vulgarisation of the famous passage in the *The Critique of Political Economy* that

> the mode of production of the material means of existence conditions the whole process of social, political and intellectual life. It is not the consciousness of men that determines their existence, but, on the contrary, their social existence that determines their consciousness.

By applying the Marxist Base and Superstructure model in an inflexible and hierarchical way, many Marxist critics committed themselves to a conception of literature which was narrowly political, reductive, tendentious and prescriptive. They were wedded to a reflectionist theory of culture, they reduced culture to the arts, and they subordinated imaginative writing to a reductive representation of 'reality'. They believed at the same time in the Romantic idea of the writer as pioneer of social progress and in a rigid subservience to 'revolutionary discipline'. And if they undervalued aesthetic experience, so they underestimated the recuperative powers of capitalism (and the power of the capitalist media to manipulate aesthetic experience).

All this is clear. But it is also clear that it was this body of criticism – flawed, uneven and immature though it was – which exercised a pre-eminent influence on the work of a later and rather better known generation of Marxist writers who freely acknowledged their debt to the native Marxist critical tradition from the 1930s. For Arnold Kettle (who remained a member of the Communist Party all his life) the work of communist critics in the 1930s like Ralph Fox, Alick West, Christopher Caudwell, T.A. Jackson, Randall Swingler, Jack Lindsay, Edgell Rickword, Roy Pascal, Douglas Garman, George Thomson and Montagu Slater was distinguished by several memorable features: 'Firstly, their work is imbued with a sense of closeness to ... the Labour Movement, and reveals a corresponding attempt to write in a simple, direct language to which working people can respond. Secondly, there is in their writing a strong consciousness of the progressive aspects of the English literary heritage, especially in the work of Shakespeare, Milton, Bunyan, the Romantic poets and the 19th-century novelists. But perhaps most significant of all is a certain suspicion of the kind of "ideological" criticism found in the work of continental Marxists trained in the Hegelian tradition.'[4] For Raymond Williams, this was a tradition 'proceeding from the Romantics, and coming down through Arnold and Morris ... supplemented by phrases from Marx, while continuing to operate in the older terms. Much of the "Marxist" writing of the thirties was in fact the old Romantic protest that there was no place in contemporary society for the artist and the intellectual, with the new subsidiary clause that the workers were about to end the old system and establish Socialism, which would then provide such a place.'[5] For E.P. Thompson, at least some of this group represented liberating 'centres of "premature revisionism"' long before 1956, their criticism avoiding *and resisting* 'the didactic methods of the Party's officers, the wooden economism of its policies and the correct pabulum offered as "Marxism"'. This was a dissenting space within a dissident tradition for Thompson, a criticism informed by their creative practice as writers and their imaginative writing informed by their heroism in action (Caudwell and Fox fought in Spain, Swingler in the Second World War).[6] Both Margot Heinemann and Eric Hobsbawm have argued that the commitment of communists such as these helped to insure that in the end it was not the Fascists that won and that their work was part of most emancipatory advances made since.[7]

   Put like this, these Marxist critics look rather more interesting. And no-one should be surprised if British Marxists blended liberal, Romantic, non-conformist and socialist utopian traditions with Marxist theory. These were simply the native traditions which best answered the desire to close the widening gap between the world as it was and the aspiration of artists and writers for a humane society. The continuity between Romanticism and Marxism lay, as Alick West put it, in the concept of 'social relations as constituting beauty in art, of a conflict and antagonism in these relations and of the same conflict reconciled in art, of poetry as the voice of humanity against oppression in ending them'. As Randall Swingler wrote in 1937 on the seventieth anniversary of the first publication of the essays which became *Culture and Anarchy*:

Arnold's was a rallying cry of the traditionalist of his time, who attempted to set the individual talent as a champion against the disintegration of emotional and moral values which the expansion of industrialism was bringing about. Now, however, we are in a better position than Arnold to see what is the true enemy of Culture. An Arnold writing in our time might well call his book *Culture and Fascism* ... Culture is the natural pattern of a growing society. Today that pattern is most clearly articulate, unified, abundant, in just those people who are the victims of the most terrible, the most unprovoked attacks of Fascist aggression.'[8]

In the face of the world economic crisis, the threat of Fascism and the seemingly successful construction of socialism in the Soviet Union, such a belief was neither dishonourable nor altogether absurd. The critical work that came out of this moment may have been damaged by the pressures of the time, written as it mostly was for publication in daily newspapers and weekly journals. And it was too scattered and too various to be easily discussed as a single canon of criticism. Nevertheless, it is possible to distinguish a number of common concerns by considering briefly seven writers who published key critical statements in 1937, work which represented the beginnings of a serious, generous and painstaking enquiry into the social possibilities of art and literature in dangerous and challenging times.

Ralph Fox

When Raymond Williams went up to Cambridge in 1939 he found that 'the central work on which most debate revolved' at the University Socialist Club Writers Group was Ralph Fox's *The Novel and the People* (1937). Fox was a journalist, novelist, critic and propagandist who had joined the Communist Party in 1925 after serving with Quaker Famine Relief in the war-torn Soviet Union. He published literary and political reviews, political and historical treatises, (*Marx and Engels on the Irish Question, The Class Struggle in Britain*), biographies (*Lenin, Genghis Khan*), a play and a number of novels before volunteering in 1936 to fight in Spain. He was killed a few weeks later, in January 1937, at Cordova.

The importance of *The Novel and the People* for the young Raymond Williams was Fox's central argument that although the economic situation formed the basis of society,

the various elements of the superstructure – political forms of the class struggle and its consequences, constitutions established by the victorious class after a successful battle, etc. – forms of law – and then even the reflexes of all these actual struggles in the brains of the combatants:

political, legal, philosophical theories, religious ideas, and their further development into systems of dogma – also exercise their influence upon the course of the historical struggle and in many cases preponderate in determining their *form*.[9]

By stressing the qualifications made by Engels (in letters to Bloch, Borgius and Mehring) to that passage from *The Critique of Political Economy*, Fox was trying to establish a space within Marxist aesthetics for the autonomy of ideas, cultural activity and artistic creation – and for literary criticism. Books were not a simple reflex production of society and therefore did not simply 'reflect' society; they were written, read and enjoyed by individuals, whose relations with the rest of their society were often complex and contradictory. Applying Engels's formula to the role of the writer, Fox argued that the novelist had 'a dual history, since he is at the same time a type, a man with a social history, and an individual, a man with a personal history. The two ... are also one, in so far as the latter is eventually conditioned by the former'. His definition of the task of Marxist literary criticism was an emancipatory one:

> to restore [literature's] great tradition, to break the bonds of subjectivism and narrow specialisation, to bring the creative writer face to face with his only important task, that of winning the knowledge of truth, of reality. Art is one of the means by which man grapples with and assimilates reality. On the forge of his own inner consciousness the writer takes the white-hot metal of reality and hammers it out, refashions it to his own purpose, beats it out madly by the violences of thought ... The whole procession of creation ... is in this violent conflict with reality in the effort to fashion a truthful picture of the world ... truth is not abstract and motionless, to be discovered by a formally logical and abstract process of thought ... Truth can only be reached through practical activity, for truth is the expression of man's own intense investigation of an object, and that investigation is above all a human activity, particularly a social and productive activity.[10]

Ralph Fox was intolerant of Marxists who dismissed half the classics of the world as 'bourgeois propaganda' or 'counter-revolutionary'. He loved the English literary tradition, which he regularly celebrated in the pages of the *Sunday Worker* and the *Daily Worker*. He was widely read too in the literature of other cultures and languages. The novel was his passionate interest, especially the English, French and Russian traditions of critical realism. Although Fox accepted Lenin's idea that the revolutionary writer must be a 'Party writer,' expressing the outlook of the 'class which is struggling to create a new social order' and fulfilling his duty to the Party by 'creating a new literature, free from the anarchist individualism of the bourgeosie in its period of decay', Fox also knew that the abstention from 'anarchist individualism' does not itself create readable novels. He repeatedly censured the unsatisfactory literary figures of contemporary 'revolutionary fiction' for being 'flat surfaces, rather than men in the round', passionately believing that the hero who had disappeared in the nineteenth-century novel needed reviving in the form of a positive working-class hero, 'who is at once greater and less than the real man.' While Fox recognised the complexity of the social, historical and ideological structures composing the unstable and changing nature of individual personality and of its role in society, he insisted (like Lukacs) that the story of an individual could not be written without the 'steady vision of the whole'. The solution for Fox (in keeping with contemporary Marxist tenets) lay in the new possibilities of Socialist Realism which sought to unite the critical tradition of realist fiction with proletarian consciousness. For Fox, 'Marxism does not deny the individual. It does not see only masses in the grip of inexorable economic forces'; 'Marxism places man in the centre of its philosophy, for while it claims that material forces may change man, it declares most emphatically that it is man who changes himself.'[11] His idea of Socialist Realism therefore implied blending critical realism and the Romantic sensibility. His decision to serve with the International Brigades was a heroic demonstration of this belief, that 'we are a part of a spiritual community with the dead of which Wordsworth spoke. We cannot stand aside, and by our action we shall extend our imagination because we shall have been true to the passion in us'.[12]

Christopher Caudwell

Four weeks after the death of Ralph Fox, Christopher Caudwell was killed on the Jarama river. A working journalist since the age of 15, Caudwell also wrote poetry, novels, thrillers, science fiction and textbooks on aeronautics. He discovered Marxism in 1934, joined the Communist Party and – unknown to other communist intellectuals – began working on an extraordinarily ambitious series of cultural and scientific studies, posthumously published as *Illusion and Reality* (1937), *Studies in a Dying Culture* (1938), *The Crisis in Physics* (1939) and *Further Studies in a Dying Culture* (1949).

Illusion and Reality ('a study of the sources of poetry') was a remarkable attempt to single-handedly invent a theory of Marxist poetics, drawing on cultural anthropology, psychology and linguistics. Caudwell elaborated a functional approach to poetry, based on a critique of mechanical Materialism and Idealism and their separation of subject and object, consciousness and reality, instinct and environment, individual and society. Caudwell's starting point was that 'art is the product of society, as the pearl is the product of the oyster'. 'Culture is a product of society made necessary by man's struggle to be freer,' he wrote, 'unlike the life of beasts, the life of the simplest tribe requires a series of efforts which are not instinctive, but which are demanded by the necessities of a non-biological economic aim – for example the harvest.'[13] For Caudwell literature and art represented the symbolic surplus generated by society, as well as social processes of influence upon the development of society. 'Science and art are neccessarily social. Through the former man becomes conscious of outer reality, through the latter he becomes conscious of his feelings;' 'Consciousness, in the broadest sense (including therefore the subconscious, which is also the product of modified instinct)) is a social product. The construction of consciousness is the socialising of the psyche.' Caudwell believed that poetry '"exposes" the endless potentiality of the instincts and the "heart" by revealing the various ways in which they may adapt themselves to "experiences";' 'art is the consciousness of the necessity of the instincts.'[14]

Literature for Caudwell was not an object of enquiry but a social practice. 'The artist in bourgeois culture is asked ... to regard the art work as a finished commodity and the process of art as a relation between himself and the work, which then disappears in the market ... The whole pressure of bourgeois society is to make him regard the art work as hypostasised and his relation to it primarily that of producer for the market.'[15] Poetry in particular was 'a specific mode of formation of the real'; 'it is in no sense a transcription either of the individual subjectivity (expression) or of "Reality" (representation): rather, it co-operated in the production of historically necessary forms of social consciousness.'[16]

Surprisingly, perhaps, Caudwell also held that bourgeois artists and writers were, by definition, incapable of grasping reality. This made him unable to do justice to much of the imaginative literature of the day and led him to absurdly reductive assessments (such as that Shaw and Lawrence were 'Social Fascists'). On the other hand, *Illusion and Reality* is a penetrating study of ideology and a utopian assertion of the 'necessity of art':

All art is conditioned by the conception of freedom which rules in the society that produces it; art is a mode of freedom, and a class society conceives of freedom to be absolutely whatever relative freedom that class has attained to. In bourgeois art man is conscious of the necessity of outer reality but not of his own, because he is unconscious of the society that makes him what he is. He is only half a man ... That everything which comes into being must pass away; that all is fleeting, all is moving; that to exist is to be like the fountain and have a shape because it is never still – is the theme of all art because it is the texture of reality. Man is drawn to life because it moves from him ... Man too must pass away. Therefore the stuff of art endures as long as man. The fountain dwindles away only when men are rent and wasted by a sterile conflict, and the pulsing movement of society is halted ... Thus art is one of the conditions of man's realisation of himself, and in its turn is some of the realities of man.[17]

Alick West

The son of a non-conformist clergyman, Alick West spent the First World War as a civilian internee in Germany. It was there that he first came into active contact with dramatic art and literature. After the war he studied classical and modern languages at Trinity College, Dublin and taught for several years at the University of Basle; in 1935 he returned to London, where he joined the Communist Party, working as a translator and English teacher at the Soviet Embassy.

In his autobiography West wrote that becoming a communist motivated him 'to express in literary form the essential truth, as embodied in Marxism, of the world in which we lived. Society was in movement, and the energy of that movement was in the conflict between capitalism and socialism. It was our responsibility to heighten men's consciousness of the freedom and abundance of life which through the socialist revolution it was now in their power to win'.[18] His major work, *Crisis and Criticism* (1937), explores the relativity of literary value, the social function of language and the relation of literary form and content. Form, he argued, represented continuity and tradition resting on past experience, while content contained the contemporary and the new. 'Form has the value, through past activity, of stimulating those to whom it is addressed, because it is a call from a social group within which ... successful activity is possible. Through its content it directs and organises the stimulated energy in the particular activity of the moment, and thereby stimulates it still further.'[19] Like Fox, therefore, West did not believe that a work of imaginative literature simply reflected history in the manner in which history actually takes place; in his best criticism he was aware that poetry, fiction and drama present the dynamics of contemporary human development in a polyphonic, contradictory and fragmentary manner, mediated by the subjective approach of the author, and the limits and possibilities of literary form and language. Following Marx and Engels's preference for Balzac over Zola, he argued that:

> Though literature is propaganda, its value ... does not depend on its manifest programme. A work may talk revolution; but if it does not show revolution through society's creative movement, it is not fulfilling its function as literature; and the consequent abstractness of presentation in what claims to be a poem or novel may repel from the aim set forth. Or a work may talk reaction: but if it conveys the sense of the social movement it condemns, the manifestly reactionary work is more valuable than the manifestly revolutionary.[20]

For West, language was an organising social activity, a cultural practice which carried constantly contested meanings, reproducing, resisting and replacing hegemonic ones. He rejected the linguistic theories of I.A. Richards, Herbert Read and T.S. Eliot which

> consider the value of language only as a means of stimulating energy through the appeal to previous social experience within a particular society, and ignore its function and value as a means of organising that energy in the new activity of the moment. The position both of Mr Eliot and Dr Richards means that the function of poetry and literature is to stimulate the energy attached to the previous forms of social activity, and to divert attention from the question of what form of social activity is to be organised now. It is fundamentally conservative: its intention is that the emotion deriving from past social experience in a group supposedly as homogeneous as the character of language appears to be, shall make the practical issues before society now seem a blasphemous question ... There can be no poem, and no response to a poem, without previous social activity. And that activity necessarily tests all utterances by their objective validity, because it is a matter of life and death to us whether what we say about the objective world is true or not. Our response to a poem derives from previous social activity; belief in our statements as truth, and not as myth, is an essential part of that activity.[21]

Unfortunately, this critical vocabulary, undogmatic and generous as it seems, also veiled its own normative intolerances. 'The criticism of our lives, by the test of whether we are helping forward the most creative movement in our society, is the only effective foundation of the criticism of literature,' he argued.[22] It sounds like common sense, but Raymond Williams for one feared that this was only a blue pencil mark away from 'the kind of literary criticism which had made Marxism notorious'.[23] Whether or not one agrees with this, or whether one prefers to name the utopian drive for human emancipation differently, West was at least consistent in his loyalty to 'the most creative movement in our society', an increasingly troubled but still loyal Party member. Shortly before his death, West wrote a long essay on Lawrence in which he addressed what he considered to be the weakness of *Crisis and Criticism* and, by implication, of his life's work. 'We did not always and necessarily represent a progressive collectivity; some kinds of collectivities might be totalitarian structures rather than truly humane communities. Totalitarian ideology', he believed, 'could only be combated by the assertion of a communist conception of totality'. And that totality could best be felt through imaginative literature:

> Literature heightens the consciousness of humanity as a totality which has reached the point in its social evolution where it can set before itself an aim and organise itself to achieve it. Humanity is not alienated from itself. And the only reality of humanity is its activity. Social change

results from the exercise by social groups of the energy of the human species ... and that energy is inseparable from the specific human powers of thought, language and the possibility of choice ... powers which have developed through an active relationship of men with nature, and between men themselves, of which the consciousness of death has been an essential part. Literature has the power to make this process of change conscious. The purpose of literary criticism must be to make explicit what in literature is implicit.[24]

T.A. Jackson

Tommy Jackson's enthusiasms were probably the most catholic of all the writers discussed here. His literary critical work reveals a passionate devotion to imaginative writing, a fine discernment of literary value and an unorthodox application of Marxism to his reading. This working-class autodidact, agitator, lecturer, propagandist, reviewer and collector of books produced remarkable works on a wide range of subjects, including *Charles Dickens: the Progress of a Radical* (1937), *Ireland Her Own: An Outline of the Irish Struggle* (1947), an autobiography *Solo Trumpet* (1953) and *Dialectics: the Logic of Marxism and Its Critics* (1936). In the last mentioned philosophical compendium he replied to those who criticised Marxism for being deterministic and then flourished their own determinism to 'prove' that Marxism was 'out of date':

> Marx said that 'ideas' individually and in their historical development were reflections of men's historically conditioned social relations [but] there are other material and social circumstances than 'economic' ones ... among other things ... the influence upon men of subjective activity – of theory and tradition ... In Marx's own material conception of history ... the differing mode of development of the economic basis of society and of its ideological superstructure is the mainspring of the whole conception and objective practice is conceived as the generating source of all knowledge ... That a world-conception must be 'out of date' because it was formulated earlier than yesterday is the most childishly uncritical affirmation it is possible to make ... Is the opinion that the Earth moves round the Sun *necessarily* false because it was held by some Greek astronomers 2000 years ago?[25]

Jack Lindsay

Although the Australian-born poet and historical novelist Jack Lindsay did not join the Communist Party until 1939, he wrote a number of Marxist historical novels in the 1930s (notably his Roman trilogy, *Adam of a New World*, *1649* and *Lost Birthright* and three books of Marxist criticism. *Anatomy of Spirit* (1937) was an early, ambitious attempt to 'fuse the basic ideas of Marx and Freud' by linking irrationality with 'false ideas about the human body and its functions', ideas which were 'intimately bound up with all that is reactionary in social life' and resistant to the idea of full human unity. *John Bunyan, Maker of Myths* (1937) was an early, influential attempt to explore the English radical literary tradition and the contradictions of English non-conformity. But it was in the massive scholarship of *A Short History of Culture* (1939) that Lindsay attempted to give a Marxist account of culture. At the end of a richly detailed and authoritative survey of over 200,000 years of cultural history, he concluded that it was 'out of the productive group, the mass' that 'the dynamic point of structure from which all cultural advance, in art or science, is made':

> This structure underlies the whole of human consciousness, which cannot be conceived without it ... The extreme inequality of the antagonists, man and nature, in the early ages, had the effect of preventing men from devising a full comprehension of reality, movement, change. The defeated part in men appeared as a need to abstract, to split, to set up static concepts to which they could fearfully cling. With the Neolithic age, when the settled life based on agriculture became possible, there was a burst of the creative forms or symbols of movement born from increased union, but there was also an increased drag, an increased splitting, from the abstraction; and from the inequality of the struggle between men and nature ... there arose an inequality of right and powers within the group, which split the original union of reciprocity and made out of increasing division of labour the deepening division of rights. Thenceforth the reattainment of equality within the group depended on the attainment of equality between the group and nature. The original union was never forgotten, for it was perpetuated at every stage by the actuality of productive union among the masses, as contrasted with the rule of privilege and power ... With the advent of class-society a deepening of conflict arose, for both the drag of the split-off and the unheaving potencies of the massed producers were accentuated.'[26]

Literary history was the story of the rise, balance and falling away of the forms and symbols representing the two impulses, shaped by their shifting points of resistance, tension and overlapping movements. If this account led inevitably to some banal conclusions about the responsibility of contemporary writers to support 'the victorious achievement of socialism in the Soviet Union', Lindsay nevertheless realised that the unity of culture lies in the continuity of man's productive energy, his courageous attempts to merge dialectically with nature through work. Culture has a unity and a persisting significance in so far as it reflects the productive tensions. Only by realising that truth can we assume the role of the defenders of culture. His approach was therefore located in culture as much as it was in politics.

Edgell Rickword

Lindsay also edited, with the poet Edgell Rickword, *A Handbook of Freedom* (1939), a hugely influential anthology of prose and verse tracing the historical lineages of dissent in England. Rickword was the Communist Party's most senior literary critic, the author of the first English study of Rimbaud, one time editor of the *Calendar of Modern Letters* and *Scrutinies*, then editor of *Left Review* and a director of the Party's publishing house, Lawrence & Wishart.

Like so many communist writers, Rickword's critical work in the 1930s was characterised by a preoccupation with historical rather than theoretical issues, devoted to the important task of making known and available a radical English literary history which had been lost. It was an educative, emancipatory, popularising project at the heart of the Communist Party's cultural work in the years of the Popular Front. *A Handbook of Freedom* is clear about the relation between writers and society, their work appearing 'like the cliffs of an iceberg that reveal the greater power beneath':

> The achievements of gifted individuals are so interwoven with the process of events that their names arise naturally at such and such points of crisis. They do not initiate the historical movements, but they clarify the issues, sustain the purpose of those in action and counter the propaganda of the backward forces; their testimony lives on to stimulate and instruct the future ... because we recognise in the combinations of recalcitrant journeymen, in the staunch bearing of farm-labourers in the felon's dock, the seed of all the formulations of the rights of man and the rhapsodies of the poets on the theme of liberty.[27]

A Handbook of Freedom successfully resisted the deterministic temptations of both the history of the Popular Front and a Marxist sense of class loyalty. Rickword developed the theoretical basis of this position in a long essay he contributed to Cecil Day Lewis's collection, *The Mind in Chains* (1937), 'Culture, Progress and the English Tradition':

> Labour as the basis of culture! What a crass idea that sounds the first time one hears it, being accustomed to the notion of our cultivated people that freedom *from* work is the necessary first condition for exercising artistic or intellectual talent ... resistance to the acceptance of the

material basis of culture is strengthened by the fact that throughout modern history the increase in the capacity to produce has been accomplished and accompanied by one of its factors, an increasing specialization and sub-division of labour ... with the rush to power of machine-industry, the specialization of intellectual work, like the minute sub-division of factory processes, is carried to its extreme. Each branch of activity is carried on in isolation from the other ... In this way the habit of thinking of culture as an independent activity becomes ingrained, and the freedom of the artist, the independence of the scientist, and the disinterestedness of the philosopher become dogmas. But the intellect is only free to solve such problems as the technical development of society provides the means of solving ... And the idea of freedom, which men have always dreamt of, and which has occupied the best minds of all ages, could only take on flesh and blood when the increase of productivity ensured a secure and adequate standard of physical well-being. At last society can afford that all its members shall be intellectuals, which does not mean, God forbid, that the world shall be turned into one vast Bloomsbury. It is not the possession of ample leisure that creates a flourishing culture ... but participation in the constructive work of society.[28]

Randall Swingler

In 1937 the poet Randall Swingler succeeded Rickword as editor of *Left Review*. Swingler was already a familiar contributor to the pages of most literary journals – *Life and Letters*, the *London Mercury*, *New Writing*, *Twentieth Century Verse*, *Purpose*, *New English Weekly* and the *Fortnightly Review*, a position which enabled him to take Marxist literary criticism into the wider world of literary London. A review in 1937 of new verse in *New English Weekly* gave him the opportunity to discuss what seemed to him to be the failings of so much contemporary English verse at the same time as making Marxist theories of poetry sound like common sense:

It must always be remembered that poetry is older and simpler than any other form of language. It fulfils, in fact, the original function of language, intended by its rhythmical character to keep people together, to organise their powers into a unity, to make them aware of their common nature and interest, their essential community one with another ... as imagination is the primary function of the mind so poetry maintains the primary function of language, of 'stimulating social activity in persons engaged together in a common task'. Hence the reaping-songs, and the sea-shanties, the ballads and the early epics, which are all of war, religious rites or navigation, the only activities which the group still pursued as a unity. The simplicity of poetry is the concrete force of its symbols: and so, much of modern verse-writing, since it does not subserve this primary function, cannot be classed as poetry at all ... a different art, if you like, but not poetry. The art perhaps of correspondence or the art of games, which may be witty, pathetic, ingenious, sentimental, within the limits of those arts. Whatever poetry is, it is not a magpies' nest ... What has happened to poetry then? Simply that in a profit-making society there is no place for it, where all social functions are increasingly divided into individual specialisation, and the function of poetry is gradually eliminated. The true poets today are those who realise this, and seek to recreate the function of poetry among all those who feel that they have been robbed of their humanity in a society of mechanical individualism; in binding these together in the common task of establishing a humane society.[29]

That year Swingler commissioned a series of articles for *Left Review* on the radical English tradition – T.A. Jackson on Dickens, Alick West on Spencer, Douglas Garman on Ibsen and Rex Warner on Swift. Swingler himself opened the series with a long essay on Blake, 'The Imputation of Madness', arguing against the popular conception of Blake as a mystic and drawing attention to the dialectical nature of Blake's thinking. For Swingler, Blake was a useful and urgent starting point for 'reclaiming our revolutionary culture', since the forces of unreason which Blake had opposed and which had distorted Blake's vision were abroad again, in capitalist crisis and in Fascism, 'making its final and open assault every day upon every kind of culture, every possible advance of human knowledge, with the burning of books, the torturing of writers, killing of poets, banishment of scientists, boycotting of musicians, suppression of teachers and philosophers.' To demystify William Blake was therefore an anti-Fascist act, unlocking the forces of poetry against the naturalising effects of ideology and the neutralising effects of education:

Consider even now the dominant associations with the word 'poet': crank, cloudy idealist, demi-god perhaps (therefore non-human), at least privileged and unreliable individual, whose licence is the measure of the impracticality and eccentricity of his speech ... These men are not to be trusted. Byron, the legendary Oedipus; Keats, the lovesick boy; Milton, the old blind theologian; Swift, the children's humorist; Coleridge, the opium addict; Wordsworth, a pious old sheep; Shelley – well, of course, Shelley was an atheist, a 'free-lover'; and Blake as mad as a hatter ... Even while it has been admitted that the values of poetry come into immediate conflict with the values of capitalist society, it is still supposed that poetry creates a world of its own, a magic world, over against the world of actuality and at no point contiguous with it. It is precisely because poets, affirming their world to be the real world and the structure of capitalism to be ephemeral and false, fought against the conditioning of their education that they are important to us.[30]

Swingler was clearly less concerned with the taxonomy of writing than he was with the politics of writers in Britain and the fate of writers in Germany, Italy and Spain. The author may not yet have been pronounced dead, but a great many authors in 1937 were facing death, torture, imprisonment and exile. If this was not the business of the literary critic, then whose was it?

Conclusion

History has since demonstrated that capitalism was able, for a period of almost half a century following the Second World War, to establish a golden age of relative economic security, in the highly industrialised parts of the world at least, while the alternative society, which was supposed to do away with exploitation and oppression, degenerated into totalitarian dictatorship. The grand historical experiment of building the New Jerusalem failed after less than a century, during which time Marxist theory degenerated from a subversive discourse into a dominant one whose main function was to keep the *nomenklaturas* in power. International communism was diverted from its one-time aim of serving the workers of the world and is now shattered. Both the golden age and the Soviet Union and its satellites have now passed away. The organised working class is no longer a challenge to the social system. Other historical agents have arrived on the stage and again made their exits. New social and cultural theories have arisen offering new ways of considering the relations of life and literature, the arts and the sciences, culture and society, and yet the cultural discourses of our time flounder no less helplessly than the much maligned cultural resistance of the 1930s. Europe is still struggling with economic and social problems unresolved 50 years ago, now in new and more dangerous forms (and with a few new ones thrown in). Vulgarised, deformed, maligned, misrepresented and now silenced, what remains of the Marxist critical tradition?

In so far as Marxism proves to be of theoretical assistance to that inexhaustible and unvanquishable minority of men and women who are not satisfied with interpreting the world, but who insist on trying to change it, it will remain part of the underground stream of cultural resistance and enrich their political, social and creative activity. Marxist literary criticism will be a productive theoretical approach so long as it continues to argue that literature is an agent of human motivation geared to probing the problems of identity, participation and power. Despite its ambiguities and inconsistencies, this was what the best of

Marxist literary criticism in the 1930s aimed at. Its most consistent spokespersons were aware of the need to help men and women exchange the status of the objects of politics to that of subjects and they tried to use their criticism to this end. For as Alick West expressed it, 'Literature expresses truths about the human condition of which political movements are unaware or indifferent.'[31]

Notes

1   *Inside the Whale* (Gollancz 1940; reprinted in *The Collected Essays, Journalism and Letters of George Orwell* (Harmondsworth: Penguin, 1968), p. 569.

2   George Watson, *The Literary Critics* (Harmondsworth: Penguin, 1962), p. 225; Terry Eagleton, *Criticism and Ideology* (London: New Left Books, 1976), p. 21.

3   Alec Brown, 'Controversy,' *Left Review*, December 1934 ; Edward Upward, 'Sketch for a Marxist Interpretation of Literature' in Cecil Day Lewis (ed.) *The Mind in Chains: Socialism and the Cultural Revolution* (London: Frederick Muller, 1937), p. 41; Rex Warner, 'Education' in *Ibid.*, p. 25 ; Philip Henderson, *Literature and a Changing Civilisation* (London: John Lane, 1935), p. 169; Cecil Day Lewis, *A Hope for Poetry* (Oxford: Basil Blackwell, 1934), p. 50.

4   Arnold Kettle, Foreword to Alick West, *Crisis and Criticism* (London: Lawrence & Wishart, 1937; new edition 1975), p. 2.

5   Raymond Williams, *Culture and Society 1780–1950* (London: Chatto and Windus, 1958; new edition Harmondsworth: Penguin, 1963), p. 268.

6   E.P. Thompson, 'Edgell Rickword', *PN Review*, vol. 6, no. 1 1979.

7   See Eric Hobsbawm, 'Address at the Funeral of Margot Heinemann' in David Margolies and Maroula Joannou (eds) *Heart of the Heartless World: Essays in Cultural Resistance in Memory of Margot Heinemann* (London: Pluto Press, 1995).

8   *Left Review*, January 1938.

9   Ralph Fox, *The Novel and the People* (Lawrence & Wishart, 1937), p. 21.

10 *Ibid.*, p. 29.

11 *Ibid.*, p. 23.

12 Quoted by Mulk Raj Anand, Preface to Ralph Fox, *The Novel and the People* (new edition, London: Cobbett Press, 1944), p. 9.

13 Christopher Caudwell, *Illusion and Reality* (Lawrence & Wishart, 1937), pp. 46, 34.

14 *Ibid.*, p. 174.

15 *Ibid.*, p. 45.

16 *Ibid.*, pp. 152, 195–96.

17 *Ibid.*, p. 328.

18 Alick West, *One Man in His Time* (London: George Allen and Unwin, 1969), p. 166.

19 Alick West, *Crisis and Criticism* (London: Lawrence & Wishart, 1937; new edition, 1975), p. 79.

20 *Ibid.*, p. 99.

21 *Ibid.*, p. 92.

22 *Ibid.*, p. 102.

23 Williams, *Culture and Society*, p. 268.

24 Quoted by Elizabeth West, Introduction to *Crisis and Criticism*, (London: Lawrence & Wishart, 1975 edition), p. 13.

25 T.A. Jackson, *Dialectics: the Logic of Marxism and Its Critics* (Lawrence & Wishart, 1936), p. 518.

26   Jack Lindsay, *A Short History of Culture* (London: Gollancz, 1939), p. 376.

27   Edgell Rickword, Introduction to Edgell Rickword and Jack Lindsay (eds) *A Handbook of Freedom* (Lawrence & Wishart, 1939; new edition, A Worker's Library, 1941 as *Spokesmen For Liberty*), p. viii.

28   Edgell Rickword, 'Culture, Progress and the English Tradition' in Cecil Day Lewis (ed.) *The Mind in Chains: Socialism and the Cultural Revolution*, p. 245.

29   *New English Weekly*, 15 April 1937.

30   *Left Review*, February 1937.

31   Elizabeth West, *Crisis and Criticism*, p. 12.

7

Kevin Morgan

King Street Blues: Jazz and the Left in Britain in the 1930s–1940s

Just before the war a young Mass-Observer, Hugh Clegg, was mingling with London's dance band players at their Archer Street meeting ground. As usual the street was buzzing, for, with its cafés, pubs, Musicians' Union office and scores of nearby clubs and theatres, it provided the capital's musicians with both an out-of-hours rendezvous and an informal labour exchange. One of them, a much-travelled saxophonist named Charles Bohm, invited Clegg back to his Ebury Street flat. There, as like any good Mass-Observer Clegg earnestly inventoried the furniture, one item stood out for special notice: a bookcase stuffed, not with *Rhythm* or the *Melody Maker*, but with Left Book Club editions and Lenin's selected works.[1]

Seven years and a world war later, a central London hall was packed solid to hear both the newest and the oldest sound in British jazz: the pioneering revivalist efforts of George Webb and his Dixielanders. Before the band could begin, a figure took the stage, a little self-consciously perhaps, on behalf of the event's organisers. 'Friends,' he began, 'and comrades,' and then read out what a sceptical observer called 'a farrago of nonsense composed by an anonymous committee ... about jazz being the music of the proletariat'. This, then, was the famous *Challenge* Jazz Club, *Challenge* being the organ of the Young Communist League.[2]

In jazz terms these two milieux, of professional dance bands and the New Orleans revival, could hardly have been further removed. For the revivalist, indeed, there was no more scornful epithet than 'Archer Street', connoting as it did a dreary, time-serving commercialism. What both had in common, however, was the significant left-wing presence attested in our opening scenes, a presence broadly but not exclusively associated with the Communist Party. Peripheral to histories of both jazz and communism, these interconnections are today largely forgotten. To some of those involved they can seem an embarrassment or professional liability, while high culture and labour history alike appear to have ruled out of consideration such frivolities. Only Eric Hobsbawm has provided some sort of serious analysis and even that appeared, under an incognito.[3] The story is nevertheless worth recovering, not just for jazz-inclined 'musico-sociological politicians'[4] but for its allusions to broader cultural dilemmas. Colliding as they often did, the worlds of Archer Street and jazz purism – 'jazz popular' and 'jazz proper' as Humphrey Lyttelton distinguished them[5] – illuminate a host of unresolved tensions as between the left and popular culture. Questions of commercialism, authenticity and professional control all play a part, along with the contingencies of communist politics in a period swinging, if one can so put it, from a broad-minded progressivism to the bigotries of Zhdanovism. Rootless and hedonistic, subversive and plebeian, no other art form inspired such passion and revulsion in the variegated ranks of protest.

Our first musical environment, however, is not at all obviously one of social turbulence. If today we think of the dance-band era, our likeliest images are those of dapper men with batons and their well-groomed orchestras, cocooning West End nightspots with their lulling arrangements. As one veteran put it, 'We were a typical society band of the 1930s, playing sweet music in a rather sedate manner, as required by the management, under soft lights in elegant surroundings.'[6] The bandleaders themselves, bearing suave and savvy names like Ambrose or Geraldo, seemed the very personification of musical escapism, a svelte divertimento in a world of constant discord. Even in their humbler manifestations, at local Mecca ballrooms where paste stood for diamonds, the dance bands' reflected musical ambience was that of Mayfair, conjuring away social barriers through the engulfing medium of radio. This, of course, is to define jazz according to its broader contemporary usage: 'one of those things,' as a 1930s wireless owner put it, 'like advertisements and modern warfare – you cannot dodge it if you want to.'[7] Nothing perhaps could have seemed further removed than this music from left-wing politics. Richard Acland, ever the optimist, did, it is true, have hopes of syncopating his Forward March. 'I wonder if it would be worth trying to convert any of these [bandleaders] to our ideas and try to get them to express them in dance tunes,' he mused. 'I can imagine, for example, an immense popularity for something with the refrain "When are they going to let us build that better world?"'[8] Any such progressive hit remained elusive, however, the worlds of aspiration and contentment seemingly proving incompatible. 'No regiment of dance band-boys marched off to the Spanish Civil War,' concludes one historian of popular music. 'No dance or jazz bands accompanied the Jarrow marchers.'[9]

So plausible a deduction is nevertheless misleading, for by the end of the 1930s leading dance-band boys were routinely engaged in precisely this sort of activity. The transformation, remarkably, was one of but a few years; from 'individualists and reactionaries', according to Charles Bohm, to political progressives, many of them active members of the Left Book Club or Unity Theatre. 'The dance musicians provided the largest section on May Day,' Bohm noted in 1939, 'yet a few years ago there was not a dance musician in the Union.' If they did not accompany the Hunger Marchers, the musicians were by no means absent from other, slighter later campaigns. The wartime People's Convention, organised by the communists, numbered bandleaders like Lew Stone, Eddie Carroll, Phil Cardew and Sidney Lipton among its supporters and enlivened the early war years with performances by the Convention Swingsters. In London, where the top dance bands were concentrated, communist spectacles had even come under criticism from King Street for featuring 'hot trumpeters' at the expense of political propaganda. For some sympathisers, the possible threat to engagements or broadcasting contracts meant that support was necessarily confined to unpublicised donations to good party causes. Nevertheless, by the 1940s it seemed that there was hardly a name dance band without its communist faction, quite literally so in the case of the Geraldo Orchestra where it was organised by guitarist Ivor Mairants. Through the help of Mairants, the *Daily Worker* news editor Douglas Hyde was even able to recruit a healthy supply of dance musicians for his CP education classes on dialectical materialism.[10]

The causes of this unsuspected politicisation lay not in the music itself but in the conditions in which it was produced. For many of the leading players, nightly exposure to the vile young bodies of class privilege provoked considerable revulsion. Billy Amstell was one such musician, a veteran of several years with Ambrose and many other prestigious engagements. 'All the luxury and all the beautiful places that we played,' he recalled, 'Ciro's Embassy Club, Café de Paris, Mayfair Hotel, people used to come and they were well fed and they used to guzzle into their food and drink, and only round the corner people were sleeping in doorways, wrapped in paper.' Van Phillips, once of the Savoy Havana Band, also recalled that 'all those rich people were beneath contempt', and similar sentiments were expressed to Hyde by his musicians' group tutees. 'If you weren't a communist already, you'd be a bloody communist if you'd seen what we'd seen of the ruling class,' they told him. The constant reminders of their own subordinate status, notably their separate and often inadequate amenities and their proscription from mixing with clients, must also have fed the musicians' sense of grievance.[11]

That was all the stronger, perhaps, because of the very different social backgrounds of so many of the musicians themselves. Typically of working-class origin, their sybaritic workplaces could taunt memories of family hardship and continuing roots among the unprivileged. Billy Amstell, who like so many musicians came from London's East End, was again a case in point. Making his daily journey from Stepney to Mayfair, a metaphor in itself for a divided Britain, his conversion to socialism came aptly enough en route from one world to the other, listening in to the soapbox oratory in the Commercial Road. Amstell was doubly a representative figure in that his parents, like those of Mairants, Harry Gold and other left-leaning musicians, were Jewish immigrants from Eastern Europe, their culture of self-improvement and educational achievement finding one outlet in rich inherited traditions of music-making.[12]

This involvement of Jews in jazz was much remarked on by contemporaries, from the Nazis, who saw it as a further proof of 'Judaeo-Negroid' degeneracy, to the American communist Mike Gold, who in the US *Daily Worker* expounded on the music's 'Afro-Yiddish' character, to a Mr Leslie Frewin, who in 1939 put a similar case to the South West London Rhythm Club.[13] This Jewish presence was also strongly marked in the British dance bands, where among the Ambrose sidemen alone there was a trumpeter son of a Canadian rabbi, a drummer specialising in 'Yiddisher' comedy numbers and a saxophonist who later recorded an album of Jewish party tunes. On Archer Street that presence met with a certain amount of anti-Semitic feeling and it may be that the hostility of some conventional musicians for dance-band players was similarly infected.[14] What seems inescapable is that the politicisation of these young musicians was part of a wider process of Jewish radicalisation to which the rise of Fascism was fundamental.

While such social factors help explain the higher than usual incidence of individuals gravitating to the left, the existence of a veritable movement of such individuals is best seen in the context of musicians' trade unionism. Formed in Manchester in 1893, the Musicians' Union was a classic example of a small craft union in which militancy and strength of organisation increasingly had to make up for the essential fragility of its craft basis. In the musicians' case, the main threats to craft control were, albeit in distinctive variants, familiar ones: new technology, foreign competition and semi-skilled labour. Of these, the first was critical, for nothing was to prove crueller to live musicians than the twentieth-century juggernaut of mechanised entertainment. Particularly damaging was the introduction of the talkies at the end of the 1920s. Where once flickering dramas had needed scores of musicians to fill the silence, now these fleapit bandsmen found themelves redundant at a stroke. Coinciding as this did with the arrival of world slump, the effects were devastating. One poignant image is of the 'Manchester Unemployed Symphony Orchestra', busking for coppers in Albert Square as no doubt its counterparts did elsewhere.[15] Musicians' employment and MU membership alike were decimated, and un- or under-employment remained an acute problem throughout the decade.[16]

Associated technologies posed a similar if less dramatic threat. Recorded sound, a blessing perhaps if confined to private consumption, became a scourge the moment it invaded the musician's public sphere. MU wrangles with the BBC had as much to do with the restriction of 'needle time' – the slots given over to records – as with the actual broadcasting rates for musicians. Another concern from just before the war was with the introduction of television to public places.[17] Later, with the spread of high-quality sound equipment, the battle was joined with public address engineers as they sought to dislodge musicians everywhere from working men's clubs to the Royal Shakespeare Company.[18] Further possible competition was threatened by incoming musicians, whether bearing the glamour of Americanism or the kudos of the European concert tradition. This could provoke strongly protectionist responses in the MU, most notably the virtual ban on US jazz musicians imposed with Ministry of Labour support from 1935. Where musicians did slip through it was either as variety artists or even, in the case of Coleman Hawkins in 1939, as a demonstrator for a musical instrument firm performing so-called 'students' concerts'.

Finally, there were the incursions of the 'semi-pro', described by the communist MU activist Harry Francis as 'our main bugbear'. That view was a widely held one. The issue was less one of dilution, perhaps, than of a beleaguered profession seeking to extend its controls to areas previously free of regulation; as Bohm succinctly put it, 'It was not the semi-pro who had invaded the pro's field, but vice-versa.' Strictly speaking the MU was not a craft union in that it had no membership requirements comparable to the literacy tests imposed by some US musicians' union locals. What it sought instead was that all remunerative engagements be paid at union rates and all musicians thus employed, whatever their main occupation, classified as professionals and thus organised in the union's ranks. The semi-pro, in other words, had no status in the union and the frank intention of union officials was that its insistence on full rates should eventually eradicate this source of competition. 'What the MU wants to see is a profession sufficiently remunerative for there to be no need for a man to have two occupations,' stated assistant secretary Hardie Ratcliffe.[19]

From its inception that had set the union at loggerheads with such leisure-time devotees as had long made up the northern brass band movement. More recently, the threat of undercutting by mere enthusiasts had become identified above all with budding dance-band players. Ratcliffe attached much of the blame to the aura of glamour with which papers like the *Melody Maker* surrounded the profession. 'Many will play just for the fun of the thing,' he noted sourly, 'and will do anything to have a seat behind a set of drums and dress up in a dinner suit.' Despite its endorsement in 1926 by the TUC, the MU's position also brought it into constant conflict with other Labour Movement bodies, concerned either to nurture their own choirs and orchestras or to hold events and benefits at less than professional rates. 'In memory of trade union martyrs, they danced to the music of a non-union band,' was the indignant reaction to a Tolpuddle commemoration by Dorchester Trades Council. The delicacy of the situation is well conveyed by the union's own contingents of top musicians at successive postwar May Day rallies, the first, in 1946, performing gratis, the second a year later marching at full union rates.[20]

Despite their particular vulnerability to the semi-pro, dance-band professionals were not at first much very much involved in the union. Nor indeed did MU officials show much hope or intention of organising this sector. 'Most of the people are young,' complained one, a professed enemy of jazz, 'and they don't see why they should be organised.'[21] It was the inadequacy of such attitudes which provided the left with its opening in the union. Moved by the uncertainty of work and erosion of wages, sometimes admittedly from very high levels, in 1935 a group of London musicians set up a so-called Voluntary Organising Committee [VOC] to circumvent official inertia. Its moving spirit, Charles Kahn, was, according to Bohm, 'officially recognised as a Communist – a strict Marxist'. Among Kahn's collaborators were other such communists or future communists as Bohm himself, a veteran of six impressionable months amidst Leningrad's 'musicians without woe'; Alec Mitchell, Bohm's companion in Russia and future MU London organiser; and two late defectors from the wage-cutting Roy Fox band, Ivor Mairants and Harry Gold. The aims, according to another communist participant, Harry Francis, were 'not only [to] enrol members by the thousand, many of whom were dance musicians, but also to teach them to think in terms of being members of a Trade Union rather than of an old-fashioned craft Guild'. The result by 1939 was that MU membership had recovered from a low point of 7000 to nearer 9000, with swinging, militant London very much leading the way. As Bohm put it, there was by then 'no outside the Union as far as London is concerned'.

With the sweeping success of a VOC slate, the union's London district committee was transformed politically, stylistically and generationally all at a stroke. Out went the 'bald-headed old guys', as Harry Gold remembered them, and in came a younger breed of dance-band leftists, gathering in the small hours in West End cafés and then setting their alarm clocks for the next morning's union business. 'It is practically a new committee with the dance musicians to the fore,' Bohm observed. 'The old reactionary element is in opposition, and a very poor opposition it is too – with the fascists trying to work through it.' As against that further suggestion of anti-Semitism among the older musicians, the dance-band boys were determinedly progressive. Their daily gathering in Archer Street, sometimes two to three hundred strong, generated its own fraternalism and opportunity for political discussion, as Lew Lewis, who was recruited there by the Communist Party, well remembers. 'You couldn't have talked politics among the rank and file 6 or 7 years ago,' Bohm reflected in 1939. 'I don't know any part of the population that has changed quicker.'[22]

While the provinces lagged far behind the capital in this respect, the 'forward movement' gradually took root across the entire country. By the late 1940s MU membership had trebled to nearly 30,000 and the communists were by now the dominant presence in the union. That was best represented by the election as union chairman and assistant secretary respectively of Van Phillips and Harry Francis, both of them veterans of the VOC. Phillips in particular was an extraordinary instance of gamekeeper turned poacher. An expatriate American and well-known broadcaster, he was briefly the highest paid musician in the British film industry, orchestrating for Jack Buchanan his 'luxurious never-never land of West End theatres, Mayfair nightclubs, Home Counties mansions, four-star hotels, Cunard liners and a Riviera where the champagne flowed without pause'.[23] Phillips's real vocation, however, which eventually led to his virtual blacklisting, was as one of life's irrepressible instigators and organisers. In this he was driven on by the strong communist commitments evidenced in 1939 by his working on Ivor Montagu's CP propaganda short, *Peace and Plenty*.

By this time Phillips was already secretary of that unlikeliest of trade unions, the Dance Band Directors' Association, and chairman and secretary of the Musicians' Social and Benevolent Council. The latter body, essentially the creation of MU militants, is remembered chiefly for its immensely popular Jazz Jamborees, held annually from just before the war. Through his West End contacts, Phillips also helped spread the ideas of the VOC to the acting profession, where, with the help of CP industrial organiser Peter Kerrigan, a Voluntary Chorus Committee campaigned to secure representation of chorus members and supporting actors on Equity's ruling council.[24]

That same year, 1940, Phillips was first elected to the MU's executive. Subsequently he was the 'prime mover' behind the union's Music Development Committee which, chaired by that 'strict Marxist' Charles Kahn, lobbied for municipal patronage of the arts as provided for by the 1948 Local Government Act. Phillips also took an active part in the founding congress of the International Federation of Musicians in 1948. By this time, he and fellow representative Hardie Ratcliffe could look back on a series of MU successes unparalleled even in the USA, particularly as regards limiting the use of recorded music in broadcasting and places of entertainment. 'The legal protection for musicians ... in Great Britain,' Ratcliffe proudly asserted, 'surpassed the provisions existing in any other country in the world.' The union had by now acquired a formidable reputation for militancy, such indeed that a threatened Yuletide strike in 1949 was widely reported as a red plot to wreck the kiddies' pantomimes.[25]

The dance players' radicalism, therefore, despite its clear political inflexion, was fundamentally an assertion of producer interests in the churning out of music as a commodity. Like other craft workers, the leading practitioners took great pride in their professional standards, while some of the better bands, like Ambrose's in the late 1930s, offered real if limited scope for creative musicianship. That was even more abundantly demonstrated in West End haunts like the Bag O'Nails, to which musicians frustrated by their paying jobs repaired to let their hair down. 'It would be typical of these Archer Street men,' writes one historian, 'to charge the rate for *one second* of overtime they worked at restaurant or hotel, fretting during this paid overtime, to hie themselves to a spot where they would blow all night for no financial reward whatsoever!'[26] That important caveat notwithstanding, the essential thrust of musicians' unionism was to combat all such unregulated or unremunerative performances. Its eventual aim, as Hardie Ratcliffe saw it, was to achieve a standing for musicians analogous to those of the legal and medical professions.[27]

One consequence of these aspirations was that the union remained on uneasy terms with mere musical enthusiasts such as characterised the new culture of jazz appreciation then emerging in Britain. Bohm's view was admittedly an extreme one. 'If they last long they are mental cases,' he explained of jazz followers. 'I was a fan for one or two years, 20–22, but I soon lost it when I learned economics and so on.'[28] The 'revivalist movement', for its part, was explicitly one of encroachment by 'collectors and enthusiasts' on to the exclusive territory of these professional musicians.[29] The paradox was that in these circles too, communists and other leftists were prominent, passably familiar with economics, no doubt, but giving voice to values that were antithetical to Archer Street's.

Although there were some adventurous precursors, the movement for jazz appreciation in Britain is best dated from the establishment in 1933 of the first local jazz club, proudly designated the 'No 1 Rhythm Club'. Within two years, some hundred or so such clubs had been established and the first 'hot' magazines produced to cater for this burgeoning interest. While the pioneering 'No 1' was very much an upmarket affair, its men in lounge suits and its women 'of the sophisticated type', jazz for rather more of its devotees had an unmistakable flavour of rebellion. 'If H.G. Wells had been in his teens in the early 1930s, he would have attended the first Rhythm Clubs,' Hobsbawm notes, and the suggestion of stifling school rules or deadening office routines to be escaped from is exactly right.[30] It was only during the war years, however, that this unfocused challenge to authority took on more overtly political forms that helped define or rationalise the visceral appeals of jazz. Central to this development were two tireless groups of young proselytisers: the Jazz Appreciation Society (JAS), based well beyond the bayou in Newark, and the more portentous-sounding Jazz Sociological Society (JSS), whose excellent publications bore the still unlikelier postmark of Neasden. Only the first of these had links with the communists, the latter leaning more towards a form of parlour anarchism, but between them the two bodies created a powerful identification between authentic jazz appreciation and the left.

It would be wrong to imply too hard and fast a line of division between the two groupings, for the 1940s jazz buffs read and contributed to each other's publications and issued no political anathemas save against their common enemies. Nevertheless, there was a very definite difference of tone between the JAS and JSS. Of the two, the JSS was the more ecumenical in its tastes, reaching beyond jazz itself to sundry other expressions of individual revolt against a mass society. In this somewhat eclectic repudiation of convention were clearly prefigured later moments of youth revolt. 'Interested in modern poetry, literature, surrealism, classical music and Eastern philosophy,' was how the society's co-founder and co-editor Albert McCarthy presented himself, not in 1963 but 1943, 'strongly opposed to haircuts and manual labour.' McCarthy's intellectual pretensions allowed some unfortunate poetry in amongst the society's jazz criticism, none of it worse than that contributed, along with enthusiasms for Henry Miller, by Nicholas Moore. 'Ping, bing, zing,' wrote Moore (who as it happened came from Tring) in a memorable evocation of the Count Basie orchestra. 'And in each line, each phrase, there is a theme, a theme of the world's madness through which there gleams that real world we would have.' McCarthy himself, to whom that poem was inscribed, described jazz as 'a sort of musical "back to nature"', appealing particularly 'to the younger person, less corrupted by the false values of our capitalist civilisation ... because it expresses their inner revolt against the acceptance of their parents' philosophy'. These were not, of course, views widely held in communist circles. Max Jones, McCarthy's chief collaborator, had at one time contributed a jazz column to *Challenge*, but on his flirting with the anarchist journal *Freedom* was cast aside, he recalled, as a 'Trotsky-deviationist'. Jones's own recollection was that he had offended as much by musical as by political heterodoxy. 'They felt that I wasn't pressing the proletarian side,' he recalled, ruefully instancing his weakness for big swing stars like Artie Shaw and Charlie Barnet.[31] Such stories lose nothing in the telling, but it is certainly true that the jazz enthusiasts associated with the Communist Party had very far from catholic tastes.

The main vehicle for these communist musical purists, the Jazz Appreciation Society, was not by any means a politically exclusive body. While one of its co-founders and editors, James Asman, was a communist, the other, Bill Kinnell, leaned away from communism and towards anarchism 'in a large-hearted way'. Contributors to JAS publications had no Party line imposed on them and its advisers even included the same Gray Clarke who so debunked musico-sociological politicians. Nevertheless, the overall tenor of the JAS was one that clearly reflected the cultural politics of the Communist Party. It worked, as it put it, 'in full co-operation' with the Workers' Music Association, and when Asman and Kinnell sought co-signatories for their 'farrago of nonsense', at least five of the seven turned out to be communists. It was characteristic that three of the five, all associated with *Challenge*, were among the list of JAS forces contacts doing their bit for the British war effort: a contrasting image to that of Albert

McCarthy, sitting implausibly in his civil defence tin hat compiling a Jimmy Lunceford discography.

Also characteristic of the JAS was its boozy masculinity. Whatever the style or location, jazz audiences and practitioners alike were in this period overwhelmingly male and Bill Kinnell, who 'look[ed] to sex as a large motivating factor in Jazz', frankly described his great love as 'a male music'. Among the communist element this preponderance of young men generated a virile camaderie that apparently was inseparable from the taproom. Asman himself set the tone, jocularly expecting 'to die young from alcoholic poisoning and foul pipe fumes' and urging the same vices on visitors to his editorial offices. The leading foursome in the *Challenge* jazz club were likewise presented as 'shady characters in many beery and pleasantly hectic episodes'. 'Now busy chasing Fascists,' the JAS's *Jazz Record* described one of them, Pete Martin, 'and, despite an extremely tough appearance ... a devil of a good fellow.' George Duffield, another of the same circle and a frequent *Challenge* contributor, was similarly depicted as 'a lengthy fellow of low habits and high principles ... Vitally interested in all forms of progressive culture while being eminently capable and ready to sink a beer with the next man.'

If real ale had needed defending in the 1940s, one feels certain that these were the people to do it, unlike the vegetarian Max Jones and non-smoking teetotaller Albert McCarthy, removed as they were from their indigenous plebeian culture. John Vyse, of *Challenge* and the RAMC, even detected in some jazz fans a 'tendency to fairyness' alien to a people's music and wished the 'precious pretty boys' and their 'abnormality' some more appropriate outlet. Artistic preferences told the same story. Tony Short, an able blues pianist returned from the forces, ridiculed the association of jazz with Surrealism. 'It is obviously objectionable to our modern pseudo-intelligentsia to rub shoulders with the ordinary sordid world,' he wrote. 'They prefer to dream vaguely of some obscure plane of their own, exclusive to shaggy hair and sandals, affected boredom and deliberate unconventionality.' Short himself, evidently sharing communist conceptions of a people's culture, carried *Piers Plowman* with him on his travels and loved Bach and the Elizabethan composers as much as he did jazz.[32]

It was the perception of jazz as a great people's art form that had such political resonance for its young aficionados. A key text in this regard was Iain Lang's avowedly 'Marxian' account, *Background to the Blues*, published during the war and shortly after it expanded to the book-length *Jazz in Perspective*. Personally Lang was more closely associated with the JSS, but his was nevertheless the definitive statement of the 'class' interpretation of jazz, acceptable enough to communists to be published under WMA auspices. Two of Lang's arguments in particular exemplified his class-based approach. The first, ineffectively sustained, was to contest conventional derivations of jazz from its underworld setting and insist instead on its roots in work as well as pleasure. In practice, it was not the world of labour that Lang depicted and he like others found irresistible the violent, exotic colours of that deep America where razor-fights were halted by hot trumpet solos and musicians hardly blinked to find their instruments 'shot full of holes'.

More consistently argued, and far more controversial, was Lang's categorical repudiation of ethnic or racial interpretations of jazz and its origins. Instead he insisted on the music's cosmopolitan sources, the offspring, as he called it, of a mixed marriage that brought together both European and African musical forms. 'Jazz is not the music of a race, black or white, but of a class – of a proletariat which includes black and white ... only a people insulated by class and poverty from cultural orthodoxy and social convention could have created a new, independent and dynamic musical language.'[33] While obviously anathema to romantics like Hugues Panassié – 'All-Black obsessionists', Lang called them – this non-racial view of jazz was contentious even among Lang's fellow Marxians, simply because the formative black contribution to the music was, except for the odd crank like R.G.V. Venables, simply unarguable.

Asman, for example, a discerning partisan of black jazz, had 'reluctantly' to be reasoned into recognising white musicians' merits and had more than once given currency to the sort of casual racial generalisations that came all too easily to the music's white devotees.[34] The JSS, perhaps, evinced a more militant political commitment in its coverage of US race politics and even on one occasion a short contribution by George Padmore. But for the communists of the JAS, the 'negrophile purist' appeared, in the 1940s, a disturbing inversion of that gravest of current perils, 'the petty racialism which in the long run destroys culture and which stems purely from the Nazi-Fascist cultural mentality.' It was thus ill-disposed to racial categories that the JAS conclusively rejected 'all-black' and 'all-white' theories of jazz alike.[35]

What these communists and left-wingers cherished in jazz was an authentic people's music uncontaminated by either state, commerce or the academy, a purity maintained by disregarding as jazz anything that was so contaminated. Thus, at several levels, was extolled a spontaneity that contrasted markedly with official communism's cult of state patronage and the artistically respectable. Lang, for example, contrasted the 'true democracy' of New Orleans polyphony, sublimely reconciling individual and collective expression, with the 'totalitarian' order of the symphony.[36] Links between audience and musician were likewise conceived as organic and reciprocal and Doug Whitton, co-founder of Collet's jazz department, trumpeted the music's independence of official patronage, ill conceiving 'anything more stifling to the production of creative music than a nationalised jazz band!'[37] The defining aversion of the purists, however, was to the commercialism and 'slick cleverness' of industrialised entertainment, not least the long-dominant strains of that 'swing' music that masqueraded as jazz.

Among the fiercest proponents of these views, best described perhaps as Jazz Against Jazz, were Lang himself and JAS leading light, Graham Boatfield. Brusquely dismissing Duke Ellington, let alone Geraldo, they identified two particular causes of musical degeneracy. One was the development of orchestration, 'the usual constipated arrangements affected by these conglomerations', in which Lang detected the influence of the sheet-music industry and conventionally trained musicians, anxious for their jobs. The other, blighting even more informal performances, was the decline into individualism, self-indulgence and mere virtuosity. 'Solo variations become exhibitions in which difficult technique becomes an end in itself, and the screaming of hundreds of high notes is held up to glory,' wrote Vyse and Duffield. 'The best of all [music] comes from groups where there is a fairly strong discipline, where no individual is purely the star,' agreed Boatfield. Their ideal was the collective improvisation of the classic New Orleans or Dixieland ensemble, to which Asman added an early, prescient appreciation of the country-blues artists who had yet to find either critics or historians.

There was something almost Rousseauian in this discovery of original virtues lost to those 'denatured', as Boatfield put it, by commercial swing and other such corruptions of taste and morals. A 'fervent' communist where Asman was a 'vague' one, Boatfield saw in the blues lyric an escape from literary mediocrity to the golden age of Chaucer and Langland, since surviving only in the subterranean traditions of the popular ballad. 'The cold and hollow splendour of the Elizabethans, the involved and clever fancies of the 17th and 18th centuries, even the high flown nonsense of our romantic poets, so beloved of some woolly-minded left-wingers, contain very little that is of use to ordinary people,' he wrote in 1942. 'It is up to the poets of today to use the fairly simple blues idiom along with other popular forms to express truly the progressive spirit of the age.'[38]

The values of a people's music were, in more complex ways than their proponents perhaps realised, sharply opposed to those of Archer Street. A characteristic sketch of Asman's set the true jazz creator in a garret-like nightspot, 'happy I guess, even if he was starved looking and kinda threadbare,' while bright lights and pay packets awaited the mercenary 'palookas' engaged in the 'music racket'. That distaste for all box-office considerations was a constant motif in the jazz magazines and Britain's dance-band palookas thus suffered the open derision of listeners indifferent to their material concerns. As for Asman's 'mugs in the dough [with] no kick except the dough', that happy state was precisely the object of the musicians' militancy.

The irony was that for all Asman's organic metaphors, of a music which 'naturally and logically had to come into being', and for all McCarthy's 'repulsion to the prevailing machine "zeitgeist"', British jazz enthusiasts were acquainted with this music exclusively through the highly artificial, industrialised medium of imported recordings. Theirs was a people's music produced not by people but by gramophone records, a commodification implicit in the enthusiasts' generic classification as 'collectors' and the endless discographical details and tips 'for your collection' found in the aptly named *Jazz Record*. The shellac 78 was at the heart of this culture, identified, listened to (preferably socially), accumulated, listed, documented and even versified ('The ping and zing of the beginning of one of the Count's records ...'). Inevitably that culture of consumption implied a certain tension with unionised musicians whose principal concern was that music, even if not a people's music, be produced by people, albeit not just any people.

At best there was a degree of mutual incomprehension. Owen Bryce, a rare case of both collector and performer, recalls how at wartime rhythm club sessions the collectors would sit rapt through the opening record recital and then disappear to the bar while home-grown musicians, themselves preferring a drink to the recital, now went through their paces. 'Generally speaking,' says Bryce, 'the collectors disliked the musicians because the musicians were all dance-band musicians and the only things that they played in the jazz idiom were things that the big bands played.' Far from supporting MU demands over needle time, the same collectors lobbied for 'good intelligent recitals by experts and a welcome end to the miserable "live" broadcasts of a dozen London Swing outfits'.

For some that betrayed a taste for older and purer jazz forms, for 'if the best jazz is not being produced at the moment,' as Boatfield put it, 'why put up with what is?' Others, less dogmatic stylistically, were nevertheless adamant as to the superiority of American jazz over the domestic productions maintained by the MU in a veritable state of autarky. This not only reinforced the fans' predilection for recordings but in due course brought them into direct conflict with the MU over the ban on visiting musicians, a protracted campaign that gave an impression of staid philistinism on the MU's part. 'Hardie Ratcliffe would say, "I thought you were one of us, mate, aren't you a socialist?",' Max Jones recalled, but the suggestion that Nat Gonella would do just as well as Louis Armstrong could not but dismay even the staunchest defender of union rights. It was noticeable that even in Lang's Marxian account, ostensibly sensitive to labour issues, musicians' unionism figured only as a baneful force of exclusion from music-making. No doubt for many left-wing fans the campaign against the ban posed a real conflict of loyalty, but only over the tactics of getting the ban lifted, not the principle itself. That dilemma remained until, after sustained pressure, the ban was finally lifted in the mid-1950s.[39]

If anything, the collectors' promotion of indigenous British jazz served only to widen the breach with Archer Street. This revivalist awakening, a minor landmark in the history of British popular music, marked perhaps the closest convergence yet of jazz with left-wing politics. Visiting London in October 1944, Asman had at first to be strong-armed into a Home Guard dance to listen to George Webb's band, then causing something of a stir in the far south-eastern suburb of Barnehurst. 'There's no such thing as a jazz band in this country,' grumbled Asman, but to his astonishment the sound he heard was like his treasured record collection suddenly made flesh and blood. The musicians showed more commitment than finesse, perhaps – 'we couldn't have got worse, it was impossible,' Webb admitted of their earliest efforts – but then the very last thing Asman was looking for was slickness of execution. Moreover, these were no gutless professionals but ordinary young workers, several from the local Vickers-Armstrong factory, who were anything but antagonistic to the left. Here then was authentic jazz, arising from the English proletariat and offering a new vocabulary for its attenuated musical traditions.

The response of Asman and his fellow communists was immediate and positive. Through Ken Lindsay, the Webb band was booked for a series of sell-out concerts for the *Challenge* Jazz Club, the first of them under the frowning Methodist busts of the Memorial Hall, Farringdon Street. Asman, meanwhile, having failed initially to get Decca to promote the band, issued its first recordings at his own expense as Jazz 0001. Prohibitively priced compared with ordinary releases, the disc nevertheless met with such immediate acclaim that Decca quickly reconsidered its position and featured the Webb band in the first commercial recordings of the British jazz revival. Reviews and radio coverage alike were broadly favourable.

Less sympathetic were the established musicians, jealous perhaps of the attention being given these hamfisted part-timers whose amateurism was a matter not just of circumstance but of ideology and ethos. An apocryphal story has the Webb trombonist, Eddie Harvey, hauled before a kangaroo court for his dance-band proclivities; and the revivalists had particular scorn for the commercial travesty of 'Archer Street dixie', best represented by communist Harry Gold and his Pieces of Eight. 'We never liked that group of people,' recalled Bryce, arranger and co-inspirer of the Webb band, 'and in many respects they not only didn't like us but were very much opposed to what we were doing because we were amateurs.' Webb himself, a veteran of Vickers-Armstrong canteen bands, did not even read music, nor had he any ambitions beyond playing for what Ratcliffe had scathingly described as 'the fun of the thing'. Though by no means anti-union, Webb was happy enough playing 'for tuppence in Vladivostock', or at least some English provincial equivalent, never troubling too much about formal MU rates. 'I was never a professional musician, I never earned any money out of jazz at all,' he later recalled. 'I feel that I'm happy to be there and I shouldn't take a penny out of it.' The unwitting threat of this new people's music to musicians' unionism could hardly have been more succinctly expressed.[40]

These tensions do not appear to have surfaced greatly within the Communist Party, although fuller records of its Musicians' Group or National Cultural Committee might tell a different story. Nor did Soviet proscriptions of jazz have much effect on British Party policy, even during the Cold War heyday of Zhdanovism, whose bayings at Americanism and cosmopolitanism could have had no more obvious target. The health of British dance music was, implausibly, among the concerns expressed at the 1951 conference *The American Threat to British Culture* and the MU's exclusionist policies fitted perfectly with the CP's Cold War cultural politics. There was, too, a day school at which J.R. Campbell confronted what was evidently regarded as the 'problem' of jazz, while for months at a time the music disappeared from the pages of the *Daily Worker* and even *Challenge*.[41] Nevertheless, it was a sign if nothing else of divided counsels that in September 1949, the very height of Zhdanovism, Collet's International Bookshop opened up its jazz department. Two months later it was prominently advertising recordings made by Sidney Bechet during his legendary clandestine visit to Britain in defiance of the MU ban.

If official responses were relatively relaxed, there were, as so often in CP history, homespun zealotries and aversions which, while owing little to Moscow, nevertheless brought to the latter's fixations their own intense moralism. In the case of jazz, this sense of outrage was provoked not so much by the music itself as by the introduction of jazz dancing. The occasion was the visit of Graeme Bell's Australian Jazz Band direct from the 1947 Prague Youth Festival. On arrival in London Bell was immediately struck by the respectful cerebration of British jazz audiences, 'chewing seriously on their pipes and sipping their beers with thoughtful expressions ... nod[ding] quietly to the beat of their "pure" jazz.' Mystified by such old-worldly solemnity, Bell linked up with a *Challenge* contingent including Lindsay, Martin and Whitton to establish the Leicester Square Jazz Club with its proud motto *Jazz For Dancing*. That message was prominently carried in *Challenge* itself under the heading 'Jazz Girls Wanted'.

Despite sceptical objections – that jazz fans preferred to listen and 'girls' preferred the treacly 'Archer Street boys' – the club soon attracted a substantial new audience including a noticeable and reputedly obnoxious art-school element. 'Hand in hand, they prance, cavort, gesticulate, stamp, whirl, sweat and laugh with the most obvious enjoyment,' the *Daily Worker* reported; 'it is a real night out from a daily round of soul-crushing self-consciousness and respectability.' One fan also chipped in: 'If boys would not stand in the corners and poke fun at the girls, we female jazzers would really show them how to jazz! ... It certainly has some go in it, even though it comes from America.'

All this was too much for those censorious elements so often found on the left. 'Dancing at its best is an emotional display and as such is to be deplored,' one of them let himself go, 'but jitterbugging is really the lowest to which anyone can sink. To turn oneself into a slobbering savage, a

drooling psychopathic horror, a jerking bundle of sensual emotions ...'
Another, no less priggish, saw dancing as 'a rather poor way ... of
consuming surplus energy', quite irrational 'from the point of view of
personal efficiency'. Stung into defending herself, our beleaguered female
jazzer could only object sniffily: 'I am no spiv (I am in the YCL). I dislike,
intensely, most of the boys I know ... ' The issue would not ultimately be
resolved, for it represented but the earliest variant of an enduring conflict
between orthodox conceptions of communist youth and prevalent forms
of postwar youth culture. At the 1952 YCL congress dance these two forces
literally came to blows when, attracted by 'the lowest and most decadent
form of Yankee Be-Bob', some hundreds of 'the St Pancras youth', many
of them working-class 'tough boys', provoked a brawl through their
extreme animosity to the country dances thrown in to keep the Scottish
and Lancashire YCLers happy.[42]

By this time we had entered a new era in which the jazz revival,
succumbing to all the insidious temptations of jazz popular, ended in the
awful apotheosis of the Trad Boom. From the ashes of the Webb band itself
had arisen a new ensemble, its star the old Etonian Humphrey Lyttelton,
personally sympathetic to left-wing causes, and its home territory the
eponymous Lyttelton Club, later the 100 Club. Behind the scenes was
leaseholder, band manager and sometime WMA lecturer Lyn Dutton,
another communist but one with a sharp eye for the main chance.
Assisting him financially was yet another CP member, the accountant
Ted Morton. Within a few years Lyttelton had, through native gifts and
careful management, become a national celebrity, while the formidable
Lyn Dutton Agency had on its books most of the top British 'trad' bands,
their talents thinly but astutely spread around a handful of 'star'
personalities. Their club, with its heart-sinking boast 'show me a banjo
and I'll show you a profit', was unquestionably the leading 'trad' venue.

In 1951 jazz had even received official recognition with a Festival Hall
concert under royal patronage, the music's left-wing promoters reportedly
showing an unseemly anxiety to brush shoulders with the present Queen.
Even skiffle, a self-made music if ever there was one, proved immensely
lucrative to Dutton in the shape of Lonnie Donegan. It was all a far cry
from the ingenuous but engaging idealism of the Webb band and JAS.
For jazz proper one now had to look to young modernists, their own
counterculture far removed from communism, or to such keepers of the
purist flame as Ken Colyer, a veritable fixture at 1950s protest marches.
That Colyer had pioneered the skiffle sound that Dutton now so adroitly
exploited only showed how apparently inexorable were the forces of
private enterprise.

For some of the early jazz converts of the austerity years it was all a little
disillusioning. Webb, a figure quite without malice, long resented the
machinations of Dutton, remembered as a 'shallow spiv'. Asman,
meanwhile, penned his own poignant valediction as early as 1950. The

rhythm club he then evoked was a place of beer, banter and fellowship, a vibrant young fraternity brought together by the turntable. Now, however, there was 'a smell around the place,' the smell of crass and insatiable commercialism. 'Bands, comperes, promoters, critics and guest artists ... fight unbecomingly for right of place,' Asman noted gloomily, 'and the real jazz lover stays at home with his collection.' That was a plaintive epitaph, but not one that everybody endorsed. Humphrey Lyttelton, as comfortable with jazz as entertainment as he was with the rewards that it brought, remembered less fondly the 'exclusive fug' of those early jazz appreciation gatherings. 'It was,' he noted pointedly, 'an audience of critics, experts, collectors, serious students – but no people.'[43]

Ungrateful as that was, it did identify a central paradox: that, despite its rhetoric of the people, early British jazz appreciation shared with so many forms of left-wing culture an eschewal of the popular, a comradeship of the elect, which was the secret at once of its richness and its marginality. Its refuge from the cash nexus, idealised even in the case of classic jazz, could be maintained solely at the expense of numbers. Only once let the actual people in, at least in postwar Britain, and the spivs and philistines were sure to follow. In the new postwar order, admittedly, it was the classes who very often aped the masses, with Lyttelton's band in great demand for debs' balls; but this was very far from the sort of social revolution the communists had had in mind. When, with a new surge of radicalism, jazz players next identifed themselves with the left, forming revolutionary ensembles and liberation music orchestras, it was in the stimulating but politically nugatory context of the artistic avant-garde. The 'people' and the popular remained as far apart as ever, and the music just as compelling.

Notes

1   Tom Harrisson, Mass-Observation Archive, University of Sussex (henceforth M-O), TC 15/4/B, 'M.U. officials in Archer St', 15 May 1939.
2   G.F. Gray Clarke, *Jazz Writing*, Jazz Appreciation Society (JAS), n.d. but 1946, pp. 20–22.
3   Francis Newton, *The Jazz Scene*, (Harmondsworth: Penguin, 1961), chs 13–14.
4   Gray's phrase; not, I take it, one of endearment.
5   *I Play as I Please*, (London: MacGibbon & Kee, 1954), p. 184.
6   Billy Amstell, *Don't Fuss Mr Ambrose*, (Tunbridge Wells: Spellmount, 1986), p. 22.
7   M-O TC 15/6/D, 'Jazz report', January 1939.
8   Acland to Tom Harrisson, 7 February 1940, M-O TC 15/6/H.
9   Ian Whitcombe, *After the Ball*, (Harmondsworth: Penguin, 1973), p. 172.
10 'M.U. officials ...'; M-O TC 25/8, '3 big shows!', c. February 1941; Marjorie Pollitt, *Party Organiser*, March 1939, p. 8; Billy Amstell, interview, October 1996; Douglas Hyde, interview, August 1993.
11 Bohm, 'MU officials ...'; Amstell and Hyde, interviews; Phillips, interview, August 1989, National Sound Archive (NSA).
12 Interviews with Amstell, Lew Lewis, May 1994, Dorothy Morgan, May 1994, Ben Birnbaum, September 1996.

13 S. Frederick Starr, *Red and Hot. The fate of jazz in the Soviet Union*, (New York: OUP, 1983), pp. 95–101; M-O TC 15/4/C.

14 See for instance, M-O TC 15/4/D, 'Archer St musicians', 15 May 1939.

15 Lewis, interview.

16 See letter to Clegg of 7 June 1939, M-O TC 15/4/C.

17 Harry Francis, 'MU officials ...'

18 MU *Report*, September–October 1949, p. 2; Birmingham Reference Library, MU Birmingham branch minutes, 11 April 1946, 14 July 1947, 28 June 1950.

19 'MU officials ...'; M-O TC 15/4/B, 'Musicians' Union', 2 May 1939.

20 Dave Russell, *Popular Music in England 1840–1914: a social history*, (Manchester University Press, 1987), pp. 230–31; 'Musicians Union'; MU *Report*, September–October 1949, pp. 4–5; Amstell, *Don't Fuss*, p. 82.

21 M-O TC 15/4/B, 'Musicians' Union. Liverpool secretary' (W.E. Skinner), 16 May 1939.

22 'MU officials ...'; M-O TC 15/4/B, 'Charles Bohm', 19 June 1939; Bohm, MU *Report*, May 1937, pp. 6–8; Harry Gold, interview, May 1987 (NSA); Phillips and Lewis, interviews; Harry Francis, MU *Report*, July–August 1948, p. 9.

23 Jeffrey Richards, *The Age of the Dream Palace. Cinema and Society in Britain 1930–1939*, (London: Routledge, 1989), pp. 222–23; for Phillips see Phillips, interview, Phillips papers, National Jazz Foundation Archive. Loughton; Dorothy Morgan, interview, May 1994; and M-O TC 15/4/B, 'Van Phillips & DBDA', 27 June 1939.

24 See Honor Blair's file in the Phillips papers.

25 MU *Report*, September–October 1949, p. 8; MU Birmingham branch minutes, 24 April 1949, 18 September 1949; International Congress of Musicians, draft minutes, August 1948; *The Times*, 17 December 1949.

26 Jim Godbolt, *A History of Jazz in Britain 1919–50*, (London: Quartet, 1984), p. 191.

27 'Musicians Union'.

28 'MU officials'.

29 James Asman, 'Thanks for the memory' in Peter Gammond, *The Decca Book of Jazz*, (London: Frederick Muller, 1958), p. 161.

30 Newton, p. 237 ff.; Godbolt, ch. 8; M-O TC 15/4/G, 'No 1 Rhythm Club', 19 June 1939; Max Jones, interview (NSA), March 1988; Laurie Green, interview, March 1994.

31 *Jazz Music*, no. 1/1942, October 1943, March–April 1944; Jones, interview.

32 *Jazz Record*, JAS, November 1943, pp. 6–7; *Jazz*, JAS, c. 1946, pp. 3–4, 9; *Jazz Writing*, JAS, 1; *Jazz Music*, JSS, June 1943 and October 1943; *Hot Notes*, JAS, c. 1944–5, pp. 17–18; *American Jazz No. 2*, JAS, 1946, pp. 20–21; Jones, interview.

33 Lang, *Jazz in Perspective*, Hutchinson, n.d., pp. 9–12, 24, 30–34, 39, 47 ff. and passim; Lang, *Jazz Music*, vol. 3, no. 2, 1946, pp. 16–23.

34 See his contributions in *Jazz Record*, nos 2/43 , 3/43, 4/43, where he crosses swords with Venables, and November 1943. Reviews in *Jazz Record* were at this time grouped under the headings 'Black Wax', 'White "Hot"' and 'Swingtime'.

35 Vyse, *American Jazz No 1*, JAS, c. 1946, pp. 8–10; *Jazz*, p. 3.

36 Lang, *Jazz in Perspective*, p. 59; other fans like Asman, however, had a great love of classical music.

37 *Jazz Journal*, May 1949, p. 13.

38 Lang, pp. 44, 54, 69 ff., 84–5, 95–7; Boatfield, *Jazz Record*, 1/43, pp. 2–3, *Jazz Music*, 9/43, pp. 4–7 and 3/42, pp. 6–7; Vyse and Duffield, *Jazz Music* 8/43, p. 8; Asman, *American Jazz No. 2*, JAS, 1946, pp. 12–14.

39 Asman, *Jazz Record*, November 1943, pp. 7–9, April 1944, p. 10, 4/43, p. 12; McCarthy, *Jazz Music*, 1/42, p. 2; Boatfield, *Jazz Music* 9/43; Bryce, interview, October 1996; Jones, interview. Godbolt's volumes provide a lively account of the campaign against the ban totally out of sympathy with the MU.

40 Bryce, interview; Webb, interview, October 1986 (NSA); Godbolt, *History*, ch. 12.

41 Birnbaum, interview; Eric Hobsbawm, letter to author, December 1996; 'The American Threat to British Culture', *Arena* (London: Fore Publications, 1951), pp. 9, 29, 37; Green, interview.

42 Graham Bell, *Australian Jazzman*, (NSW: Child & Associates, 1988), p. 105; *Challenge*, 21 February, 20 March, 10 April, 1 and 22 May, 5 June 1948; *Daily Worker*, 10 December 1948; George Bridges to Dennis Goodwin, 10 November 1952, NMLH.

43 Webb, interview; Roger Horton, interview (NSA), April 1992; Asman, *Jazz Journal*, June 1950, p. 3; Lyttelton, *Second Chorus*, (London: MacGibbon & Kee), 1958, pp. 70–71.

8

Andy Croft

The Boys Round the Corner: the Story of Fore Publications

'Poetry is the most intense and intimate form of communication between men,' wrote the poet Randall Swingler in the *Daily Worker* in 1950:

> Apart from any other significance it may have, it is therefore a thermometer of the condition of the human commonwealth. If you find contemporary poetry difficult, it may well be because in the present decadent condition of capitalist society the relation between men and women and their world are difficult and complicated. It may also be because the mechanism of modern life tends to squeeze out the creative spirit and the personal equation.[1]

Swingler was introducing 'Key Poets,' a series of one-shilling poetry pamphlets aimed at 'breaking down the barriers between poet and audience, and giving poetry a chance to rediscover itself as activity'. The series was published by Fore Publications and edited by Swingler and Jack Lindsay, two of the Party's most prolific and widely published writers, both regular contributors to the *Daily Worker* (Swingler had been literary editor from 1939 to 1941). Five books in the series were by Party members – Lindsay's *Three Letters for Nikolai Tikhonov*, Swingler's *The God in the Cave*, *Gentle Exercise* by Maurice Carpenter, one-time editor of the YCL magazine *Alive!* Dorian Cooke's *A Fugue for Our Time*, and *Aspects of Love* by Jack Beeching, an ex-merchant seaman. The others were *Twinter's Wedding*, a long poem in Cumberland dialect by the late Jonathan Denwood, *The Common Festival* by Stanley Snaith (an old friend of Lindsay's from the 1920s), Norman Cameron's poised and sardonic *Forgive Me, Sire*, Edith Sitwell's post-Hiroshima *Poor Men's Music* and George Barker's most famous long poem *The True Confessions of George Barker* (rejected by Faber on the grounds of obscenity, the poem later became the subject of questions in the House of Commons when part of it was broadcast on the Third Programme).

It was a distinguished, if uneven, project, a brave attempt to intervene in the widely perceived crisis of postwar English poetry, bringing together some of those poets who were not in thrall to the late Bloomsbury Modernism of Eliot-Auden-Spender-Lehmann but whose achievements had already been marginalised by it. The Key Poets demonstrated that even at the height of the Cold War communist writers still enjoyed some influence, respect and reputation in London literary life (the next series was to have included Dylan Thomas), that communist poets did not always only write about 'politics' (the most personal collections were by Beeching and Swingler) and that the Cold War settlement was still opposed by writers – like Edith Sitwell – a long way from communism. The series was well reviewed in the *Manchester Guardian*, while the poet John Pudney called it 'the only practical attempt I saw in 1950 to break the poetry crisis and reply to those who say that poetry is dead because poets are remote, wilfully obscure – and expensive'.

Unfortunately readers of the *Daily Worker* were less impressed. Four days after Swingler's article appeared, the paper published the first of a series of letters denouncing the general condition of contemporary verse and Swingler's perceived defence of its 'unintelligibility', holding up the Key Poets as examples of everything that was wrong with it. 'If Randall Swingler were familiar with the outlook of the workshop,' wrote one reader, 'he would know that we do not read a lot of "modern" poetry, simply because one needs to be a university don or a personal friend of the writer to get the hang of it.' Instead the Key Poets were urged to 'turn with more determination to the struggle for a better society. Let them furnish such poems as our Chinese comrades chant on the march; satire for our pamphlets; works which might put life into a public meeting; songs our young Communists could brighten a ramble or a demonstration with'. By the following week this correspondence had become a regular 'Forum on Poetry'. 'For the working class,' wrote one reader, 'things are and always have been fairly simple – for the class-conscious workers, extremely so.' 'Get a grip lads !' wrote another. 'If the ideas and hopes you express are clear, so should be your style. From the poets who are on our side we want verse we can shout and songs we can sing to help us in our struggle.' One reader dismissed the series as 'the musty blowings of an obscure and unintelligible clique of key-less poets'; another wanted to know 'why the poetry that the workers failed to understand at 7s 6d should be any clearer for being sold at 1s'.

None of the Key Poets were reviewed in the paper. The features editor 'John Bridger' (Michael MacAlpin) published only three letters defending the series from Lindsay, Ewart Milne and Edward Thompson who tried to raise the stakes by arguing that the context of Key Poets was the general failure of the Party (and the *Daily Worker* in particular) to support the Party's own writers. The debate was closed by Maurice Cornforth who observed that there was no point treating communist poets 'as tender shoots which wilt at the fresh wind of critical comments' from the working class, adding that if they 'want to stop writing for a narrow clique of aesthetes, they have got to change their ways very considerably ...'[2]

By 1950 readers of the Party's press were becoming familiar with this public-schoolmaster manner (the following month Cornforth opened the assault on Christopher Caudwell in *Modern Quarterly*, an attack for which the Key Poets controversy now looks like a dry run). For the previous two years the *Daily Worker*, *World News*, *Communist Review* and the *Modern Quarterly* had been urging Party intellectuals – writers especially – to join the front line in the 'Battle of Ideas'. Readers of the *Daily Worker* had been entertained to a series of vivid 'controversies' on cultural issues – *A Streetcar Named Desire*, Picasso, Ilya Ehrenburg, Lallans poetry, Caudwell, Shakespeare and the 'lively Soviet musical controversy'. In an attempt to bring these discussions into some sort of ideological order, the paper published a long article on 'The Fight for Culture' by Emile Burns (chair of the Party's National Cultural Committee) coincidentally on the same page as the 'Forum on Poetry'. There was nothing to be learned, Burns wrote, from the 'decadent culture of capitalist society'; 'it is absolutely vital to the working class that it should see that culture for what it is – the culture of a decaying class. To accept it as just "culture" in general, to allow oneself to be influenced by it, is to pass over into the camp of the class enemy ...'[3]

The affair demonstrated the vulnerability of the British Party to the exhortations of Zhdanovism (the Stalinist cultural line identified with the late A.A. Zhdanov) at the same time as it undoubtedly tapped a genuine and popular suspicion of post-Georgian poetry. But it also looks like a stage-managed attempt to clarify the Party's emerging Zhdanovite war on its own literary intellectuals (not surprisingly, the next series of Key Poets was never published). To use Swingler's metaphor of poetry as a thermometer of the condition of the human commonwealth, the temperature was falling fast. In the context of the Battle of Ideas, the inclusion among the Key Poets of non-Party writers was not a virtue but a heresy. Worse, some were *Bohemian* writers, associated with pre-war Modernism and postwar Fitzrovia; one reader thought Edith Sitwell's verse was 'tommy-rot'; another wanted to know 'what in the name of Burns and Gorky' was 'key' about the 'unsavoury scratching-the-itch' poetry of George Barker. Moreover, the accusation that the Key Poets constituted a 'narrow clique' and that the Party members responsible for the series represented interests that were not subordinate to the Party was related to the issue of the ownership of Fore Pubs. For the controversy was also part of a series of unequal contests between Party Centre and the generation of literary intellectuals who had joined the Party in the early 1930s and who were gathered around Fore Publications.[4]

Beginnings

Fore Pubs began before the war inside the Ralph Fox (Writers) Group of the Communist Party. The group did not itself engage in any public activity, but tried to co-ordinate the work of communists working in the Left Book Club (particularly in the Poets Groups and the London Writers and Readers Group) in the Association of Writers for Intellectual Liberty (FIL), the London PEN Club, Unity Theatre, the Workers Music Association and the magazine *Left Review*. In the summer of 1938 the group was looking for new ways to develop the Party's influence among British writers in order to strengthen the emerging radical and anti-Fascist literary culture in Britain:

> The two main projects instituted by the Group are the Monthly magazine of the Arts and Sciences which is to succeed 'Left Review', and the company for Pamphlet Publications. The 'Left Review' was brought to a dignified close in May, and since then negotiations which are now on the point of settlement, have been carried on with Allen Lane of the PENGUIN PUBLICATIONS, with a view to publishing the magazine as a PENGUIN MONTHLY. The first issue of the magazine in this form should appear in October. Cde. Maurice Richardson is now in charge of the Editorship of the magazine. The Pamphlet Publications Company is in charge of Cde. Randall Swingler, and will be in working order in August. A full memorandum of both schemes has been submitted to the Secretariat and approved.[5]

Left Review was no longer able to respond adequately to the rapidly deterioriating international situation and the Party was not in a position to fund the expansion which the editor, Randall Swingler, considered necessary. So long as it was identified with the Communist Party, *Left Review* was unlikely to increase its circulation much beyond 5,000 a month. To make the magazine more popular, more secure and more professionally produced, Swingler (clearly with the sanction of King Street) closed *Left Review* in order to put it at the disposal of the wider movement it had helped to bring into existence. Conceding control over the most successful literary magazine on the left was of course a risk, but Allen Lane had a reputation as a left-wing publisher and the presence of Maurice Richardson as editor would ensure the Party's links with the new magazine. Anyway, these were minor considerations set against the prospects of the capital investment and bookshop sales that Penguin could deliver.[6]

What happened to the negotiations is not clear but the new magazine never happened[7]. Not for the last time, Randall Swingler had lost a magazine and the Party a key point of contact with London literary culture, caught between the impossible economics of an independent radical magazine and the uncertain loyalties of commercial publishing.

Negotiations with Lane were certainly over by October, when Swingler was trying to launch a new, weekly cultural paper 'to be put at the disposal of organisations such as FIL for the expression of their news and views'.[8] But FIL were uncertain about the financial liabilities of such an ambitious publication and it never appeared.

The relaunch in July of the LBC Poets Group news-sheet as a monthly magazine called *Poetry and the People* suggests that negotiations with Penguin may already have broken down by then. But *Poetry and the People* – 20 badly duplicated pages inside a hand-drawn cover – was a poor exchange for *Left Review*. The first issue, edited by Philip Ongley, John Isserlis and John Manifold, sold only 400 copies. Despite its amateur appearance, however, by the end of the year it was selling 1,000 copies a month, aiming 'to stimulate and encourage the poet to write out of his experience, to reflect the life and feelings of his fellow-men', 'to arouse an interest in such poetry among the people' and 'to bring the poet and the people into as close a contact as possible for their mutual understanding and enjoyment'.[9] And yet there was something curiously defensive about the magazine, which repeatedly defended its existence on the grounds that poetry had a potential for attracting new people to the movement and that 'it is high time the written and spoken propaganda in the progressive movement had a poetic quality, that is to say became humanised'. This argument was made often enough to sound like a coded disagreement with King Street (presumably with either R.W. Robson or Emile Burns, then responsible for cultural matters). It might explain why in only the second issue (August 1938) *Poetry and the People* carried the extremely odd confession that 'many of our readers are far from convinced of the need for the journal', believing that, 'to put it mildly, we could be just a little better employed than with writing and reading poetry ...'

Meanwhile, Swingler and his brother Humphrey had combined part of their inheritance to launch the Pamphlet Publications Company – Fore Publications – in September 1938. Fore Pubs had a share capital of £1,000 and the Swingler brothers each acquired a £1 share in return for loans of £1,000 to the company. Unlike other communist publishing operations – Martin Lawrence, Modern Books, the Utopia Press, Lawrence & Wishart, the Cobbett Press – Fore Publications was never owned or controlled by the Communist Party (though the Party often behaved as though it was). Instead it remained the property of a group of communist writers and artists gathered round the Swinglers. Their loyalty to the Party was not in doubt, but their professional reputations and experience gave them a sense of an audience well beyond the Party. The other shareholders were the Australian writer Jack Lindsay, the actress Ann Davies (star of the Unity hit *Babes in the Wood*), the concert pianist and Unity stalwart Jimmy Gibb, Randall Swingler's wife Geraldine Peppin (also a distinguished concert pianist), the poet and critic Edgell Rickword and the *Daily Worker* circulation manager Charlie Castro. The Swingler brothers were the firm's first directors.

From an office on Great James Street, five minutes' walk from King Street, Randall Swingler began commissioning 'Key Books', a bi-monthly series of pocket-sized 64 page pamphlets – 'fiction, biography, history, science and topical information by the best modern writers.' Attractively designed and illustrated, Key Books certainly did not look like Communist Party propaganda. And they were not written exclusively by Party members; Geoffrey Trease contributed two children's books, while Swingler commissioned the novelist and critic Walter Allen to write an anti-Fascist novella for the series. The first six appeared in March 1939, covering a range of issues identified with the Communist Party's campaigns, but not advocating Party policy – Lindsay's *England, My England* (on the English radical tradition), Richard Goodman's *Britain's Best Ally* (the Soviet Union), Salme Dutt's *When England Arose* (celebrating the centenary of the People's Charter), *Science and You* by J.B.S. Haldane and two novellas – John Sommerfield's *Trouble in Porter Street* (about a rent strike) and Geoffrey Trease's *North Sea Spy* (a children's story about running food ships to Republican Spain).[10] Two months later they published Steven McGregor's anti-Munich polemic, *Truth and Mr Chamberlain*, and a political fable by Egon Erwin Kisch, *The Three Cows*. Key Books was a strikingly successful project, raising the technical standard of communist publications, a characteristic product of the Popular Front market for well-written, undogmatic, 'progressive' books which the Left Book Club had opened up so successfully. *Trouble in Porter Street* and *England, My England* both sold over 80,000 copies, and Fore Pubs sold nearly half a million pamphlets in their first year.[11]

Wartime

By the time the next Key Books appeared however, delayed for four months by the outbreak of war and the subsequent *volte-face* of the Party, the market for 'progressive books' had considerably narrowed. So had Key Books, now devoted to current political events – Desmond Greaves's *Ireland, Whose Ireland?* was written in response to the recent IRA bombing campaign. They were also less reluctant to argue for Communist Party policy; Edmund Paul's *A Warning to Europe* sought to justify the Soviet occupation of Eastern Poland, while both Hymie Fagan's utopian *England for All* and Wilfred Willett's *British Farming* were tailored to the Comintern's 'imperialist war' thesis (the latter somewhat improbably).[12]

As Popular Front institutions like the Left Book Club fell apart, poetry represented one of the Party's last surviving links with the mainland of British intellectual culture. As late as February 1940 an appeal for money in *Poetry and the People* attracted the signature of Stephen Spender (and by way of encouraging other readers, the magazine was pleased to announce that George Bernard Shaw had taken out a subscription to the magazine for the next eleven years). In May, *Poetry and the People* announced that it was planning to expand (though Swingler was quick to assure readers of the *Daily Worker* that this did not mean the magazine was becoming 'highbrow')[13] and was extending its coverage to the 'four arts', with Swingler, Rickword, Tom Wintringham, A.L. Morton, Sylvia Townsend Warner and Cecil Day Lewis joining the editorial team. *Poetry and the People* was taken over by the Arts and Entertainments Committee of the People's Convention through 'Newport Publications', another company established by Swingler, Davies and Jimmy Gibb (named after the WMA offices on Great Newport Street from which *Poetry and the People* was published); Jimmy Gibb was the proprietor. Turning *Poetry and the People* into a more substantial-looking publication – typeset, with an illustrated cover and carrying reviews and adverts – gave Swingler access to an increased paper ration. So many London literary magazines had folded since the start of the war – the *Criterion*, the *London Mercury*, *Twentieth Century Verse* and *New Verse* – and Swingler saw an opportunity to launch a broad, cultural journal which would be to the People's Convention what *Left Review* had been to the Popular Front. Early in 1941 Swingler wrote to Edgell Rickword, outlining plans for the new magazine:

> The paper will cover architecture, medicine, education, art, literature, etc., and the general plan is to devote the space to four or five quite substantial pieces per month rather than attempt by scraps and bits to cover the whole ground every time. One should, for instance, include a central article every month up to about 6000 words, with critical and constructive work really thoroughly done ... The great thing is that the field is now ours undisputed. Poor doddering old *Horizon* gives out a plaintive moan this month about nobody really liking them and if somebody doesn't buy a copy soon they will have to shut down! We can make a go of this paper in spite of the fact that our resources are now so scattered.

There was a small inaugural committee, consisting of Swingler, James Boswell and Allen Hutt, with Charles Ringrose as administrator (replaced by Honor Arundel when Ringrose was called up). Montagu Slater, John Banting, Cliff Rowe and Laurence Bradshaw were also involved.[14] The first issue of *Our Time* eventually appeared in February 1941, incorporating *Poetry and the People*. Edited for the first seven issues by Swingler, Beatrix Lehmann, Banting and Ben Frankel, the magazine ran to 28 pages and cost just 6d. At first *Our Time* was written wholly by communists, within the terms of the People's Convention. But it was clear from the start that Swingler was hoping to recreate the success of *Left Review*. A short editorial in the first issue announced the magazine's wider remit, arguing that the arts 'are not luxuries or decorations on the border of social life', but 'necessities to its development as essential as food and sleep. And like food and sleep, there is now too little of them'. In June 1941 *Our Time* moved to an office on Henrietta Street; the following month Fore Pubs also moved there. Ann Davies replaced Humphrey Swingler as a director and became chair and administrator of the company.

Shortly before Swingler was called up at the end of 1941 he bought the magazine *Seven* (with his own money) for £25, in order to acquire its paper ration for Fore Pubs.[15] Swingler installed Gordon Cruickshank as editor, and Cruickshank quickly established *Seven* as a bestselling quarterly magazine of stories and poems by men and women in the armed forces. When *Seven* was acquired, the accumulated losses of Fore Pubs amounted to nearly £2,000; within twelve months the firm was out of debt for the first time, returning a profit of £700. That year Fore Pubs left Henrietta Street and bought the lease on 28–29 Southampton Street (just round the corner from Great Newport Street, Henrietta Street and King Street), a first floor office, three second floor rooms and four third floor rooms. By 1943 *Seven* was selling 60,000 copies a quarter, running at a profit of £1000 per issue and enabling the firm to expand its operations. That year Fore Pubs took over Newport Publications and *Our Time*.

Meanwhile, with so many of the Party's best writers in the Forces, *Our Time* had fallen into the hands of the Party's Cultural Groups Committee formed at the end of 1942. The Party decided 'to try and give the magazine a firmer direction' and turn it into a kind of cultural *Labour Monthly*. Edited by the LPO manager Thomas Russell (calling himself 'A Sharp') it was aimed at arts professionals with the intention of expanding the Party's already considerable presence in the arts and entertainments industries. The move was a disaster; by the beginning of 1943 *Our Time* was selling less than 1,000 per issue.[16] Party members at Unity Theatre and the WMA persuaded the Cultural Groups Committee to intervene and Russell was replaced, first by Honor Arundel and Peter Phillips, then by R. Vernon Beste (Secretary of Unity Theatre) with instructions to make *Our Time* a more popular publication aimed at the new audiences created by ENSA, the Council for the Encouragement of Music and the Arts (CEMA) and the Army Bureau of Current Affairs (ABCA).[17] The first issue in the new format (August 1943) sold 5,000 copies; by April 1944 it was selling 9,500 copies.[18]

The economic success of *Our Time*, *Seven* and Fore Pubs coincided with the expansion of the Party during the war, and with the dramatically expanding demand for reading material, particularly in the forces. In 1943 Fore Pubs published the text of Ted Willis's Unity hit, *Buster*; in 1944 they published a critical pamphlet by Lindsay, *Perspective for Poetry* (Key Essays no. 1) and two collections of poems, *Trident* (by John Manifold, Hubert Nicholson and David Martin) and *Rhyme and Reason* (a selection of poetry, edited by Martin, from *Our Time*). They set up 'Lightning

Cartoons' to supply cartoons to other publications. By now Fore Pubs employed a full-time 'space salesman' and, thanks to Charlie Castro, they knew they could distribute any magazine or paper they published. In 1944 Lindsay and A.L. Lloyd began planning a series of popular essays (modelled on the WMA 'Keynote' series) celebrating the artistic and organisational gains of the war and looking ahead to postwar possibilities. Other plans included a new poetry quarterly, a radical dance-band music weekly and what Vernon Beste solemnly described as a 'Broad Woman's paper' ('to interest women in the achievements of women, with the idea of getting them to feel their equality with men'). After the success the previous year of Geoffrey Trease's *Undercover Army* (Key Books no. 15) Fore Pubs also planned an ambitious publishing programme aimed at children, launching two six-penny comics for children, *The Young Hero* and *The Young Comrade*.

The possibilities for expansion were however severely restricted by a paper quota of only six tons per annum (representing 40 per cent of Fore Pubs' paper consumption in 1938–39). And the distribution of Fore Pubs' magazines were always more successful than its books, which depended on sales inside the Party. On a print run of 2,500 copies, *Buster* sold only 800 copies in twelve months; over half of these were through Central Books and Collets, while sales through W.H. Smith accounted for only six copies. Reliance on the Party was not a problem for Vernon Beste, who considered Fore Pubs to be 'under Party control'. While he was on the board he established regular, weekly meetings with Emile Burns at King Street and defined the firm's role as publishing 'cultural magazines and books necessary to the Party, i.e. those which did not come within the definition of Marxian theory and which therefore would be put out by L & W'.[19] When Gordon Cruickshank left to work full-time for the Party he was succeeded as editor of *Seven* by an ex-*Mirror* journalist called Sidney Tremayne. Although *Seven* continued to go from strength to strength, Beste felt it had a 'none too clear line' (Tremayne was not in the Party) and was alarmed that Tremayne 'flatly refuses to accept what he calls "any control"'.[20] There were fights over the contents of the magazine; on one occasion Beste removed a four-page poem against Tremayne's judgement. When Tremayne refused to accept the imposition of an editorial board he was replaced in 1944 by John St John, a Party member with no experience of publishing (he also became a director of Fore Pubs).[21] Beste wanted to co-opt 'culturally conscious workers' on to the *Our Time* editorial board and tried to veto the publication of Lindsay's *Perspective for Poetry*. When Lindsay and assistant editor Arnold Rattenbury published (in Beste's absence) a May Day poetry supplement in *Our Time* including verse by Dylan Thomas, David Gascoyne and Hugh MacDiarmid, Beste published a letter the following month from 'an average industrial worker who is taking part in the fight for Socialism' protesting that he 'could not make head nor tail of them' or see 'how they could possibly help the struggle against fascism and for progress', 'a waste of paper because to the widest masses it is Greek.' In case the point was missed, Pat Sloan wrote in from King Street to demand that *Our Time* should 'print nothing that would not be understood by the ordinary reader who picks up the magazine on W.H. Smith's bookstall ...'[22] In order to preserve the autonomy of Fore Pubs and the integrity of *Our Time*, Rattenbury, Beatrix Lehmann, Slater and Lindsay appealed to Geraldine Peppin to remove Beste. She became a director, along with Lindsay and A.L. Lloyd.[23] In September 1944 the editorial board of *Our Time* was replaced by an editorial panel of Sidney Cole (films), Ted Willis (theatre), Francis Klingender (art) and H.G. Sear (music), with Beste as editor and Rattenbury as assistant editor; two months later the new board replaced Beste as editor with Edgell Rickword, and Emile Burns lost his weekly meeting.

Peacetime

Our Time expanded rapidly under Rickword's editorship. By the end of the war the magazine was selling 18,000 a month and attracting substantial advertising revenue. When Swingler was demobbed and returned as assistant editor to Rickword, he was amazed to discover that Fore Pubs not only owned a building but paid their contributors (£1 4s per thousand words). With estimated assets of £3,500, Fore Pubs had every reason to believe they could ride the peacetime 'cultural upsurge' which they assumed would follow the end of the war.[24] In March 1946 they launched *Theatre Today* (edited by Slater and Rattenbury) with sales of 20,000, the first of a series which they hoped would include *Film Today*, *Music Today* and *Art Today*. That year Lindsay and Krishna Menon launched Meridian Books and another radical literary magazine, *Anvil*, from the Southampton Street offices.[25]

But the continued rationing of paper made sustained expansion impossible. The problem was so acute that Rickword, Lindsay and St John entered negotiations with the Pilot Press (run by Charles Madge) to find ways of sharing their paper ration. Madge offered Fore Pubs his paper supply for *Cinegram Review* and for their *Achievement* series (which included Lindsay's *The British Achievement in Art and Music*) with a view to it being published by Fore Pubs as a monthly magazine. In return, Fore Pubs booklets would in future be published by Pilot Press. *Seven* was to become an occasional publication (which would then have access to Fore Pubs' book paper quota). They discussed setting up a new limited company with a joint board and an independent, non-Party figure as chairman (Julian Huxley's name was suggested) in order to launch a new group of periodicals. Rickword even tried to persuade Pilot Press to take over Fore Pubs (with places on the board of the expanded firm reserved for himself, Lindsay and Swingler):

The advantages as I see them are that we hitch our wagon to the star of an experienced businessman who will naturally want the company to be a success and who has as far as one can make out no political axe to grind beyond a general progressive one; that we should have the usual advantages of a concentration with which to face the dark and stormy days of postwar competition – in which the continuance of our present financial solvency is only problematic; and the wider contacts in the intellectual world which P.P. would bring us ... Of course the whole scheme would have to be vetted by experts on our side before a final decision were taken. Robbie doesn't like the idea much and of course that weighs a lot.[26]

Presumably either 'Robbie' (R.W. Robson) or the 'experts' at King Street were against the move, since it never happened. A year later Rickword again tried to increase Fore Pubs' paper ration by reviving, unsuccessfully, 'Left Review Publications' (the company which before the war had published *Left Review*). Fore Pubs was now in serious difficulties. Sales of *Our Time* had halved since 1945, as its wartime audience was demobilised. In the spring of 1947 Fore Pubs were forced to sell *Theatre Today* and the title *Film Today* to the Saturn Press and *Seven* (for £1,000) to the Dryden Press. Having commissioned a 'New Developments' series dealing with the contemporary cultural scene – including James Boswell's *The Artist's Dilemma*, Thomas Russell's *Music*, Fernau Hall's *Ballet*, Ann Lindsay's *The Theatre* and Arthur Calder-Marshall's *The Book Front* – Fore Pubs did not have the paper to print them and were obliged to sell the series to the Bodley Head.[27] In 1948 they published just two books, Roy Pascal's *The German Revolution of 1848* and Albert Soboul's *The French Revolution of 1848*.

Meanwhile Swingler called a meeting, chaired by Emile Burns, to discuss the future of *Our Time*. Rickword wanted to open the pages of the journal still wider while Rattenbury, Edward Thompson and David Holbrook wanted a more aggressive, *political* magazine. Chastised for the decline in circulation, Swingler and Rickword resigned, and for the next twelve months *Our Time* was edited by various 'commissions' including Rattenbury, Holbrook, Slater, Sommerfield, Russell and Charles Hobday.[28] Published by 'Our Time Publications' (and not Fore Pubs) *Our Time* was now recognisably communist once more. But if it was sufficiently anti-American to damage its circulation even further, the magazine also displeased King Street by refusing to endorse the Zhdanov and Lysenko 'controversies'. Rows with King Street meant that publication was sometimes delayed and W.H. Smith refused to handle distribution. By the end of 1948 Swingler was asked to return to *Our Time*, a far from irresistible prospect, as he explained to Rickword:

OUR TIME, ironically seems to be reverting on to my hands. What is one to do? It seems no one else is prepared to do anything about the paper. I've said that I'll take no interest at all unless it is on a fairly sound financial basis (the paper, I mean). But I can't at present make up my mind whether it ought to be allowed to die quietly, or whether we should really take it over and try to make something good of it again. It is because you made something so good of it (in everyone's opinion) that I am reluctant to let it die.[29]

Swingler returned as editor in January 1949. Sharing offices with Lindsay's Meridian Books on Garrick Street (still only round the corner from King Street) he and the artist Paul Hogarth immediately made *Our Time* more *literary*, devoting less space to criticism and more to new verse and fiction. The magazine's political provenance was heavily disguised by the range and distinction of its contributors and by a determinedly sprightly tone. In what sounds like a nod to King Street, Swingler acknowledged in his second editorial that he was often asked 'What sort of audience are you really addressing? Who is your magazine intended for?'; his answer was 'to anybody and everybody'. But Burns still insisted on trying to vet each issue and Swingler was fast losing heart. A last attempt to put the magazine on an independent financial basis with some 'Indian money' (the source of which was presumably Krishna Menon) failed. *Our Time* folded in August 1949 and Swingler lost another magazine.[30]

A Thankless Business

Anticipating the end of *Our Time*, Swingler and Lindsay had already started planning a new quarterly journal with the writer John Davenport. Fore Pubs were to publish it, although Rickword had serious misgivings about the economics of the project. Advertising itself as being 'especially interested in the work of the New Europe, in the roads blazed by resistance poetry, and in the new directions of postwar developments in the cultural field', the first issue of *Arena* was published on 1 May 1949, publishing work by Paul Eluard, Tristan Tzara, Albert Camus, Boris Pasternak, Jean Cassou, Hugh MacDiarmid and Edith Sitwell. *Arena*, declared Lindsay in an editorial note,

neither seeks to label our culture as 'decadent' nor to acclaim it as securely progressive. We believe that the culture of our world is rent by intense conflicts, and for that very reason is full of the most violent potentialities for good and evil, for integration and disintegration ... The work in which *Arena* is interested is the sorting out of these confused and often vital trends of resistance ... This work involves a give-and-take between Marxism in its critical aspects and the free play of the creative elements in our culture.

But the idea of a dialogue between communist and other writers in 1949 was a heresy on both sides. Emile Burns informed them that they were 'absolutely wrong' and should drop the formulation, and Derek Kartun in the *Daily Worker* called on the editors to 'start writing intelligibly' in future.[31] Despite publishing new work by Neruda, Montale, Aragon, Nancy Cunard, Malcolm Lowry and Angus Wilson, the next four issues of *Arena* were ignored by both commercial wholesalers and Party bookshops. Describing the magazine as 'European, with no Iron Curtain' was a brave but commercially suicidal position in 1950, when London literary culture was on one side of the Iron Curtain and the Party on the other. Presumably in the hope of placating King Street, an editorial board was created, containing 'reliable' names – Slater, Arnold Kettle and Alick West (chair of the Party's new, loyalist Literature Group) – and the magazine began to articulate the Party's Cold War cultural politics (Slater and John Lewis denouncing the Americanisation of British culture and Swingler ridiculing the 'Freedom of the West').

Just when it seemed that *Arena* had to either follow *Our Time* or surrender to the attentions of Emile Burns, Davenport suddenly found a source of unexpected finance from a young man called Tony Hubbard whom he had taught at Stowe School. Swingler wrote to Rickword in cautious disbelief:

> The old firm of Fore Pubs is hovering on the unusual crisis of being flooded with capital! John D has found some young millionaire protégé who is excited in a youthful dilettante way by ARENA and wants to back it. John D, who is penniless and also without other prospects, spies the possibility of a job in this and has persuaded him that what we want is a monthly magazine. I said (too modestly I now think) not less than £5000! And the fish seems to be biting. So here we may be with a firm, premises, and five thousand capital committed to the production of another literary monthly. What do you make of that? I must confess the prospect slightly appals and depresses me, but I suppose I am still disillusioned and cynical from recent experiences with OT. Not at all sure myself that we actually have the intellectual resources to run such a thing successfully – quite certain that I'm not a bit keen on editing it. Maybe John would knuckle down and make a job of it. I don't know. Wish I could discuss the whole thing with you. I suppose your feeling may well be too like mine, weary of the whole thankless business. One thing already established, we shall get no help out of the boys round the corner whose philistinism seems to be hardening rather than otherwise ...[32]

In the end they decided to launch yet another magazine and *Arena* was effectively left to the 'boys round the corner' at King Street. Swingler, Davenport and Paul Hogarth immediately set up another company,

Hubbard Pubs, operating from the Fore Pubs offices on Southampton Street. *Circus* appeared with a fanfare of publicity (including an advert in the *Daily Worker* inviting readers somewhat improbably to 'Join Circus and See Life on Stilts'):

> *Circus* is the magazine which Britain has always declared she wanted, and has never yet had. Wit, wisdom, sanity and enjoyment of life, without pomposity, exclusiveness or wailing self-pity will be the ingredients of this medicine for the public conscience. 'Health-giving and pleasant to take!' Why not?
>
> But you will find that *Circus* is not merely a gay diversion from the serious concerns of living. Very far from it. This *Circus* is at the centre of the whirl of the world, even giving impetus and vitality to its movement. Our purpose is profoundly serious, our method irresistibly cheerful. Where we find targets for attack, we shall hit hard and certainly; where we find cause for mockery our laughter will be uninhibited; and where we discover new paths to enjoyment, we shall open them up to common usage.
>
> We believe in life, and in man's capacity to extend his control and his appreciation of it. We believe in literature and the arts as the widest and readiest means towards that extension. We do *not* believe in appealing to any clique of the Best People, or in making dark ways even darker. To us the current cult of despair has become one of the funniest jokes in the West.
>
> So *Hoop-la!* Here we shall be in the first of every month, with the starriest troupe of performers ever gathered under one big top.

In order to attract advertising revenue they persuaded advertising agencies to loan them the stereotypes of their leading clients' adverts to use as bait for paid advertising, and so *Circus* appeared – on April Fool's Day 1950 – carrying adverts for Guinness, Shell, BOAC and Jamaica Rum, as well as contributions from Dylan Thomas, Angus Wilson, Gavin Ewart, Andre François, Keith Vaughan, John Minton, Ronald Searle, Augustus John, Lindsay and Swingler, *Circus* was an immediate success, a lively, pocket-sized humorous, radical literary magazine costing 1s for 64 pages. With a circulation of 10,000 a month, they moved into new offices on the Strand.[33] 'The intention, one gathers,' reported the *TLS*, 'is to produce a slightly higher-toned *Lilliput* but most of these left-wing Gullivers are ill-at-ease in their chosen *Lilliput*.' So successful was the imitation that Edward Hulton (owner of *Lilliput* and *Picture Post*) offered to buy them out after the second issue. When they refused, Hulton threatened legal action on the grounds that they had poached the character of *Lilliput* as well as some of his best contributors.[34] Ronnie Scott, Constant Lambert, Reggie Smith and Laurence Scarfe contributed to the magazine, and work was commissioned from Jocelyn Brooke, Joyce Cary, Dan Davin, Louis

MacNeice, Olivia Manning, Edith Sitwell and Edward Ardizzone. But Hulton's legal action never reached court. With only three issues published, Tony Hubbard discovered that his magazine was being edited by communists; two days later the bank account was closed. With a further six issues in proof and the contributors unpaid, *Circus* closed and Swingler lost yet another magazine.

The Damned Elusive Cash Basis

After the row over Key Poets, the patience of the 'boys round the corner' with the Fore Pubs 'clique' was running out. When Fore Pubs published a biography of the Polish poet Adam Mickiewicz, the *Daily Worker* ridiculed Lindsay's introduction (with its 'elitist' quotation from Czeslaw Milosz) as 'the sort of criticism which survives only because nobody has the courage' to say they cannot understand it; 'humbug is humbug, no matter where we find it,' added a helpful reader the following week. The paper returned to the attack on *Arena* two months later, which Michael MacAlpin thought made too great a claim 'on the concentration of its readers'. An essay on Coleridge by Lindsay was written, he said, in the 'jargon' of a 'snob-intellectual' 'coterie' who were 'guilty of ignoring the reader to whom *Arena* should appeal'; in future, the paper insisted, 'Mr Lindsay should write in the English language.'[35] Soon afterwards the Party's National Cultural Committee instructed Lindsay and Swingler to transform *Arena* into an expanded journal of Socialist Realism:

> a vehicle for the fight to develop a Marxist attitude in relation to literature and art, to combat reactionary trends, to provide a platform for writers and artists fighting for peace and socialism ... It must be a fighting journal of popular culture, breaking completely with the narrow cliquish trends of the past, fighting not only open reaction but also sectarianism on the part of our own writers and artists ...[36]

The NCC announced that in future it would appoint the editor, who would be paid by the Party and required to report to the NCC. Even the usually loyal Lindsay was dismayed, as he explained to Swingler, 'This is clearly not my cup of tea – though I'll possibly be on the Editorial Board. *But what about yourself?* I am sure that all the ouvrieristes would hate it. But we might well be able to get it through if Emile agrees. With your permission I'll take it up with Emile.'[37] Swingler refused to have anything to do with it, and *Arena* was allowed to die a slow and undignified death in three 'special issues' reprinting the main speeches from NCC conferences – *The US Threat to British Culture* (1951), *Britain's Cultural Heritage* (1952) and *Essays on Socialist Realism and the British Cultural Tradition* (1953). When the 'fighting journal' eventually appeared as the grim-looking

Daylight, it was with the announcement that this was one magazine which was 'NOT a journal for a clique ...'

Paradoxically, after the disasters of *Our Time*, *Circus*, Key Poets and *Arena*, Swingler and Lindsay began to turn Fore Pubs towards the Party. Because they knew the firm could not survive outside the distribution system of Party's bookshops, they began publishing books which would be acceptable to King Street. In 1950 they published a book of *Contemporary Chinese Woodcuts* (with a preface by Joseph Needham), Joseph Revai's *Lukacs and Socialist Realism* (with an introduction by Eric Hobsbawm), Neil Stewart's *Background to the New Hungary* and Lindsay's glowing account of his visit to the 1949 Pushkin celebrations in the Soviet Union, *A World Ahead*. Fore Pubs' list in 1951 consisted entirely of imports from the socialist countries – Ksawery Pruszynski's *Adam Mickiewicz*, Rena Moisenko's *Realist Music: Twenty Five Soviet Composers*, *Songs of Peace* by the Czech poet Nezval Vitezslav, Pierre Courtade's *Albania*, *Barefoot* by the Romanian novelist Zaharia Stancu and *Report from the Gallows* by the Czech communist Julius Fucik. In 1952 they published a collection of poems by the Welsh communist A.H. Evans, *I Face the Sun*; in 1953 Harold Watkins's account of working in the Peace Movement, *The Dove and the Sickle*, the Reverend Stanley Evans's *East of Stettin, Trieste* and *Mitrea Cocor* by the Romanian novelist Mihail Sadoveanu; in 1954 they published *Music in Rumania* by Leonard Cassinti. They were distributed through the Party and advertised and handsomely reviewed in the Party press (Edward Thompson reviewed *I Face the Sun* in the *Daily Worker* and Pollitt himself reviewed *Report from the Gallows*). But sales were disappointing to say the least; no copies of *Albania*, for example, appear to have been sold.

Fore Pubs' anomalous position, half inside, half outside the Party, was now a position of weakness. Towards the end of 1952 Lindsay tried to persuade Emile Burns to take Fore Pubs 'into the system', to become in effect an imprint of Lawrence & Wishart, offering King Street and Central Books a veto on all new publications in return for the Party's investment in a new literary magazine. But the NCC were not interested in supporting another magazine edited by Lindsay and Swingler. Anyway, Fore Pubs was by now inescapably 'in the system', their list distorted by the need to find books which could be 'guaranteed by party'. Lindsay was still optimistic that the firm could survive with the backing of the Party:

On this programme it will be seen we can't lose and must make something. But there is of course no income in it for anyone. However, we could certainly get more of the R[omanian]-novel type if we were more active and set ourselves to it. I think that in the definite effort to reinforce the peace overtures, etc. the new democs are likely to go more in for such things and if we can show that it is useful. But that alone won't suffice. What would is a programme linked with the party and the new efforts that the writers' group will be making – i.e. short novels etc., poems. The field would certainly be open to us, with very strong party backing for sales, etc., if we could step into it in the near future. What we need is the damned elusive cash basis to start a few of the non-directly-financed ideas off. I am convinced that the situation is totally different from 1950–1 when we flopped – the bottom of the wave-trough. In turn the hypothetical magazine could be linked to this. This ought all to be in your hands – because its just what you need and because in any event I haven't the time.[38]

But Swingler was no longer prepared to tolerate King Street's interference. When Ann Davies (now Lindsay) died in January 1954, Fore Pubs lost its administrator and one of its most able and energetic founding spirits. Without her, Lindsay and Swingler appear to have lost interest in the firm.[39] That year Fore Pubs published its last book, *The Transition from Feudalism to Capitalism* (the documents from the Dobb-Sweezy debate). The American *Science and Society* bought 500 copies, but US sales did not cover even half the printing costs. By now Fore Pubs was earning less from sales than from collecting rents and extensive repairs to 28/9 Southampton Street ate into even this. In 1953 Hyman Levy started a Socialist Book Club (a late attempt to revive the spirit of the LBC) renting offices from Fore Pubs. But reproducing the intellectual culture of the Popular Front was never likely to succeed at the height of the Cold War, and People's Books appears to have folded in 1955 after publishing only two books. Rent on the other parts of the building brought them £169 a quarter but the rent on the lease was increased in 1955 to £1,388 per annum, and then again to cover land tax; the rates on the building were £282 a year. By 1955 the sale of publications was earning Fore Pubs less than £200 a year. When the Czech authorities declined to publish a book which they had commissioned from Swingler and Hogarth about a visit to Czechoslovakia (on the bizzare grounds that it was not critical enough) Fore Pubs agreed to publish it. The publication date was supposed to be March 1956. By then, however, Swingler had left the Communist Party and the book was never published.

When Swingler joined the editorial board of another new magazine in 1957 – the *New Reasoner* – he borrowed £50 from Fore Pubs to help launch it. Edward Thompson even suggested that Fore Pubs might publish the magazine and, when it merged with *Universities and Left Review* in 1959, he enquired about the possibility of renting the offices on Southampton Street. But Fore Pubs had left Southampton Street in November 1956, surrendering the lease the following June (because of the costs of decoration, Swingler had to pay £25 of his own money to be rid of the lease). Swingler tried, unsuccessfully, to sell the firm's title (Henry Parsons suggested an asking price of just £25). On 13 June 1957 Fore Pubs – owing £13 to the bank – finally closed and Central Books pulped their remaining Fore Pubs' stock, including the bulk of the Key Poets. None of Edith Sitwell's poems had been sold.

As a long-running footnote to the cultural history of the Communist Party in the middle decades of the century, the rise and fall of Fore Pubs reflects the richness of the Party's literary life as well as the poverty of much of its cultural organisation. Between 1938 and 1956 Fore Pubs demonstrated both the possibilities and the limits of communist literary publishing in this country, occupying a shifting space – sometimes expanding, sometimes narrowing – for radical artists and radical writing. Its successes and its failures were characterised by an unresolved tension between literary ambitions, political loyalties and commercial realities. It was an autonomous, creative space outside the Party which was nevertheless the site of much inner Party conflict. The Party was not slow to share in the success of Fore Pubs, but neither was it slow to condemn its failures. If communist writers did not always enjoy as much autonomy from the Party apparatus as they wished, the story of Fore Pubs demonstrates that they still enjoyed rather more than historians have usually allowed. A communist publishing house that was not run by the Communist Party, Fore Pubs tried to use the Party to protect itself from the market and the market to gain a kind of independence from the Party; in the end it fell victim to both, being too political for literary London and too literary for the Communist Party.

Notes

This account is reconstructed from papers in the possession of Randall Swingler's daughter Judy Williams, and from conversations and correspondence with Jack Beeching, Jimmy Gibb, Charles Holday, Paul Hogarth, David Holbrook, Arnold Rattenbury, Charles Ringrose and John Willett. I am grateful to Judy Williams, Helen Lindsay and Jane Grubb for permission to quote from their fathers' correspondence.

1 *Daily Worker*, 19 October 1950.
2 *Daily Worker*, 23 October, 30 October, 2 November, 9 November, 15 November, 28 November 1950.
3 *Daily Worker*, 9 November 1951; Jack Beeching remembered Burns playing at Zhdanov at a meeting called to discuss the Key Poets series, 'Randall, Jack and I being put on a cockshy at Marx House as effete literary intellectuals to an audience of hard liners' (letter to the author, 4 March 1993). For British communist writers in the Cold War see Andy Croft, 'Walthamstow, Little Gidding and Middlesbrough: Edward Thompson the Literature Tutor', *Socialist History*, no. 8 1995, and 'The End of Socialist Realism: Margot Heinemann's *The Adventurers*' in Mary Joannou and David Margolies (eds) *Heart of a Heartless World: Essays on Culture and Commitment in Memory of Margot Heinemann* (London: Pluto Press, 1995).
4 On the same page as Burns' article, the paper published an uncharacteristically churlish piece by Swingler, attacking Ezra Pound for being a 'decadent' and 'cosmopolitan' Modernist, and a very warm review by MacAlpin of *Peace is Our Answer* (by Lindsay and Noel Counihan) which he welcomed as 'a challenge to others'. Thompson submitted two letters to the 'Forum on Poetry', only one of which was used and moreover in a heavily 'mutilated' form.

5   Report of the Ralph Fox (Writers') Group of the Communist Party, written in June or
     July 1938.
6   A note in the April issue that 'the opportunity now exists for the launching of a
     monthly in a highly popular form addressed to a wide public' suggests that negotiations
     with Lane must have been progressing well as early as March; Lane contributed an
     article on the paperback revolution to the last issue in May, when Swingler explained
     that the closure of *Left Review* was to be temporary:

> Paradoxically it comes to an end at the height of its success, and because of that
> success. Its history has been a gradual mounting graph of influence and position.
> Now it is felt by the Editorial Board that the present basis of editorial work, production
> and distribution, is too narrow to cope adequately with the job and the opportunities
> that press so urgently upon us ... Today we find almost universally writers and artists
> profoundly disturbed by the crisis with which we are faced. In every possible form
> the two questions – 'What is my job?' and 'What can I do?' – are activating in the
> minds of all workers in the domain of culture. To answer these questions, to give
> expression to the enormous and varied voice of those who will not be deceived and
> tricked, nor allow themselves and the treasures of their past civilisation to be
> bombed into nothingness, to provide an organ for the life-utterance of a people's
> will in the people's interest, is now beyond the task of a review privately run on
> voluntary labour ... Consequently with this issue, LEFT REVIEW as you have
> known it, and as it has established itself in the cultural world, will close, so that
> we may give all our energy in support of a wider project, which can reach a vastly
> greater mass of the people, and establish in the popular mind that principle which
> has been the working basis of LEFT REVIEW throughout its history, that the vitality
> of a whole culture depends upon the unity of interest of a whole people, and the
> opportunity for free expression of their unity and their will.

7   Two years later Lane began the negotiations with John Lehmann which were to turn
     New Writing (first published by Lawrence & Wishart, but by then in flight from its origins)
     into *Penguin New Writing*.
8   FIL minutes, 13 October 1938 (I am grateful to David Bradshaw for this information).
9   The LBC Poets Group had begun life in late 1937 as a loose corresponding network
     for LBC members interested in poetry. Within a few months members in London were
     meeting regularly at Honor Arundel's flat in Belsize Park. While the LBC Writers and
     Readers Group never really established itself outside London, there were 20 Poetry Groups
     outside London by March 1939, including those in Manchester (where the secretary
     was a young art student called Ray Watkinson), Cambridge (George Scurfield) and
     Hastings (F.C. Ball, then Jack Beeching).
10   An abridged version of *When England Arose* was later reprinted as a wartime Marx House
     syllabus, *The Chartist Movement*; *Trouble in Porter Street* was republished in 1954 by
     Lawrence & Wishart; although Geoffrey Trease claims not to have been a member of
     the Party, he was then best known for his fiercely pro-communist children's books,
     Bows Against the Barons (1934), *Comrades for the Charter* (1934) and *Missing from Home*
     (1937); neither of Trease's books for Fore Publications is mentioned in his autobi-
     ographies, *A Whiff of Burnt Boats* (1971) or *Laughter at the Door* (1974).
11   There is a 1940 Mass Observation report on Key Books which nicely describes its
     marketing and political strategy:

> Hardly advertised at all, except DW and Reynolds.
> Not mainly sold at party meetings at all, but at small stationers. Stocked in small
> country villages.
> Initial publicity deliberately not done through party organs so as not to be identified
> with party. Circularised booksellers and advertised in booksellers weekly.

Bought mainly by working class – not the Penguin market. Postbag cheifly [sic] working class.
Not pushed through left-wing channels and not identified with the CP.

(report by HDW, 19 February 1940, in M-O TC25/9/1, Mass Observation Archive, University of Sussex.) I am indebted to Kevin Morgan for this information.

12   By the time Key Books nos 13 and 14 appeared in September 1941 – Pat Sloan's *Country With a Plan* and Anna Louise Strong's *China's New Crisis* – events had of course overtaken them again.

13   *Daily Worker*, 27 January 1940.

14   According to Charles Ringrose, Swingler produced the starting capital of £250 himself.

15   Originally edited by the poet Nicholas Moore, *Seven* was then owned by Philip O'Connor; Swingler put another £500 into Fore Pubs to fund *Seven*.

16   'It became so intellectual, so remote and so Soviet, difficult for the unprivileged to read, that people at Unity were moaning that they had no voice outside the theatre. They were very proletcultish. Ted Willis was the only bloke I ever met in the Communist Party who was a fully paid-up Zhdanovite. The Tom Russell thing, by being so stand-back and disengaged and wordy, reproducing great documents from Moscow, really set up the situation in which anyone wanting something commoner and more available, could leap in. And that's exactly what happened' (Arnold Rattenbury, interview with the author, 28 November 1995).

17   The new look *Our Time* had an editorial board consisting of Honor Arundel, Phillips, Charlie Castro, Diana Hutber, Vernon Beste, Mira Harmer, Francis Klingender, Mulk Raj Anand, the well known typographer Tony Froshaugh and Maurice Carpenter.

18   Sales of *Horizon*, usually considered the representative literary journal of the war, had peaked at 8,000 in April 1940.

19   Vernon Beste, undated 1944 policy paper on *Our Time*.

20   Vernon Beste, undated 1944 policy paper on *Seven*.

21   John St John was later a novelist and an influential figure at Heinemann.

22   *Our Time*, June, August 1944; Rattenbury suspected that some of the letters were written by Beste himself in order to police the magazine.

23   A.L. Lloyd's anthology, *Corn on the Cob: Popular and Traditional Poetry of the USA*, was published by Fore Pubs in 1945.

24   For *Our Time* see Andy Croft 'Writers, the Communist Party and the Battle of Ideas, 1945–50', *Socialist History*, no. 5, 1994; the place of *Our Time* in the London literary scene is evident in Denys Val Barker's *Little Reviews Anthology* 1945 and 1946, which reprinted pieces from the magazine next to work from *Penguin New Writing*, *Horizon*, the *Cornhill Magazine*, *New English Review*, etc.

25   Between 1946 and 1958 Meridian Books published 23 titles. It ran a much more commercial – if eccentric – looking list, including books on ballet, ghosts, contemporary Europe, Hampton Court and Indian philosophy, books by Konni Zilliacus and Philip Lindsay (including his bestselling *The Secret Life of Henry the Eighth*), collections of poetry by Swingler and Maurice Carpenter and *The Year of Revolutions 1948* by James Eastwood and Paul Tabori; *Realist Music: 25 Soviet Composers*, by Rena Moisenko (with a foreword by Sir Adrian Boult) was published jointly with Fore Pubs.

26   Edgell Rickword to Randall Swingler, 19 June 1945.

27   The board of the 'New Developments' series included Lindsay (as 'executive editor'), Rickword, James Boswell, Arthur Calder-Marshall, Basil Wright and Pamela Hansford Johnson.

28   The job of liaising with King Street was given to Rattenbury; 'Edgell wanted peace, and said, "I'm not going to go round, you go round." So I used to go round monthly. And I got all this bullshit from Emile. There was always a survey of the back issue and projected articles about Zhdanov or something that he wanted in. I thought he was horrible, his whole attitude to *Our Time* was venomous. I remember going in to see

Gary [German] who used to take over if Emile was away, and he threw a book at me, because I was just another middle-class intellectual' (interview with the author, 28 November 1995); see also Charles Hobday, *Edgell Rickword: A Poet at War* (Manchester: Carcanet, 1989) and the recollections of Thompson and Rattenbury in *PN Review*, vol. 6, no. 1, Supplement XXIV.

29   Randall Swingler to Edgell Rickword, 17 September 1948.

30   Jimmy Gibb remembers Swingler once saying that *Our Time* was 'killed off by Emile Burns and his bloody fish-cakes ... Burns went to the same cafe for the whole of his life in King Street where he had one fish-cake! He must have done it for twenty-five years and Randall thought of presenting him with a silver fish-cake' (interview with the author, 11 January 1992).

31   *Daily Worker*, 12 May 1949. In *Meeting with Poets* (1968) Lindsay significantly remembered Kartun's review as even less favourable than it really was; while Lindsay was being criticised for speaking over the heads of the working class, he was giving advice about writing to a young YCL member called Arnold Wesker; Arnold Wesker, *As Much As I Dare* (London: Century, 1994).

32   Undated 1949 letter from Randall Swingler to Edgell Rickword; Hubbard's mother was an American heiress whose money had established the International Music Club in South Audley Street.

33   See Paul Hogarth's autobiography, *Drawing on Life*, (Newton Abbot: David & Charles, 1997) re *Circus*.

34   *Lilliput* was then edited by James Boswell (a Communist Party member) and Richard Bennett.

35   *Daily Worker*, 18 January, 23 January, 22 March 1951.

36   'Cultural Journal,' NCC papers, May 1951; NCC minutes, 11 May 1951.

37   Undated 1951 letter from Jack Lindsay to Randall Swingler.

38   Undated 1952 letter from Jack Lindsay to Randall Swingler.

39   In a memorial volume published after Davies' death, Montagu Slater paid tribute to her work as 'secretary of Fore Publications, and consequently secretary, general manager. advertising manager and Lord High everything else of both *Our Time* and *Seven* ... She raised the capital for Fore Publications and managed its affairs single-handed with such political and business sense that in those few months the foundations were laid for the respect this little publishing house commanded during what we used to call the "cultural upsurge" of the later war years.' *Nothing is Lost* (published by Edgell Rickword for the Writers Group of the Communist Party, London, 1954).

9

Hamish Henderson

The Edinburgh People's Festival, 1951–54

When the political decision was made in 1946, under Clem Attlee's government, to inaugurate an International Festival of the Arts in an attempt to counterbalance the effects of world war weariness, the likeliest venue seemed to be not Edinburgh, but Bath. Indeed the latter appears to have been that most favoured by the Festival's guiding spirit, Rudolf Bing. The rival claims of these two handsome cities were by no means based on their respective cultural qualifications or backgrounds; the context was purely a matter of the number of undamaged buildings which would be at the disposal of the organisers. It was a close run thing, but Edinburgh came out on top.

There was a club on the go in Princes Street at the time, International House, which had been founded during the war by the British Council to cater for the off duty needs of officers of the Polish Forces, and the 'arty' sections of the Edimbourgeoisie were encouraged to join it. After the war it widened its appeal somewhat, and for practical reasons – I used it for years as a *poste restante*, when I was 'in the field' collecting songs and stories up north – I eventually applied for membership myself. Not long after the end of the war, while I was still 'sounding the joint out' I overheard a priceless conversation between H. Harvey Wood, who was an official of the British Council, and an ex-army colonel who had been co-opted to join the organisation. They were discussing the opportunities that this new projected International Festival of the Arts offered the local branch of the British Council and they were talking entirely in terms of which celebrated foreign orchestras, opera companies, ballet light-footers and suchlike they might be able to attract to Auld Reekie. Right enough, it was to be an *international* festival, but the idea that the host nation, Scotland, might be considered as one of the participant nations seemed not to enter into it.

Inevitably, news of this and similar discussions soon reached the ears of the great Hugh MacDiarmid, Scotland's leading poet, and one of the outstanding poets writing in Europe at that time. His reaction was not difficult to forecast. He regarded the entire International Festival project as a sort of English/cosmopolitan plot to subvert our native Scottish culture and thus to put paid to the Scottish Renaissance in literature which he had inaugurated – almost single-handedly – way back in the 1920s. In 1949 he wrote a virulent article for an Edinburgh-based magazine called *The Galliard*, the implicit tenor of which was that all nationally committed Scottish poets and cultural figures should unite to oppose the International Festival and try to ensure its eventual failure.

This appeared to me and to several other left-wing intellectuals an entirely self-defeating attitude. The Communist Party had welcomed the festival, which had been covered in the *Daily Worker* since 1947 (when Sir Hugh Roberton, conductor of the Glasgow Orpheus Choir, had reported on the first festival for the paper). And for all its faults the festival did bring to Edinburgh, in its first five years, a great many films from the Soviet Union and the 'New Democracies'. The Party's support was not unqualified, however. The announcement, during the second Edinburgh Festival, that the Arts Council of Great Britain was to withdraw funding from Glasgow Unity Theatre, confirmed our feelings of a widening gap between what the festival was and what it could have been. So long as the festival relied on 'big names' (mainly non-Scots) it isolated itself (by high admission prices) from the Scottish people and therefore from new cultural developments in Scotland. The Communist Party was greatly interested at the time in helping to develop a national cultural identity for Scotland. I was asked to review books by and about Scottish writers (Sorley MacLean, Burns, MacDiarmid, Boswell, Stevenson) for the *Daily Worker*, which also gave generous space to a number of literary controversies among Scottish readers at this time (notably regarding Burns, Lallans and Gaelic).[1]

Shortly before Christmas 1950 a meeting was convened by Martin Milligan, a Communist Party member and a man of great brilliance. He had just returned a short time before from Oxford, where he had studied philosophy, although his philosophy was hardly the establishment kind. The meeting took place at the Scottish Miners' HQ in Rothesay Place, Edinburgh.[2] The central idea behind the discussion was that, far from opposing the 'big' festival, the left should welcome its existence, take advantage of the presence of so many five-star foreign actors, singers, etc. on Scottish soil, and try to present an Edinburgh People's Festival which would complement its senior brother, and in some select zones of cultural enterprise, actually outdo it. And this in fact is what actually happened.

The Edinburgh Labour Festival Committee soon comprised 40 people, representing 17 trade union branches, five Labour Party organisations, the WMA, the Musicians Union, the local Labour League of Youth and the Edinburgh Trades Council. There were various poets, artists and story-writers belonging to the Cultural Committee of the Scottish District of the Communist Party – Norman and Janey Buchan, Hugh Paterson, Simon and Ella Ward, Bill Maclellan; several left-inclined Labour Party members (and indeed, one or two who turned out to be right-wingers) and last, but not least, one or two non-attached cultural figures such as John MacDonald, a Highland psychologist who originally hailed from Sutherlandshire and who spoke up vigorously for a Gaelic component in any future People's Festival. He it was who in the event, with his wife, did a great deal of the donkey work of organisation when the People's Festival got going. The organiser was Martin Milligan. Under the slogan 'By Working People For Working People', we wanted to show the International Festival what it still could be,

> To initiate action designed to bring the Edinburgh International Festival closer to the people as a whole and to make it serve more fully the cause of international understanding and good will; and also to initiate action such as will more generally make what is best in the cultural life of our country more accessible to working people, and will secure fuller facilities for the development of the cultural activities of working people.[3]

Attracting people who felt excluded by the International Festival, keeping the admission prices low and including children – it was Gramsci in action! One of the things that attracted me to Gramsci was his great interest in popular culture. He was a Sardinian, and the Sardinian folk song is rich and bountiful and vigorous to the nth degree. When he was in prison he wrote to his mother and sisters asking for details about their folk festivals. Gramsci in action *was* the People's Festival!

The committee set its sights high. The festival ran for a full week, from 26 August to 1 September. Glasgow Unity Theatre performed Joe Corrie's *In Time of Strife* and there was a Theatre Workshop production of Ewan MacColl's brilliant historical gallimaufry, *Uranium 235*, which, when first produced in London, had been accorded great praise by both Bernard Shaw and Sean O' Casey. There were performances by Barrhead Co-op Junior Choir, the Tranent Fa'side Players (winners that year of the NCB drama festival), the Lesmahagow Male Voice Choir, and a production by the Ferranti Drama Group of Ena Lamont Stewart's *Starched Aprons*. There were 'film-strip lectures', coffee-time lectures and 'tea-time lectures' (given by Ralph Bond, Tom Driberg, Ewan MacColl, Helen Cruickshank, Hugh MacDiarmid and myself, among others) designed to show 'how all forms of cultural activity, at their best, depend on ordinary working people and also how much the happiness of the people as a whole depends on the condition of science and the arts'.[4] There was a festival club and a day conference, 'Towards a People's Culture', attended by over 170 people.

Abe Moffat, Secretary of the Scottish Area NUM, spoke on the last night, an evening's entertainment of drama, song and poetry by Scottish miners and their friends.

One of the committee members was very insistent that the festival should not only provide a platform for 'Hamish's folksy finds'. However, as things turned out, it was the Oddfellows Hall Ceilidh, drawing on native Gaelic and Lowland Scots folk singers, which drew the most appreciative comments from the press. One critic even asserted that the most interesting musical experiences of the entire festival period were not to be found on the 'high heid-yin' (or official) side of the event but on the non-official side. The singing began at 7.30 p.m. and finished, rather hilariously, about two o'clock in the morning. It was an event of incalculable importance, because from it sprang a hundred other fruitful cultural enterprises in subsequent years. Instead of 'Muckin' the Byre' in white tie and tails and Kelvinside accents, there was the glorious singing of Flora MacNeil and Calum Johnston from the Isle of Barra, John Strachan singing the classic ballads 'Clyde's Water' and 'Johnnie of Breadislee', the expert piping of 19 year old John Burgess and, above all, the unparalleled artistry of Jessie Murray, a Buckie fish-wife, whose incomparable 'Skippin' Barfut Throw the Heather' enjoyed its city debut at that same 1951 Ceilidh. Over from Glasgow to witness the event was the Communist Party cultural stalwart Norman Buchan, who was overwhelmed by the Ceilidh. He said he had never heard anything like it, and afterwards admitted that his folk song enthusiasms and his resolve to propagate authentic singing styles among West Country children dated from that moment. In the festival programme I wrote:

> In Scotland, both north and south of the Highland line, there is still an incomparable treasure of folk song and folk music. Very little of it is known to the ordinary Scottish public, and even less to the world public which is patron to the Edinburgh International Festival. What is known is often irredeemably spoilt by normal 'concert-hall' technique and arrangement.
>
> The main purpose of this Ceilidh will be to present Scottish folk song as it should be sung. The singers will all without exception be men and women who have learnt these splendid songs by word of mouth in their own childhood, and who give them in the traditional manner. This fact alone will make the *People's Festival Ceilidh an absolutely unique thing in the cultural history of Edinburgh*.[5]

To explain the background of this truly fabulous event, we must go back six months, to February 1951, when I received the following letter from Ewan MacColl, the brilliant singer/playwright and Communist Party activist, who was the intrepid 'battle-post' of Joan Littlewood's Theatre Workshop. 'Dear Hamish,' he wrote,

Just a brief note – there is a character wandering around this sceptered isle at the moment yclept Alan Lomax. He is a Texan and the none the worse for that. He is also just about the most important name in American folk song circles. He is over here with a super recording unit and a girl, Robin Roberts, who sings like an angel. Columbia Gramophone Co are financing his trip. The idea is that he will record the folk singers of a group of countries (he has already covered Africa – America – the West Indies – the Central European countries). And Columbia will produce an album of discs – an hour for each country. He is not interested in trained singers or refined versions of the folk songs. He wants to record traditional style singers doing ballads, work songs, political satires, etc. It occurred to me that you could help him in two ways.

1   Record some of your soldier songs and add any other songs you know. You sang some to me in the little cafe opposite the Epworth Hall.
2   Introduce him to other Scots folk singers. You know the kind of thing he wants: bothy songs, street songs, soldier songs, mouth music, the big Gaelic stuff, weavers' and miners' songs, etc.

This is important, Hamish. It is vital that Scotland is well represented in this collection. It would be fatal if the 'folksy' boys were to cash in. If you can help, write to him – Alan Lomax c/o BBC, London. He intends coming to Scotland in about a week's time.
Do try and help.
Yours aye, Ewan.
PS If and when you meet him, get him to sing some of his American coal miners' songs. They are terrific.[6]

I dropped a note to Alan – a member of the US Communist Party – and in the summer of 1951 spent two or three months with him collecting folk songs, especially in the Scottish North East (Aberdeenshire, Moray, etc.) and most of the singers we found then nearly all expressed readiness to make the journey to Edinburgh, to appear at the Ceilidh I was already planning. It will be seen, therefore, that the powerful stimulus behind the whole People's Festival enterprise was that splendid character Ewan MacColl. Ewan – real name Jimmy Miller – although born in Salford, was the son of two formidable working-class Scots. His father was an iron-moulder from Falkirk, his mother from Auchterarder, and (a fact I can vouch for) a really bonny singer. Ewan knew all about German agitprop troupes and had formed the Red Megaphones in Salford ('A Propertyless Theatre for a Propertyless Class') named after a German communist troupe from Red Wedding. So the People's Festival could claim a distinguished ancestry – both Gramsci, and the KPD's *Rote Sprachrohr*!
Encouraged by the success of the first People's Festival, the committee immediately began to plan for the 1952 event. This time it ran for three

weeks, from 17 August to 7 September, under the banner 'That the People's Voice May Be Heard and the Needs of the People Met'. The committee appealed in the *Daily Worker* for new songs, poems and plays, and the festival included a 'People's Art Exhibition', including a 'People Like Us' photography exhibition. There were poetry readings by Sydney Goodsir Smith, Alexander Trocchi, Norman MacCaig and Sorley MacLean; a series of lectures (including James Gibb on Beethoven, Desmond Greaves on James Connolly, myself on Scottish folk song, Ewan MacColl on MacDiarmid, and MacDiarmid himself on David Lindsay and on the 'Radical Tradition in Scottish Culture'). We had an ambitious programme of foreign films, including *Bicycle Thieves*, the award-winning Polish classic, *That Others May Live*, and the first full-length film from the new China, *Daughters of China*. There was also a People's Festival Ball; a series of Beethoven concerts; and three plays, *Flatter No Flesh* by the People's Festival Players, *Out of Bondage* by Lanark CLP and a new Theatre Workshop production, Ewan MacColl's *The Travellers*. The festival concluded with a day conference on 'Our Cultural Traditions and Their Advancement Today' and among the speakers were Hugh MacDiarmid, Ewan MacColl, Naomi Mitchison and several Labour MPs.[7]

There was now no question but that the Ceilidh had to be one of the central features of the festival. By this time Hugh MacDiarmid had generously acknowledged the wisdom of our approach to the festival question and had accepted the post of People's Festival chairman. Furthermore, as 1952 was also the year of his sixtieth birthday, we resolved to dedicate that year's Ceilidh to him. In the event, this second Ceilidh was an even more resounding success than the first one. The aim was again 'to present the finest flower of our folk song tradition', but this time the emphasis was 'upon young singers who are carrying on the splendid tradition in its integrity'. 'We are convinced,' I wrote in the programme, 'that it is possible to restore Scottish folksong to the ordinary people in Scotland, not merely as a bobby-soxer vogue, but deeply and integrally.'[8] The veteran Barra singer Calum Johnston again sang splendid Gaelic songs and played the pipes; the famous Lewis sisters Kitty and Marietta MacLeod enthralled the audience with 'Cairistiona' and 'Agus Ho Mhorag'; an excellent bothy ballad singer from the North East called Frank Steele sang 'Come All Ye Lonely Lovers'; the young Arthur Argo, great-grandson of the famous Aberdeenshire folk song collector Gavin Greig, sang 'The Souter's Feast' in a boyish treble; 18 year old Blanche Wood sang songs she had learned from her aunt Jessie Murray; and Jimmy MacBeath gave of his best with 'Come All Ye Tramps and Hawkers' and 'The Moss o' Burreldale'. Hugh MacDiarmid, in whose honour they were performing, had been invited to sit on the platform and at the beginning the entire audience rose while Calum Johnston played 'Blue Bonnets over the Border' as a tribute to Scotland's greatest living poet and most celebrated Borderer. MacDiarmid was obviously deeply moved and at the end of the Ceilidh he rose to propose a vote of thanks to the performers:

> As you all know, my personal vanity has always been notorious – but it is quite unequal to the present occasion. I've been absolutely overwhelmed by the honour that has been done me and by the honour that the various artists, and this magnificent audience, have done to themselves, and to Scotland, in doing it.
>
> It would be wrong of me, even in proposing a vote of thanks, if I didn't point out that our tremendous treasury of folk song in Scotland, whether in Lowland Scots or in Gaelic, is a treasury that has been occluded, very largely for political reasons, from the knowledge of the majority of our people. This Edinburgh People's Festival, and the movement in which my friends on the platform and others in the audience are concerned, is a re-assertion of that tradition, against the tide of all the things ... all the cultural enemies that are besetting us at the present time.
>
> One thing must have struck you, I think, in the programme tonight – that is, the extent to which all the items on the programme have been correlated to the lives of the common people, to the work of common people, the daily darg of the common people.
>
> We are not going to be taken from that – we're not going to be persuaded by the advocates of snob art, that some mystical palaver is better than that which comes from the working life of our own people.[9]

Unluckily, Ewan MacColl's *The Travellers* played straight into the hands of the right-wing minority on the committee – two vociferous ladies who almost from the start had claimed to identify Communist Party propaganda in even the most innocuous events. Drawing on Theatre Workshop's travels in the New Democracies, *The Travellers* was the subject of an emergency committee meeting called at the insistence of the same ladies in October 1952.[10] The result was that in December 1952 the Scottish TUC placed the festival on its long list of proscribed organisations and withdrew its support for future festivals. Two weeks later the Scottish Labour Party declared that association with the festival was incompatible with membership of the Labour Party (despite the fact that the chair of the festival committee, councillor Jack Kane, was also chair of the Labour Party in Edinburgh).[11]

Thus the two main financial props of the enterprise were knocked from under us at a blow. This was in spite of – or possibly because of – the staunch outspoken support of Hugh MacDiarmid, who was later to rejoin the Communist Party in the wake of the Soviet invasion of Hungary. In 1950 I had been expelled, probably under US pressure, from Italy, where as a guest of the PCI I had been lecturing on folk song traditions; apparently folk song was now deemed a subversive activity even in Scotland.

Despite this disabling setback, the committee prepared to plan for a People's Festival in 1953, holding meetings at factory gates and building sites to raise support, interest and money. Organised by Norman Buchan and myself, the third festival was inevitably a much smaller event. Hitherto the *Daily Worker* had maintained an even-handed approach to the 'two festivals'. Now it only mentioned the International Festival (which it pointed out was 'neither international nor Scottish') to pour scorn on the way 'Edinburgh breaks into tartan' once a year to the 'rustle of crisp dollar notes'.[12] Theatre Workshop returned with two new plays, adaptations of *Lysistrata* and Molière's *Le Malade Imaginaire*; the Glasgow YCL Choir sang and Ewan MacColl gave a memorable three-hour performance of unaccompanied folk song. The 1953 Scots-Irish Ceilidh was in many ways the most memorable of all, principally because it was the one which introduced the recently discovered Jeannie Robertson (universally acknowledged now as the greatest Scottish ballad singer of the twentieth century) to a wider public. It also featured the renowned Tennessee diva Jean Ritchie, singing her own people's version of 'Guide Me O Thou Great Jehovah', a truly glorious, spine-tingling rendering.

The People's Festival limped on into 1954, supported largely by contributions from personal well-wishers, but later that year was forced to acknowledge defeat. However, the spirit of the festival continued in the Scottish folk revival which it had helped to start. And the far-off repercussions of those early proposals from the cultural committee of the Communist Party can still be felt in the Fringe today.

Notes

1 The correspondence columns of the *Daily Worker* were once filled for several weeks with letters taking sides for and against an article of mine on the poet Sorley MacLean (30 March, 4 April, 12 April, 17 April, 18 April 1950).

2 For other accounts of the People's Festival, see Antaire MacAnair, 'Democracy, Intellect and the Muse'; *Cencrastus*, no. 57, Summer 1997; Hamish Henderson, 'Folk Champions', *The Carrying Stream*, vol. 1 no. 2, 1991 and Hamish Henderson, *Alias MacAlias: Writings on Songs, Folk and Literature* (Edinburgh: Polygon, 1992).

3 *People's Festival Week, 1951*, programme, p. 12.

4 *Ibid.*, p. 10.

5 *Ibid.*, p. 8; see the coverage of the first People's Festival in the *Daily Worker*, 22 and 31 August, 10 September 1951.

6 Ewan MacColl to the author, 16 February 1951; see Hamish Henderson, *The Armstrong Nose* (Edinburgh: Polygon, 1992, pp. 46–7)

7 See the coverage of the second festival in the *Daily Worker*, 27 August, 1, 5, 6 September 1952.

8 *Edinburgh People's Festival 1952*, programme, p. 13.

9 *Cencrastus*, no. 48, Summer 1994, p. 9.

10 See Joan Littlewood, *Joan's Book* (London: Methuen, 1994).

11 The ban was reported in the *Daily Worker*, 1 December and 17 December, 1952.

12 For coverage of the third festival in the *Daily Worker*, see 17, 21 and 29 August, 1 and 4 September 1953.

Gerald Porter

'The World's Ill-Divided': the Communist Party and Progressive Song

In recent years, larger claims have been made for the role of the Communist Party in the field of vernacular song than in almost any other area of cultural life. In *One for the Money* (1980) and *Fakesong* (1985), Dave Harker argued that 'the history of the Second Folksong Revival ... was closely involved with the cultural policy of the CPGB'.[1] He saw this as a crude attempt to manipulate a cultural phenomenon in knee-jerk reponse to Zhdanovite exhortations to rediscover (fake) national traditions. Traditional song was seen as directly reflecting 'reality', while mass culture was regarded as a capitalist drug.[2] In Harker's scenario, dedicated Party workers fanned out across the country from the capital to set up folk clubs and encourage the growth of other clubs in neighbouring towns. They 'softened' the political edge of their music in a crude attempt to win new allies and audiences. Paradoxically, he claims that the most successful of these performers, like A.L. Lloyd and Ewan MacColl, were at the same time financially self-seeking. Harker contrasts communist performers unfavourably with the singer-songwriter Alex Glasgow, who was 'not on the market for a fee'.[3]

In fact, while the revival was strongly influenced by individual communists and the work of some branches, the Party never had a coherent or effective policy towards the political song. The role of Party activists depended less on decisions made at the centre about a 'cultural Popular Front' than on a principled response to the constantly changing field of values, beliefs and practices competing for dominance within a social formation dictated by capitalism and industrialisation. In contrast to the Labour Party, the Communist Party paid considerable attention to cultural matters, but most of the impetus came from regional cultural committees. The activity and composition of these committees seems to have varied from area to area. In Birmingham, for example, the committee had 18 members from 1962 onwards, representing industrial and professional workers (such as teachers, artists and musicians) as well as homeworkers or housewives. Meetings were held monthly and were practical in purpose as well as offering a forum for ideological debate. They put on folk concerts, helped the YCL run sessions of folk dance and song, and organised the music at social events and on demonstrations.[4]

However, in the end, as so often, it was the work of individual communists, working at the district or branch level, who made the difference, not merely implementing cultural committee resolutions but struggling to put in place once more the radical culture that had been so battered by the capitalist institutions.

The Invisibility of Working-class Songs

The view that song could offer a challenge to bourgeois versions of working-class history was not by any means universally accepted in King Street. After Ewan MacColl left the Party in 1953, he claimed that it was because he had asked a Party official what sort of songs he should sing at a rally 'and the bloke replied along the lines of, "It doesn't matter a toss what you sing, just pack the people in".'[5] This attitude to song, treating it as mere entertainment, a diversion from the real struggle, was rooted in a long-standing ignorance of the progressive song tradition.

Traditional working-class songs were not strongly supported in Party circles in the 1920s and 1930s, as they were regarded as a form of popular culture that was dead, at least temporarily. Even A. L. Lloyd shared this view. As he put it in the *Daily Worker* in 1937, 'It is true that capitalism has put an end to folk-art, for the time being.'[6] He was soon to revise this opinion, which was based on the work of the collectors of the first English folk song revival (the bourgeois-Romantic movement steered by Cecil Sharp), who routinely marginalised industrial and progressive songs in their published work.[7] Most folk song collections ignored, and still ignore, the fact that many English songs are urban and also that many deal with exploitation and the prospect of revolutionary change.[8]

It is true that Britain was without a tradition of militant trade union songs like the one in France and Spain until after the Second World War. However, in Scotland, William Motherwell showed the importance of song in working-class culture in and around Glasgow in the early nineteenth century, and so did John Harland in Lancashire.[9] About half the traditional songs in English from the seventeenth to the nineteenth centuries at least mention the occupation of one of the protagonists. Many go further. They look to the sweatshop or building site for their settings, to the blacksmith, lacemaker or collier for their protagonists, and to the act of working itself for their metaphors. And they constantly challenge the bluff certainties of the prevailing ideology.[10]

The first English folk song revival, at the turn of the century, coalesced around the Cecil Sharp canon of English folk music, including songs like 'The Raggle-Taggle Gypsies-o' and 'A Frog He Would A-wooing Go' suitable for school or drawing room arrangements for piano. As a contributor to the progressive folk magazine *Sing* noted, 'Cecil Sharp saw folk song as something that could be re-grafted (after censorship, of course) on to the population rather than something which could be a vehicle for its expression.'[11]

The marginalisation of the progressive song tradition in England that Sharp and his contemporaries achieved can be compared in scale to the neglect of women in historical and cultural studies. It resulted from the fact that collectors and editors (often the two roles were combined in the same person) had the final say as to what was a true 'folk song'. They believed that such songs were to be sought from non-literate informants in rural settings. They made their recordings where possible from solitary individuals singing unaccompanied in domestic settings. Since it was almost universally believed that 'true' folk song had more or less died out by the early nineteenth century, younger singers were neglected. Folk songs basically dealt with love relationships or the exploits of folk heroes. The most prestigious oral tradition of all was the tragic narrative, the ballad.

The songs of the radical tradition, on the other hand, often originated from urban or industrial settings, among people who were highly articulate and made considerable use of published material from the popular presses. The songs were sung above all as *group expression*, in pubs, clubs and workplaces, often noisily accompanied. Far from the tradition being on the point of extinction, the nineteenth and twentieth centuries have been among the most productive, with new songs not only from the great established industries like weaving, farming and coal, but coming for the first time from engineering, transport, service industries and the Peace Movement. While often showing anger or despair, the songs may also be provocative, ribald or parodic. Finally, they have a high degree of sexual reference and a characteristic stance of being in resistance to the status quo.

It was these songs that the initiators of what has come to be called the Second English Folk Revival aimed to set up as the new national tradition of 'radical Englishness'. As early as 1924, the setting up of the Woodcraft Folk (effectively the youth wing of the Co-operative Movement, which had many communists as members) was an attempt to wrest traditional dance and song for children from the hegemony of the English Folk Dance and Song Society (as it was later called) and enlist it in the cause of inter-nationalism and world peace. As such, it helped to make generations of leftists aware of an alternative tradition of popular song, although by clinging to the Romantic concept of the 'folk', the project was caught up in the same simplified and middle-class concept of 'one nation' as the EFDSS.

It was A. L. Lloyd who first emphasised the class nature of the suppressed struggles of 'the singing Englishman', as his first book on the subject was called.[12] His most famous example of such a reclaimed song was 'The Cutty Wren', a song which had always been cited as an example of a children's song with deeply embedded ritual elements. Lloyd related it, on slender evidence it must be said, to the popular resistance to the feudal order that culminated in the Peasants' Revolt, the wren representing the tyrant ruler.[13] In this way he could claim that song was as much a part of democratic struggle as those traditionally confrontational popular arts, dance and drama. Lloyd would have been on stronger ground if he had cited 'Little Jack Horner', which refers covertly to Henry VIII's seizure of church property at the Reformation.[14]

There was a wider purpose in this recovery of the suppressed singing tradition. Progressive folk song, however it was defined, was not only displacing schoolroom pieces like 'Widdecombe Fair', but was also felt to be the answer to the American threat to British culture. After 1948, the Party championed folk music so as to distance itself specifically from what was seen as the ice blue suits and chewing gum culture of the USA. This, of course, wrongfooted the Party when, eight years later, rock and roll brought with it influences from both black and white traditional music such as Country and Western and the blues.

Ewan MacColl (1915–89) and Political Songwriting

Both before and after the setting up of the Popular Front, active Party involvement was directed towards new political songs, particularly in defence of the Soviet Union and the young Spanish Republic. Songwriters like Ewan MacColl were able to come up with the right stuff:

> Fly higher and higher,
> Our emblem the Soviet star,
> And every propellor is roaring 'Red Front'
> Defending the USSR.[15]

MacColl, whose energy and didacticism made him a central figure in the folk revival, was born Jimmy Miller, a member of a Scottish singing family which had settled in Salford, the original 'dirty old town'.[16] In the 1930s and 1940s he worked with progressive groups like Red Megaphone and Joan Littlewood's Theatre Workshop. His early play, *Johnny Noble*, loosely based on *Romeo and Juliet*, was set in Hull in the Depression and already showed his interest in songwriting. MacColl became actively involved with the folk revival after the war through countless initiatives like the cultural pluralism of the *Ballads and Blues* radio programmes, the teaching of practical performing skills at the Singers Club, and the synthesis of form and content in performances of the Critics Group.[17] By the time of his death in 1989, he had made over a hundred recordings.[18]

In addition to being a composer and performer, MacColl helped to make industrial songs more widely known. In *The Shuttle and the Cage* (1954), which he edited for the Workers Music Association, he included songs which express the alienation of groups like the miners, the railway workers and the Irish navvies. As he pointed out, a mining song on an accident in a Welsh pit in 1934, sung to him by a young Sheffield miner, is typical of the new note struck by industrial song:

> The fireman's reports they are missing,
> The records of forty-two days;
> The colliery manager had them destroyed
> To cover his criminal ways.
> 'The Gresford Disaster' 17–20

It makes it clear that compensation is seen in terms of class interests:

> The owners have sent some white lilies
> To pay for the colliers' lives. (27–28)[19]

Exercising the right of any song-gatherer, MacColl printed a song of the Irish navvies, 'Poor Paddy Works on the Railway', with two melodies which speak antithetically for the constantly changing lives of the digging gangs.[20] They were successfully combined by MacColl in a single, tension-filled performance which rapidly entered the repertoire of the folk revival. MacColl was also one of the first to recognise the importance of the singing tradition of marginalised groups like the travellers.

The Workers Music Association

In 1936, at a time when the Party was, in the words of its most recent historian, 'in the vanguard of culture',[21] the Workers Music Association (WMA) was founded. Alan Bush was its first president and it had the active support of progressive composers like Benjamin Britten, Hans Eisler and John Ireland. It had an ambitious programme which included 'the promotion of socialist and communist song from national and international sources',[22] making performance skills available to all and defending the rights of professional musicians. However, as the roll-call of sponsors suggests, the WMA saw its main task as being 'to bring "proper" music – that is, classical music by composers like Beethoven and Mozart with an (obviously or implicitly) progressive bias – to a working-class audience'.

For a long time, interest in plebeian or popular culture smacked of Proletkultism.[23] Folk song was disapproved of because, as Charles Seeger pointed out, it was 'pre-Marx'.[24] Even after the war, the WMA booklet *Policy for Music in Post-War Britain* (1945), the nearest the Party came to a specific cultural strategy in the field, concentrated on choral and orchestral groups, the dance band, the concert party and the brass band. It made no mention of folk music or even political song. It did, however, highlight the music hall (which treated workers as mass consumers for the first time), for its 'element of realism'.[25] Ironically, such songs were to be marginalised by the later revival.

Nevertheless, within ten years the WMA had become closely associated with the rapidly growing interest in political song. It supported the London Youth Choir, which was an offshoot of the Young Communist League. It published popular songbooks to make available not only the finds of the early collectors, hitherto buried in elite journals, but also industrial songs and new compositions by progressive songwriters. These compilations included A. L. Lloyd's *Coaldust Ballads* (1952) and MacColl's *The Shuttle and the Cage* (1954). For many communists who were later to become outstanding singers in the revival, like Harry Boardman of Manchester, the WMA's summer schools brought an awareness, impossible through the patronising channels of the English Folk Dance and Song Society, that democratic politics had a cultural dimension in song. However, the movement was now outgrowing the WMA as it had left behind the English Folk Dance and Song Society: 'The WMA as an organisation or a source of ideology meant little to the erstwhile fans of Lonnie Donegan now crowding into folk clubs.'[26]

The Second English Folk Revival

The rise of the Second English Folk Revival has sometimes been dated from 1950, when Alan Lomax arrived in the UK looking for songs for the *World Library of Folk and Primitive Music*. Lomax actively suppported Party cultural work, taking part, for example, in the cultural and musical tribute in 1951 to Joe Vaughan, communist mayor of Shoreditch, where he joined Ewan MacColl in singing 'One Big Union'. The CP, according to legend, then called on Lomax to join forces with Lloyd and MacColl to start the revival. This classic 'top-down' account of cultural change is not supported by any first-hand sources. In the first place, the dynamic for the new interest in the country's vernacular music did not arise in London, nor even in England. Several alternative 'People's Festivals' were organised by the trade unions and the left at the time of the Festival of Britain in 1951. In Scotland, the first People's Festival Ceilidh, organised by various interested left-wing groups including the Communist Party, was held in Edinburgh, and the interest in Scottish music generated there was sustained by the setting up of the School of Scottish Studies in the same year. Hamish Henderson, employed at the school from the beginning, was himself an active collector and composer of songs, and, in making known the astonishing repertoires of singers like Jeannie Robertson and the Stewart family of Blairgowrie, he showed that 'the tradition' was very much a living one. Given the male-dominated image of the pubs and clubs of the later revival, it is important to emphasise that the tradition was being actively maintained by women.

This public recognition of the strength of the alternative singing tradition in a democratic working-class culture was quickly recognised south of the border. The discovery of vigorous local singing traditions offered a natural counterweight to the American domination of popular music. Once again, much of the activity was concentrated outside London, the reverse of Dave Harker's scenario of a conspiracy hatched in King Street.[27] The first folk music festival was held in Sidmouth, Devon, in 1954, Manchester's first folk club was started by local Party members Lesley and Harry Boardman in the same year, and two years later, the Young Communist League choir in Bradford, a city with a strong tradition of industrial song, became the basis of a similar club. All are still in existence. As Karl Dallas comments,

> while MacColl, Lloyd and Lomax were the great polemicists and philosophers of the revival, its shocktroops were the products of the 1944 Education Act, working-class kids who came pouring out of the grammar schools after the war equipped with the hunger to do for their generation what Mayakovsky and Brecht had done for Russia and Germany before the war, grabbing hold of folk song not so much for the inherent beauties that had charmed the prewar romantics, but because it was a convenient tool.[28]

As in the United States, Party branches were beginning to seize on the power of progressive songs not only to build solidarity but to make socials, political meetings and picket lines more lively. Roy Palmer, unquestionably the leading editor of English folk song in recent years, recalls singing 'The Coal Owner and the Poor Pitman's Wife' at one such meeting in the early 1950s. At a Party social in Birmingham at about the same time, quizzes and party games were interspersed with performances of 'Westering Home', 'The Wild Colonial Boy' and 'Joe Hill'.[29]

It is clear from such personal accounts that the singing took second place to the larger political agenda at such meetings. However, the work of A.L. Lloyd, Woody Guthrie and others was giving the progressive song a more central role, not only in the history of progressive movements but in current political struggles. The setting up of folk clubs, often with the active support of Party members, naturally accelerated this process. Birmingham's Partisan and Peanuts folk clubs (the latter named after Hugh

Gaitskell's dismissive term for CND), both with close Party ties, were examples of this. New songs were tolerated, but the great majority were traditional.[30]

The Clarion Singers (taking their name from Robert Blatchford) were formed in Birmingham in 1940 to raise funds for Spanish refugees. A visit to Czechoslovakia in 1957 led to an emphasis on folk-based music and they took part in the Centre 42 festivals (as The Leaveners) and the recording of Ewan MacColl's radio ballad 'Singing the Fishing'.[31] They sang at demonstrations and meetings (including anti-racist songs from the back of a lorry in Enoch Powell's Wolverhampton constituency) and showed an early interest in the tradition of songs of resistance that was to underpin the later revival. The revival of interest in progressive song in London also began with Party choirs. The London Youth Choir was set up in 1951 for the Third World Youth Festival in Berlin, and continued to perform on its return, singing in streets and markets. In 1954, for example, it was collecting signatures for the Ban the H-Bomb Appeal. It often opened its performances with a dance such as the Yorkshire Square, following it up with a topical peace song. John Hasted, lecturer in physics at the University of London, introduced the choir.[32]

When folk clubs did develop in London, Party members were once again closely involved. Malcolm Nicholson, who was active in the World Federation of Democratic Youth, opened the Ballads & Blues Club, where Ewan MacColl's Ramblers Skiffle Group were to appear. From 1958 onwards Dominic Behan, Stan Kelly and Shirley Collins helped Doug Moncrieff to run the famous club Folksong Unlimited, which met in the Cranbourne pub in Long Acre. Here again Hamish Henderson's role was central: he introduced Isabel Sutherland to the club, which was run on democratic lines, as Doug Moncrieff remembers:

> We paid trade union rates (3 guineas) to our booked professional performers, when we had them. The agreement was that we shared any profits among our resident singers. However, I can't remember that happening. We seldom made a profit and ended up fourteen pounds in debt (to me, the only regular wage owner!)'[33]

Such were the 'clutches of commercialism' commented on by Dave Harker.[34] As Moncrieff says,

> These were performers who needed a platform and an audience. Our singers were all left-wing and had a respect for the folk tradition and a real urge to protect it. They also needed a way to make a living. The performers were the Club and were in control, not us three with our names on the notepaper, and certainly not the Communist Party.[35]

This reality was not always clear to the Party centre. Bruce Dunnet, who organised the Scot's Hoose folk club at Cambridge Circus, London, says that 'one of the hardest tasks was to get the CP to accept that this was a genuine natural Communist-inspired but not dominated revolution'.[36]

The revived interest in new political songs led to the WMA taking an active role in setting up *Sing* (1954–66), the first magazine of the folk revival. Although the first issue announces itself as 'published for the London Youth Choir', its editor, Eric Winter, declared its independence from the Party: 'The public of SING must control its own magazine.'[37] This policy had only mixed success. One of the first songs it printed was Ewan MacColl's hymn to Stalin's achievements, which won the *Sing* Prize for the best song of 1954:

> There was a range of mountains that was standing in the way
> So Stalin put his hand out and he smoothed them all away;
> For Joe he was determined to make the land all green
> And that's the biggest project that the world has ever seen.[38]

In the following year, *Sing* printed a 'call to international action' based on an idea floated at the Warsaw Peace Congress in 1950. This included exchanging songs between the WMA, the London Youth Choir, People's Artists in Australia, the Jeune Equipe in Montreal and others; setting up an international magazine of progressive song; and organising concerts by People's Artists at the World Youth Festivals, which could be recorded.[39] Two years later, the proposal was repeated, with the added condition that participation should be limited to affiliates of the World Federation of Democratic Youth and the International Union of Students.[40] This international project, which restricted itself to work in bodies where the Party's role was decisive, was never realised. It was the nearest the Party ever came to intervening in the folk revival. These close ties between *Sing* and the Party were given as the reason for setting up a rival magazine *Spin* in 1961.[41]

While *Sing* concentrated on printing new songs for its readers to learn, there was a great need for reliable texts of traditional songs that would replace the heavily mediated songs of the first collectors. Some books were already available. A. L. Lloyd's *The Singing Englishman* (1944) was one of the few titles dealing with vernacular song in the Workers Music Association's ambitious 'Keynote Series'. Like MacColl, Lloyd was simultaneously a performer, producer, collector and editor of songs.[42] A journalist by profession, he saw his role as a communist as radicalising institutions like the English Folk Dance and Song Society. He performed frequently in Cecil Sharp House and sat on the editorial board of its *Journal*. While this arguably made him, with Picasso, the best-known communist in English cultural life in the 1950s, his position was paradoxical. Vic Gammon maintains that Lloyd's Sharp-based folk song scholarship was incompatible with his support of the radical tradition.[43]

After 1945, Lawrence & Wishart took the lead in publishing works that brought forward the radical songs that Lloyd and others had championed. That year they reprinted *Marxism and Poetry* by George Thomson, Professor of Greek at the University of Birmingham, who argued that work songs contributed to the rise of poetry, since 'human rhythm originated from the use of tools'.[44] His analysis owes much to Marx's provisional description of culture and ideology as reflexes in the brain of real life-processes. He showed how the earliest, pre-industrial songs, of which very few survive, have links with ritual ceremonies. Such songs have from the earliest times acted as mouthpieces for social criticism.

It is known that corn-grinding songs were being adapted for political purposes as early as in classical Athens, where a song survives about the Tyrant Pittakos 'grinding' the people. Thomson summarised his case in this way: 'The three arts of dancing, music and poetry began as one. Their source was the rhythmical movement of human bodies engaged in collective labour. This movement had two components, corporal and oral.'[45] Thomson's approach is a purely functional one, in which work songs are regarded as 'primary' (and by implication, superior). This view was very influential among folk singers, and songs like 'Sixteen Tons' and 'Pick a Bale o' Cotton' remained in vogue when singers were being urged by Ewan MacColl to 'sing your own country's songs'. MacColl himself recorded 'Sixteen Tons' and sang a black prison work song at a benefit for the *Daily Worker* in the mid-1950s.[46]

A. L. Lloyd (1908–82) and Industrial Song

The most important industrial song project was, ironically, management-not union-led, but once again A. L. Lloyd was the driving force. His book *The Singing Englishman* (1944) had contained no strike or union songs, but in a 1946 article he suggested that they would be worth looking for and warned 'Comrade Cleverdick' against saying that 'you can't have folk in a capitalist society'.[47] Five years after the nationalisation of the mining industry, the National Coal Board got Lloyd to run a competition to find the best mining songs. Although there were earlier American examples from the industry, such as George Korson's collections,[48] this was the first systematic attempt to collect industrial songs anywhere in Britain.

In 1952, they were published by Lawrence & Wishart as *Come All Ye Bold Miners: Ballads and Songs of the Coalfields.* The book was important in creating a consciousness of an achieved tradition. In particular, it established the importance of Tommy Armstrong of Tanfield, 'the Pitman Poet' (1848–1920), as a central figure in the tradition of progressive song-making.[49] *Come All Ye Bold Miners* was the first important new collection of English traditional song for nearly 30 years. Although Roy Palmer estimates that less than a third of the mining songs appear to come directly from oral sources, this collection gave great impetus to the search for industrial songs, both to provide singers with progressive songs and to rewrite Britain's oral history.[50] Lloyd's success (his book was reissued in a much expanded version in 1978) led to trade unions producing books of fighting songs – a recent example was the NALGO collection *Songs that Make us Strong* (1991).

Lloyd's editing was interventionist in the sense that he attempted to provide versions for singers to learn and perform. He often printed composite versions and married broadside texts to suitable melodies. Dave Harker maintains that in the process much of the political edge of the songs was lost.[51] However, it has also been asserted that he rewrote traditional songs to make them more class-conscious. Referring to 'The Greenland Whale Fishery', Tony Davis of the Spinners claimed that 'political elements in the Folk Revival' had sought to change it in their own interests, to make the captain more interested in profit than in the welfare of his crew.[52] In fact, the version to which he refers, in the *Penguin Book of English Folk Songs* (1959) edited by Lloyd and Ralph Vaughan Williams, said the opposite, and Lloyd only remarked in a footnote that 'in some more modern versions, the two sources of grief are put in reverse order'.[53] Contrary to what Tony Davis alleges, oral sets presenting the captain in this light have been known since at least the beginning of this century, as in this version which the poet Edward Thomas collected around 1907:

> Now the losing of that prentice boy
>> It grieved our captain sore,
> But the losing of that great big whale,
>> It grieved him a damned sight more.[54]

This example points to a serious obstacle to the recovery of the 'alternative tradition', the very strength of the prevailing ideology itself. Changes made to source texts in conformity with such ideology are justified as 'standard editorial practice', while attempts to restore an authentic reading are seen as 'interference'. Ironically, Dave Harker has shown that Lloyd tended to soften the class hatred of songs that he edited.[55]

In 1967 A. L. Lloyd's *Folk Song in England* appeared, a book which even Harker acknowledges as 'the most important single book on English workers' songs ever written'.[56] Harker has criticised Lloyd's *Folk Song in England* for its negative attitude to pop music.[57] It is true that many Marxists in the folk revival looked on pop in this way, and both Lloyd and MacColl rejected Bob Dylan, for example, out of hand.[58] This attitude goes back at least to the scepticism about popular music in the WMA pamphlet *Policy for Music in Post-War Britain*. Harker also scorns Lloyd's 'mechanistic conception of the relationship between cultural practice and capitalist social relations'.[59] It is difficult to recognise in this description Lloyd's complex accounts of the relationship of occasion to function in songs of ceremony or the workings of sexual metaphor,[60] for example, still less to see how a book published in 1967 could have taken account of Marxist positions in cultural theory that were only evolved in the 1970s. In fact, Lloyd anticipated modern theories of popular culture by refusing to dismiss the broadside ballad. He saw it dialectically, not as a purely bourgeois and commercial genre but as also a key instrument of working-class expression, the third stage in a progression leading from popular epic and the traditional narrative ballad to the modern folk revival, and was one of the first to show the centrality of broadsides in the transmission of nineteenth-century industrial ballads.[61]

In other respects, Lawrence & Wishart's list in 1967 still reflected the Party's 1930s preoccupation with presenting classical music as the people's culture, a position quite at odds with the work of Lloyd and George Thomson (though Thomson's wife Katharine had herself written on Mozart and the masonic tradition). Sidney Finkelstein's *Composer and Nation: The Folk Heritage of Music* (1960), for example, doggedly traces folk themes through countless classical compositions.

With the exception of *Folk Song in England* and the enlarged edition of *Come All Ye Bold Miners*, no books on vernacular song were published by Lawrence & Wishart after 1960, in line with the Party's wider under-estimation of the progressive implications of popular song. At the same time, however, communists were able to take their interest in folk song into wider spheres, such as David Craig's important book *The Real Foundations* (Chatto & Windus, 1973), which includes chapters on radical song, and Roy Palmer's anthology of songs of social change *A Touch on the Times* (Penguin, 1974).

New song collections appeared which attempted to eliminate, or at least recognise, the degree of control routinely exercised by earlier editors over their material. The most consistent and principled of these attempts to print unmediated versions of traditional English and Scottish songs is undoubtedly Ewan MacColl's and Peggy Seeger's *Travellers' Songs from England and Scotland* (1977), and the high standard of their editing stands as a model for representing song performances in another medium. Their collection includes many songs which would have been considered fragmentary and incomplete by most editors, who preferred publishing composite or 'clean' texts in the interests of providing a version suitable for performance.

In the field of recordings too, the Party had at first a considerable role. Before the war the WMA had set up the 'Topic record club' – one 78 rpm disc a month, available only to members. Many of the records had historical or international themes. Records were chosen by a WMA committee which included its patron, Alan Bush, and A. L. Lloyd. With its repertoire of both working-class and revival singers, and with Lloyd as artistic director, Topic became a welcome source of material for singers. In the 1950s and 1960s, as Dave Harker comments resentfully, just as Lloyd and MacColl had 'cornered the market for "folk" broadcasting ... they dominated the recording of folk songs'.[62] Topic had a policy pioneered by Moses Asch of Folkways of keeping all its records available as far as possible.

The first task, to create a nationwide consciousness of songs that only had local currency or had been forgotten altogether, was carried out by Lloyd, MacColl and others. Their recordings *The Iron Muse*, first released in 1956, and *Steam Whistle Ballads*, from 1958 onwards, provided performing versions of industrial songs for the first time, and the songs became standards in the repertoire of revival singers.[63]

Union Songs and the Radio Ballads

The main project was not, however, one of recovery but the creation of a new and militant song repertoire. On the initiative of individual communists who were often working autonomously from the Party, new political songs were written and recorded with the co-operation of the trade union movement, which was moving towards a situation like that in the USA in the 1930s and 1940s, when singer-songwriters like Woody Guthrie were sponsored by unions.[64] Such songs punctuated NUR annual conferences and AUEW picket lines.[65] Ewan MacColl describes how, every week for nearly a year, he and Alan Lomax used to go to the meeting of the NUR National Executive in London:

> It was the political *machine*, if you like, in, certainly in London, that gave the final edge to the beginnings, to the burgeoning revival. There was hardly a meeting, there was hardly a [political] meeting that took place at all at that particular time which wasn't graced by somebody singing a song specially written to traditional tunes.[66]

When MacColl wrote an anthem for the AUEW in the 1960s, 'We are the Engineers', 'Unity is Strength' provided the opening image:

> Two joined hands was our device when our banner first unfurled,
> Hands that know the feel of tools and helped to build a world,
> Two hands became a million hands and fashioned down the years
> The machines that make the world go round.

Despite its occasional stereotyped language ('our banner first unfurled', 'fashioned down the years'), 'We are the Engineers' summarises in its dramatic devices the changes in the industrial song since the early steam and machine ballads. It is rhetorical, more of an anthem than a traditional song. The tone is collective, as in the 'we' of the title, and newly authoritative. Machines retain their world-transforming powers, and workers are still perceived as 'hands', but both have been newly situated. Machines are no longer autonomous entities or agents of the Other but the last link in a chain of construction that is firmly under the control of those who physically make them. Through the polyvalence of the central metaphor, the engineers are simultaneously 'two hands' and 'a million'.

MacColl's song addresses the problem of the threat to solidarity presented by media attempts to split unions during a strike. He counters the threat from outside by offering a new occupational identity which, because larger than the experience of any shipyard floor or workshop, is itself 'outside', a piece of high ground for the engineers to occupy with pride. The following stanzas bristle with answered challenges:

> We tamed the fire,
> ... we fought the cruel laws
> And when we lost, we rose to fight again
> For the right to work and live like men.
> ... we, the youngest engineers, now march to claim
> our rights.
> > 'We are the Engineers', lines 8, 18–20, 29.

Since every engineer stands for all ('We are the Engineers'), the comic and heroic role-types of early union stereotypes like The Big Hewer and 'Big John' have been subsumed into a new identity, although one in which women are still invisible ('the right to work and live like men').[67] The early muddle about individual and collective resistance seen in nineteenth-century songs like 'The Poor Cotton Weaver' has been superseded by the new discourse which makes every engineer both the *representative* craftsman and part of a much larger force with the will and the means to defend itself.

Industrial song forms a huge resource of oral expression in the years dominated by the growth of heavy industry. The title of an important source of new occupational songs which Ewan MacColl helped to edit, the *New City Songster*, confirms that today the impetus for song-making remains, as with the broadsides of earlier centuries, in the cities.

The best-known examples of the often close co-operation between unions and Party members were the eight Radio Ballads (1957–63). A.L. Lloyd's radio drama-documentary, *The Voice of the Seaman* (1938), had already put songs in their working context, but the Radio Ballads gave new status to their subjects, which ranged from the fishing industry to the travelling people, by using the actual voices of those interviewed instead of actors. *Singing the Fishing* won the Italia Prize. In *The Ballad of John Axon*, MacColl and Charles Parker received help from the National Union of Railwaymen to produce a significant new cultural genre that suggested how radio might become a medium that served progressive rather than Establishment interests. Karl Dallas has remarked how parts of *John Axon*, such as the sequence describing the passage of steam through the engine, are reminiscent of Brechtian *Lehrstücke*, which is hardly surprising when one considers the influence of German expressionist theatre on the English agitprop groups in which MacColl found his first medium of expression during the pre-war Popular Front days.[68]

Some of MacColl's songs from the Radio Ballads were taken up by traditional singers. Travellers all over Britain sing the 'Moving-On Song', and 'The Shoals of Herring' was published as a traditional folk song by an American professor who heard it being sung on the west coast of Ireland.[69]

The Growth of Mass Movements

As Party choirs and ensembles began to take on board not only the new songs of the revival but also the progressive tradition of political songs, members also called for this version of 'radical Englishness' to become part of the international youth movement. Eric Winter proposed that a British Folk Dance and Song Ensemble should be set up to go to festivals such as the Sixth World Youth Festival in Moscow in 1957 and participate in what he called (in an early use of the term) 'world music'.[70]

From the mid-1950s onwards, the CP created for itself a new role in 'rainbow' movements like CND and (later) the Anti-Nazi League. The Communist Party regarded the international Peace Movement as central to its activity after the war, but its position on the 'worker's bomb' meant that it came late to CND, and once again the Party functioned most effectively at the branch and district level. Eric Winter wrote in an early *Sing* editorial, 'To print peace songs is one of the reasons for our existence.'[71] The first song the magazine printed was 'The Atom Bomb and the Hydrogen' and the second issue called for material and experiences which would be of use in the campaign against US testing of nuclear weapons: 'The hydrogen bomb may be able to destroy singers, but can't destroy songs.'[72] A CND march was featured on the cover of *Sing* as early as 1958, when the Party's attitude was still ambiguous.

Individual communists, on the other hand, were in no doubt that this was one of the most important mass movements of the day, and there was a close link between their support for CND and the establishment of new folk clubs. The Hoy at Anchor in Southend, one of the first generation of folk clubs, is typical in that it was set up by Myra Abbott, a communist and active trade unionist, for 'singing between marches'.[73] Ian Campbell, Lou Killen and Leon Rosselson had an influence that the Party as a whole could not have. Such was the centrality of the Peace Movement that, at one point in the early 1960s, it was virtually obligatory for singer-songwriters to have a 'peace song'. Walter Benjamin had seen that new media could divorce songs from ritual and open them up to politics, and Bob Dylan demonstrated this in his reworking of the old love and death ballad 'Edward' into the anti-Bomb 'A Hard Rain's Gonna Fall'.

The individualist variety of progressive music known as the 'protest song' became sanctified in the 1960s as the only true song of rebellion, and the autonomous protest singer, absurdly, became its only recognised transmitter. This creation of music journalism was, as Karl Dallas puts it, 'the showbiz establishment's attempts to package up the expression of our determination to resist war and social injustice, and sell it back to us at a profit'.[74] The protest song has not only survived into the 1990s but has become almost the only channel for songs about racism, green politics and gender issues to penetrate the mass media. It has had the effect of marginalising communist singers or sympathisers like Dick Gaughan and Ewan MacColl who have worked within the parameters of organised movements.

To use Engels's distinction, the protest song treats those involved as a mass of individuals rather than as a class.[75] As politicians know, the grievances of such individuals can be dealt with by a combination of carrot and stick in the way that an organised strike or mass movement could not. In fact, songs of individual protest live in a symbiotic relationship with labour anthems and sponsored recordings. One will often grow into the other, as in the case of Ian Campbell's 'The Sun is Burning', which became virtually an anthem of the Peace Movement and was recorded by Simon and Garfunkel, and Dick Gaughan's semi-official *True and Bold: Songs of the Scottish Miners*, which was released during the nationwide miners' strike of 1983–84.

Progressive Song Without the Politics

Despite individual successes, the Party was becoming terminally estranged from a whole constituency of possible activists by its rejection of the popular culture and the mass media. Pop music in particular was criticised as individualistic, crudely commercial and an arm of American foreign policy, a gross simplification of its actual cultural role. This negative attitude had a long history. In an article on music and ideology that appeared in *Our Time* in 1943, Christian Darnton had attempted to distinguish between folk, art and commercial music. Only folk music, he maintained, satisfied the criteria of anonymity and rebelliousness that characterised the people's music.[76] Part of the problem was the continuing view of America as a cultural imperialist that could produce only trivia. In the folk clubs, Ewan MacColl's hostility was very influential. He insisted that singers should stick to the music of their own culture, and effectively policed that decision in the clubs and pubs.

Although it was represented as an attempt to avoid ludicrous imitations of Balkan folk music styles in English working-class settings, its main thrust was directed against American music: 'Send the Yanks back home again,' MacColl sang in 1955.[77] The active interventions of American foreign policy against British communist and progressive organisations at the time made this seem an urgent necessity. Musicians, as highly visible role models, were being singled out for discrimination in jobs and in the granting of visas, and the rapid growth of interest in folk music, almost by definition at odds with the status quo, inevitably made it the object of 'Red scare' investigations. Anticipating Dave Harker by more than 20 years, McCarthyites often cited the folk revivals in England and Scotland as examples of Communist Party cultural policy in action. It became extremely difficult for progressive singers to move freely between Britain and America. In 1957, Paul Robeson, then vice-president of the Workers Music Association, was obliged to perform for them by amplified transatlantic telephone because he was forbidden to enter Britain.[78] Three years later, Ewan MacColl was refused an American visa for a concert tour. It was not until 1961 that popular pressure had relaxed controls to the point where Pete Seeger was able to visit Britain again. As late as 1963, the Los Angeles Fire and Police Research Association requested that the Committee for Un-American Activities

investigate Communist subversive involvement in the Folk Music Field, that the continued effective misuse of this media ... may not be further used as an unidentified tool of Communist Psychological or Cybernetic Warfare to ensnare and capture youthful minds in the United States as it has so successfully and effectively captivated them abroad.[79]

These fears of foreign subversion were no doubt based on the knowledge that, at the Jug o' Punch, Birmingham, the communist Ian Campbell Folk Group was running the biggest folk club in Britain. This very influential band, which succeeded the Clarion Skiffle Group in 1957, was the first British group of the folk song revival. As well as being the prototype for later groups like the Corries and the Dubliners, it has recorded 19 albums of traditional songs (and two of Ian Campbell's own songs) which laid the foundations of the popular revival repertoire.[80] However, the touching concern of the Los Angeles police was misplaced, as the folk revival was by this time rapidly changing, under the very commercial pressures that early activists had warned about, into a much more middle-class movement, to the point where a recent analysis of folk club audiences can comment on the very low representation of manual workers, comprising 60 per cent of the general population but only 18 per cent of the folk club sample.[81]

The effects of this change were soon seen. Patrons like the British Council and the brewers began to show interest in sponsoring tours and festivals. There was a change of emphasis away from the songs themselves to refinements of instrumental technique. Ewan MacColl's Critics' Group, in attempting to raise the standard of singing, worked themselves into an elitist position by their determination 'to counter the view ... that anyone, indeed everyone, could sing folk songs'.[82] Nevertheless, the folk boom of the 1960s showed many regional variations: above all, the importance of song in shaping ideology and forming cultural identity was being recognised for the first time. E. P. Thompson, who himself left the Party in 1956, made a pioneering use of song and ballad at this time as a way of recovering working class history in *The Making of the English Working Class* (1963). Songs of struggle could be regarded as 'movement culture', part of a secret verbal tradition which passed on the practices of the disempowered and opposed the untrammelled ascendancy of individualism, the market, private property and the other orthodoxies of patrician society.[83] They offered a place to stand, an arena for ideas that could not yet be realised in the dominant culture.

This revaluing of the tradition of progressive song has become widely accepted and applied, but the same importance was not attached to the modern music of the working class, pop. The rejection of pop music led to the almost total marginalisation of the Party when, for example, Rock Against Racism was set up in 1976, and again when Paul Weller and Billy Bragg put together Red Wedge in the 1980s. Ewan MacColl, who had himself had a sizeable hit in 1973 with 'The First Time I Ever Saw Your Face', sang in Anti-Nazi League concerts, but two of the most politicised singers of folk songs in the 1980s, Billy Bragg and Shane McGowan, had never been to a folk club. The focus of popular songwriting had changed to the point where the great anthems of the closed shipyards in the northeast were written by Sting and Elvis Costello.[84] Meanwhile, two of Ian Campbell's sons, Ali and Robin, were playing reggae in the significantly named band UB40, and *Marxism Today*'s considerable coverage of popular music in the 1980s hardly mentioned progressive song.[85]

However, for more than 40 years there was a convergence between Party political struggle at the grass roots and a recognition of the importance of progressive song. Far from being an instrument of Party policy 'until ... a Russian fleet is permanently anchored in the Thames', as a hostile critic put it,[86] the central role of communists in the folk music revival after the Second World War was a result of such music being itself almost uniquely radical and determinedly non-commercial. Working-class song was a major means of contesting attempts by other classes to establish social and cultural hegemony. As Niall MacKinnon comments,

The folk scene seeks to celebrate continuity and participation, itself a protest against musical passivity, spectacle and commodity. As a form of protest it marks itself off quite differently to punk, where the protest against the ephemeral values of commodification have insufficient capability to resist incorporation into captalist forms of musical production.[87]

The revival was not a self-conscious or factitious one but part of a wider movement to reclaim areas of culture that had been marginalised by education and the media. As such it is a continuing project.

Notes

1 Dave Harker, *One for the Money. Politics and Popular Song* (London: Hutchinson, 1980) pp. 146–158; *Fakesong* (Milton Keynes: Open University Press, 1985) p. 250.
2 Harker, *Fakesong*, p. 250–253.
3 Harker, *One for the Money*, pp. 154, 188.
4 Katharine Thomson, personal communication, 1 November 1996.
5 Ian Watson, personal communication, 13 March 1996.
6 *Daily Worker*, 10 February 1937.
7 See Gerald Porter, *The English Occupational Song* (Umeå, Sweden: University of Umeå Press, 1992), pp. 39–51.
8 For this perspective, see 'All Things be Dear but Poor Men's Labour' in V. de Sola Pinto and A. E. Rodway, *The Common Muse* (Harmondsworth: Penguin, 1965), pp. 165–168; 'We Dear Labouring Men' in MacColl and Seeger, *Travellers' Songs*, pp. 309–310 and the many songs entitled 'The World Turned Upside Down', Roy Palmer, *A Touch on the Times* (Harmondsworth: Penguin, 1974), pp. 321–322.
9 John Harland, *Ballads and Songs of Lancashire* (London: Whittaker, 1865).
10 See Porter, *The English Occupational Song*.
11 Hylda Sims in *Sing*, vol. 1 (1954) p. 75.
12 A.L. Lloyd, *The Singing Englishman* (London: Workers Music Association, 1944).
13 Lloyd, *The Singing Englishman*, pp. 7–9. This interpretation of 'The Cutty Wren' was used in the communist 'Music and the People' Pageant (1939) written by Randall Swingler.
14 David King Dunaway, 'Music and Politics in the United States', *Folk Music Journal*, vol. 5, no. 3, 1987, p. 268.
15 Quoted in Robin Denselow, *When the Music's Over. The Story of Political Pop* (London: Faber, 1989) p. 19.
16 MacColl wrote the song of that name for the play *Landscape with Chimneys*.
17 See Karl Dallas, 'MacColl – the Man, the Myth, the Music' in *English Dance and Song*, vol. 51, no. 4, 1989, p. 13.
18 There is as yet no full-length study of the life and work of Ewan MacColl. His autobiography, *Journeyman*, was published in 1990 (London: Sidgwick and Jackson). Ian Watson devotes a chapter to his songs in *Song and Democratic Culture in Britain* (London: Croom Helm, 1983) pp. 179–203.
19 Ewan MacColl ed., *The Shuttle and the Cage* (London: Workers Music Association, 1954) p. 12.
20 MacColl, *Shuttle*, pp. 20–21.
21 Francis Beckett, *The Enemy Within* (London: John Murray, 1995) p. 68.
22 Ian Watson, 'The Achievement of A. L. Lloyd' (working title), unpublished MS, University of Bremen, Germany, p. 7. I am very grateful to Ian Watson for making this important study, ranging much more widely than its title suggests, available to me.
23 Ian Watson, personal communication, 13 March 1996.
24 Quoted in Denselow, *When the Music's Over*, p. 9.
25 Ian Watson, 'The Achievement of A. L. Lloyd', p. 8.

26   Georgina Boyes, *The Imagined Village* (Manchester: Manchester University Press, 1993) pp. 235–236.

27   Harker, *One for the Money*, p. 154.

28   Dallas, 'MacColl', p. 11. The first Scottish folk club was set up in a Glasgow school three years earlier.

29   Roy Palmer, personal communication, 24 July 1996.

30   Roy Palmer, personal communication, 24 July 1996.

31   Katharine Thomson and Roy Palmer have given great assistance in these and other details of the progressive song movement in Birmingham.

32   *Sing*, vol. 2 (1955), p. 37.

33   Doug Moncrieff, personal communication, 6 March 1996.

34   Harker, *One for the Money*, p. 188.

35   Doug Moncrieff, personal communication, 6 March 1996.

36   Bruce Dunnet, personal communication, 19 February 1996.

37   *Sing*, vol. 1 (1954), p. 2.

38   *Sing*, vol. 1 (1954), p. 92.

39   *Sing*, vol. 2 (1955), p. 2.

40   *Sing*, vol. 4 (1957), p. 11.

41   *Spin* editorial, October 1961.

42   Although Dave Arthur has been collecting the materials for a life of A. L. Lloyd, there is as yet no biography available. Ian Watson's unpublished paper, 'The Achievement of A. L. Lloyd' has already been mentioned, and Ian Russell's *Singer, Song and Scholar* (Sheffield: Sheffield Academic Press, 1986) includes articles on Lloyd by Leslie Shepard, Roy Palmer and Vic Gammon, and a preliminary bibliography of his large output by Dave Arthur. Dave Harker's highly critical account is in *Fakesong*, pp. 231–253.

43   Russell, *Singer*, p. 160.

44   George Thomson, *Marxism and Poetry* (London: Lawrence & Wishart, 1945) p. 15.

45   Thomson, *Marxism and Poetry*, pp. 17, 19.

46   Denselow, *When the Music's Over*, p. 23; Boyes, *Imagined Village*, p. 237.

47   'This "Folk" Business: Review of *The American People* by B. A. Botkin', *Our Time*, September 1946, pp. 4–6. I owe this reference to Boyes, *Imagined Village*, p. 201.

48   Beginning with *Ballads of the Anthracite Miners* (Philadelphia: University of Pennsylvania Press, 1927).

49   For Tommy Armstrong, see Ross Forbes, ed., *Polisses & Candymen* (Consett: Tommy Armstrong Memorial Trust, 1987).

50   'A. L. Lloyd and Industrial Song' in Russell, *Singer*, p. 135.

51   Harker, *One for the Money*, pp. 162–77.

52   'Music from the People' (BBC Radio 4, 5 October 1986).

53   Ralph Vaughan Williams and A. L. Lloyd, eds, *Penguin Book of English Folk Songs* (Harmondsworth: Penguin, 1959) p. 51.

54   Edward Thomas, *Pocket Book of Poems and Songs* (London: E. Grant Richards, 1907).

55   Harker, *Fakesong*, p. 250.

56   Harker, *Fakesong*, p. 252.

57   Harker, *Fakesong*, p. 250–253.

58   A. L. Lloyd, *Folk Song in England*. First published 1967 (St Albans: Granada, 1975) pp. 12, 385.

59   Harker, *Fakesong*, p. 251.

60   Lloyd, *Folk Song*, pp. 86–126, 187–97.

61   Lloyd, *Folk Song*, p. 128. See also Gerald Porter, 'Cobblers All: occupation as identity and cultural message' in *Folk Music Journal*, vol. 7, no. 2 (1996), pp. 43–61.

62   Harker, *One for the Money*, p. 153. Topic is today an important distributor of more than 130 independent labels – but has had no connection with the WMA for 40 years: it was sold off to avoid bankruptcy. As Ian Watson comments, 'with folk song the

Cinderella of left music, when institutions did emerge ... they were squandered' ('The Achievement of A. L. Lloyd', p. 11).

63   *The Iron Muse*, Topic 12T86 (1956, 1963) and *Steam Whistle Ballads*, Topic 12T104 (1958, 1964).

64   See Archie Green ed., *Songs About Work. Essays in Occupational Culture* (Bloomington, Indiana: Folklore Institute, 1993) pp. 208–220.

65   Karl Dallas 'MacColl ', p. 12.

66   Quoted by Ailie Munroe in 'The Role of the School of Scottish Studies in the Folk Music Revival', *Folk Music Journal*, vol. 6, no. 2, 1991, p. 152 (punctuation revised).

67   The explicit maleness of this image of the engineer was challenged on the other side of the same record by Peggy Seeger in 'I'm Gonna be an Engineer', produced by the AUEW (Engineering Section), London, undated.

68   Karl Dallas, 'MacColl', p. 15.

69   'Ewan MacColl 1915–1989', *Folk Music Journal*, vol. 6, no. 2, 1991, p. 122.

70   *Sing*, vol. 3 (1956), p. 94.

71   *Sing*, vol. 1 (1954), p. 112.

72   *Sing*, vol. 1 (1954), pp. 2, 14.

73   Niall MacKinnon, *The British Folk Scene. Musical Performance and Social Identity* (Buckingham: OUP, 1993) p. 25.

74   Quoted in *English Dance and Song*, vol. 56, no. 3, p. 16 (Autumn 1994).

75   Friedrich Engels, 'Socialism: Utopian and Scientific', in Karl Marx and Friedrich Engels, *Selected Works*, 2 vols, (Moscow: Foreign Languages Publishing House, 1958), vol. 2, pp. 120–121.

76   Christian Darnton, 'Ideology and Music', *Our Time*, vol. 3, no. 1 (August, 1943) pp. 18–19.

77   A 1955 song against the US atomic bomb, quoted in Boyes, *Imagined Village*, p. 222.

78   Boyes, *Imagined Village*, p. 223.

79   MacKinnon, *British Folk Scene*, p. 22.

80   Katharine Thomson, personal communication, 1 November 1996.

81   MacKinnon, *British Folk Scene*, pp. 43–44.

82   'Ewan MacColl 1915–1989', *Folk Music Journal*, vol. 6, no. 2, 1991, p. 122.

83   Bob Bushaway, Review of E. P. Thompson's *Customs in Common* in *Folk Music Journal*, vol. 6, no. 3 (1992) p. 306.

84   Elvis Costello, 'Shipbuilding' (1985); Sting, 'Island of Souls' (1991).

85   Notable exceptions were Karl Dallas, 'The Unhipness of Folk', January 1984, and Andrew Goodwin, 'Beating the Defeat' (on the songs of the miner's strike), December 1985.

86   Cyril Tawney, review of Musical Traditions, *Folk Music Journal* (1989), p. 662.

87   MacKinnon, *British Folk Scene*, p. 134.

11

Bert Hogenkamp

The Sunshine of Socialism: the CPGB and Film in the 1950s

> Films from the Soviet Union, China and Eastern Europe are the sunshine
> of Socialism. We must ensure that as many members of the working
> class as possible see them.
>> Colin Siddons (Bradford) at the 1952 Congress of the CPGB[1]

'Of all the arts,' Lenin once said to Lunarcharsky, 'for us the most important
is cinema.'[2] Since the late 1920s, the British Communist Party had made
strenuous efforts to use film as a 'weapon in the struggle'. Film was the
most authoritative and utopian art form of the century, offering audiences
a glimpse of the future through its rapidly increasing technical
sophistication. It was the most important form of mass cultural
consumption, a hugely popular source of entertainment and information,
a shared, collective cultural experience and a site of symbolic – and
ideological – representation of the hopes and dreams of the audiences.
Although the British Party could never even begin to compete with
Wardour Street or Hollywood in either the making or the distribution of
films, it nevertheless tried bravely, energetically and imaginatively, to use
the medium to 'get its message across' to the British working class in the
1920s and 1930s.

By the late 1940s however, nothing demonstrated more clearly the
Party's estrangement from British society than the failure of its film
culture, a failure which both represented and confirmed the Party's
isolation, partly self-imposed, in the early years of the Cold War. During
the 1950 General Election, when the Party needed all the support it could
muster to defend its two Parliamentary seats, it had no communist film
organisation to fall back on. Kino and the Progressive Film Institute
which in the 1930s had played such an important role in stimulating the

exhibition of films within the British Labour Movement, were both disbanded during the war.[3] To some extent their work had been taken over by the Workers Film Association, supported by the Labour Party, TUC and Co-operative Movement and renamed National Film Association (NFA) in 1946. But in the deteriorating conditions of the Cold War, the NFA became less and less inclined to distribute those films in which the communists were primarily interested: films from the socialist countries.

Shortly after the German invasion of Russia in 1941 the communist zoologist/journalist/film-maker Ivor Montagu had helped to set up a Soviet Film Agency in London to make dubbed versions of Soviet films available and liaise with British distributors. For a time the agency even ran its own film shows in the Tatler Cinema in London. Although it proved hard to run on a commercially viable basis, the agency played an important part in satisfying the needs felt by newsreel companies, the Ministry of Information, non-theatrical exhibitors and others for Soviet film material.[4]

After the end of the war the situation changed quickly. The Soviet Union became an enemy and the film trade was no longer interested in Russian films. Negotiations over an exchange of ten films each between Britain and the Soviet Union, proposed in 1949 by the President of the Board of Trade, Harold Wilson, ended in failure.[5] In vain too were the efforts of Montagu to find the Soviet Film Agency a cinema in central London, so that there would at least be a 'shop window' for Soviet films in the country.[6] This left the British-Soviet Society (known as British-Soviet Friendship Society from 1950) as the only active exhibitor of Soviet films, screening these to members and their relatives in cinemas such as the Scala, off Tottenham Court Road, or in halls hired for that purpose. On a similar basis other friendship societies showed films which had been made available to them by their adopted country.

Film and the Battle of Ideas

By adhering rigidly to the policies of the Soviet Union, in the second half of the 1940s the CPGB isolated itself more and more from so many of those whom it had fought hard to win over to its side during the previous years. This was particularly noticeable in the field of the arts, where the Party's increasing sectarianism as well as its defence of Zhdanov's dubious inter-pretations of Socialist Realism had led to disenchantment among sympathising intellectuals and artists, writers in particular.[7] A determining part in what communist artists and intellectuals had to think and how they had to act was played by the National Cultural Committee (NCC), chaired by Emile Burns with Sam Aaronovitch as Secretary.

At the Party's 1948 National Cultural Conference the latter outlined their role in the 'Battle of Ideas', that is, 'the battle of classes as it is fought out in men's consciousness.' Aaronovitch's analysis of a capitalism wanting to forestall another world economic crisis by starting a war against the Soviet Union and the People's Democracies sounded remarkably like a rehash of the 'Class against class' position of the late 1920s. The NCC secretary pointed out that the people of Britain and Western Europe had to be won over first for the idea of such a war. Cultural products coming from the USA such as detective stories, comic strips and Hollywood movies were designed to weaken the resistance of the British people. Therefore the fight against the 'cultural subjection' by the USA was a direct contribution to peace. But by extolling freedom Soviet-style as being of a higher order and dismissing the idea of a 'Middle Way', Aaronovitch firmly closed the doors to possible allies who might have shared the concern of the communists over the Americanisation of British culture.[8]

The NCC co-ordinated the work of a substantial number of specialist groups consisting of Party members active in professions like history, science, writing, etc. The Film Workers too had their own group, but they felt more involved with the CPGB's industrial department than with the NCC. This made sense, given the leading positions held by communist film-makers Ralph Bond, Sidney Cole and Ivor Montagu within the Association of Cine-Technicians (ACT). Through the union the Film Workers campaigned for measures of support to the British film industry which in 1948–49 was undergoing one of its recurring crises. In May 1949 the group published a pamphlet, *The Great Film Lock-out*, in which it linked the film crisis directly to Marshall Aid and demanded a package of State interventions including a state-owned and operated fourth cinema circuit.[9]

The Battle of Ideas logic may have implied that 'the fight for Britain's films [was] a part of Britain's fight to live',[10] but this did not mean that British films as such – with rare exceptions like *Chance of a Lifetime*[11] – played any role of importance in communist thinking and campaigning. It was the influence of Hollywood movies which worried the Party, coupled with the boycott by the film trade of films produced in the Soviet Union and the People's Democracies. As letters to the editor in the *Daily Worker* or the YCL paper *Challenge* witness, the Party press was facing the dilemma of either condemning or even simply ignoring American films and being accused of elitism, or accepting the fact that it was primarily Hollywood movies that working-class people were seeing and reviewing them like any other film. Both papers chose to print brief plot synopses of films on general release as a service to their readers. Only a few overtly anti-Soviet Hollywood films such as William Wellmann's spy drama *The Iron Curtain* (1948) came in for ideological (and consequently damning) criticism.

Positive Leadership

By the end of 1949 the unsatisfactory state of the Party's film work had become the subject of much internal debate. Leading members of the Film Workers group discussed new structures which would make the film work not only more efficient but also more accountable to Party organs. A memorandum circulating inside the Party suggested among other things the establishment of our 'own national film library'.[12] But when it came to contributing to the election campaign, it was only 'at the last moment and in a great hurry' that the Party's film technicians 'managed to film two Youth Brigades'.[13] It was this 'slough of despondency' and lack of 'positive leadership' which prompted Peter Brinson, Tony Simmons and a couple of other youngsters, all either relatively new in the film industry or eager to enter into it, to found the New Era Film Club in February 1950.[14] This new enterprise was to act as a film society, a 16mm projection service for clubs and trade union branches and a production outfit.

On 3 March 1950 the New Era Film Society showed its first programme comprising English and Polish shorts plus a French feature film in the Hammer Theatre in Wardour Street, London.[15] The idea proved a great success and at its first AGM in July 1950 the society claimed a membership of 440.[16] To accommodate all its spectators it was eventually forced to move to a bigger cinema. Soon New Era Film Society branches were established in Birmingham, Leeds, Bradford and Ilford. In Glasgow the Clydeside Film Society operated along similar lines, screening the same film fare as New Era.

Brinson and Simmons then managed to assemble a group of film technicians, among whom were some experienced ACT members willing to do the job free of charge, in order to make a film of the May Day demonstration in London. In defiance of a ban on marches by Labour Home Secretary, Chuter Ede, the London Trades Council (LTC) had called for a demonstration to celebrate the 'workers' holiday'. When the police started to disperse the procession, serious clashes followed. The New Era camera teams tried to cover these as well as circumstances (and the police) allowed them. Among the 69 men and women arrested were cameraman Sam Napier-Bell and his assistant.[17] New Era gratefully accepted the offer of £10 for a print of the May Day film, made by LTC secretary, Julius Jacobs. The film, entitled *May Day 1950*, was therefore premiered at an LTC meeting on 8 June 1950 in Beaver Hall, London.[18]

So unusual was the way this production had been financed that the ACT organiser present at this screening first suspected foul play from the members of his union who had participated in the film, but was eventually persuaded of the truly non-commercial nature of this venture.[19] For an old-timer like Ralph Bond though, the project must have had a strong *déjà vu* aspect: after starting the Workers' Film Society movement in 1929 he went on to make a series of *Workers' Topical News*.[20] The subject of the second of those newsreels was ... a May Day demonstration. The parallel went even further: on both occasions the May Day parade shown was one organised by the left without sanction from the 'official' Labour Movement.

Having acquired a taste for filming demonstrations New Era cameramen were once more present in Trafalgar Square, where a peace demonstration was held on 1 July 1950. There were no disturbances, but Film Polski showed interest in the footage which was shot and eventually paid New Era £36 for its use in Joris Ivens's film on the Warsaw Peace Congress, *Peace Will Win*.[21] This deal had been brokered by Ivor Montagu who thereafter presented New Era in late 1951 with the cameras and equipment belonging to his now defunct Progressive Film Institute (PFI).[22]

Another beneficiary of the definite winding up of the PFI was Plato Films to whom the sum of £41 17s 7d was bequeathed. Montagu justified this generous act with the argument that Plato were 'distributors of films of a similar type to those with which formerly PFI was concerned'.[23] Plato Films Ltd., registered in May 1951, could be considered the outcome of the desire for the Party to have its own film library. Strictly speaking Plato was not a Party organisation, but it certainly had the blessing of King Street. Plato shareholders included communist luminaries like Eva Reckitt (of Collet's bookstore fame), trade union official Bill Ellerby, secretary of the British-Soviet Friendship Society Bill Wainwright, composer Alan Bush and singer Martin Lawrence. British-Soviet Friendship Houses Ltd. made a substantial investment of £500.[24] The managing director was Stanley Forman, who had previously had a career with the YCL, the British-Soviet Society and the Civil Service Union. Using the slogan 'See the other half of the world' Plato distributed films from the Soviet Union, the People's Democracies and China on 16mm. These were obtained through official channels, costing Plato only the Customs duties.

Hardly had Plato started its activities than it faced competition from an unexpected source. Charles Cooper had been active in Kino and the Film & Photo League in the 1930s but then emigrated to the United States. Being a communist he was forced to leave that country as a result of the McCarthy witchhunt. He returned to London with a collection of 16mm American Labour films and Soviet and other 'classics' that he had been distributing in the USA through his company, Contemporary Films Inc. In the spring of 1951 Cooper founded Contemporary Films Ltd., resumed his distribution activities and started adding films from Eastern Europe to his library. Some Party officials were less than happy with this situation, but Forman and Cooper soon came to terms with each other, each finding a particular niche for his company.

On the theatrical front too there were positive developments. Kenneth Rive who ran the Continentale Cinema on Tottenham Court Road, London, realised that there was an audience for a certain, non-political type of film that the Russian studios were also producing: ballet films, musical 'biopics', opera films. After years without any sales at all Sovexportfilm was only too willing to oblige Rive. In May 1951 *Ballerina* was premiered at the Continentale, in the presence of the Soviet ambassador.[25] Other titles followed, including the Soviet super production *The Fall of Berlin*. Finally Ralph Bond started Bond Films as an outlet for 35mm films of a more political nature such as *The Last Stage*, Wanda Jakubowska's moving film about life in the Auschwitz concentration camp.[26]

Behind the Scenes

This sudden burst of activity brought new difficulties. First there was the problem of finding the most suitable films among the output that the film studios in the socialist countries had to offer. Then English-language versions had to be made, either by dubbing or subtitling. A crucial role in this was played by Ivor Montagu who, through his membership of the World Peace Council, was a regular visitor behind the Iron Curtain and happened to find dialogue translation a congenial source of extra income. Typical of the kind of troubles Montagu had to face is the case of the East German feature film, *Council of the Gods*. In March 1951 Montagu wrote to Kurt Maetzig, director of the film, asking him to send a copy. After a long wait Montagu appealed to his old friend, historian Jürgen Kuczynski, who made it clear that he did not know the first thing about films but was nevertheless willing to pull the right strings. On 22 June the East German film company DEFA sent a print of *Council of the Gods* by airfreight via Prague and Brussels to London. As Board of Trade officials interpreted the place of origin on the import application form in their own peculiar way as being West Berlin (Montagu had written 'Berlin, Democratic Republic'), an import licence was refused.

Montagu contacted Labour MP Elwyn Jones to put matters right for him, but it was not until September that Customs finally cleared the film. Montagu then had to negotiate with the British Board of Film Censors (BBFC), knowing how controversial the film's message was (that the Americans intervened in the Nuremberg trials to prevent German-American wartime collaboration from being exposed). In East Berlin, however, these talks about alterations and cuts raised the suspicion that Montagu was giving in to the BBFC. In no uncertain terms he was told that 'cuts which would change the meaning were under no circumstances allowed'. But when Montagu answered that one particular scene might lead to a libel charge, the DEFA backed down. After the final version had been agreed on and the subtitles made, Montagu arranged the distribution of the film: Contemporary was allocated one 16mm and one 35mm print, Plato one 16mm print and Bond Films one 35mm print. In the end *Council of the Gods* was released in April 1952, more than a year after Montagu had first written to East Berlin![27]

The quality of prints and the English dubbing or subtitling was a recurring cause for concern. Films such as *Donets Miners* had originally been shot on colour stock but were released on 16mm black and white prints for financial reasons. The quality of the copy that Plato held of the Bulgarian feature *Danka* was such that it had to include a warning in its catalogue that the 'print is rather dark'.[28] Even more serious were the complaints received by Pat Sloan, secretary of the British-Soviet Friendship Society, from members of his society about the print of Pudovkin's *Storm over Asia* distributed by Contemporary. Sloan decided to go and see for himself and discovered that the film only contained a few explanatory titles at the beginning but otherwise lacked any translation. As far as he was concerned this made *Storm over Asia* 'far from being intelligible to the ordinary British 16mm audiences'. He appealed for help to Ivor Montagu, who suggested distributor Charles Cooper have the film titled at the cheap Ideal Film Labs and until then 'not to book the picture to political groups'; 'non-political film societies interested in art only are rather a different matter.'[29]

The banning of a film in its entirety for political reasons was a rare occurrence in the early 1950s. But negotiations with the BBFC over cuts and alterations – Montagu was a master in the art – were normal practice. What Montagu did not know was that the Labour Government was then considering steps to enable Customs officials to seize imported films of a 'dangerous propaganda nature'. Herbert Morrison, now Foreign Secretary, proposed to use the Royal Prerogative, but the idea was rejected in Cabinet in April 1951.[30]

The sudden flood of films from the socialist part of the world also placed new demands on the communist press. For a while short reviews of the films distributed by Plato and Contemporary were printed alongside those of American and British films on general release in the weekly film column of the *Daily Worker*. But in November 1951 a fortnightly column was started to draw attention to films from the socialist part of the world. Their superiority was continually stressed: 'With this film [the Soviet colour film *Donets Miners*] it is obvious that the Soviet screen industry has advanced enormously ahead of Rank or Hollywood.'[31] But communist film critics found it harder to put into words what exactly made the difference. *Daily Worker* film critic Thomas Spencer (the pen-name used by Paddy Goldring) probably came closest to expressing the feeling generally held in the movement, when he attributed to films produced under socialism 'the ability to give a character or an incident a light which helps you to see the whole social landscape a little more clearly and to understand life a little more deeply'.[32]

Lastly the films had to be screened. In the 1949 memorandum it had been pointed out that as far as equipment was concerned Party districts had neither the funds to buy 16mm film projectors nor the political conviction that this was a sound investment, let alone the knowledge of how to use them.[33] For that reason Plato – whose advertising slogan was 'It's easy to run your own film show' – provided a projection service on demand, first in the London area only but from 1953 covering the whole country through a network of agents.[34] New Era too advertised its 'first-class' projection service, offering special rates for youth organisations.[35]

Cultural Struggle

Within a short time the film medium had made a remarkable comeback in the Party. For the election campaign in the autumn of 1951 a five-minute film was shot, in which Harry Pollitt outlined the communist programme and exhorted the viewers to vote communist.[36] Its newly found status was confirmed at the 22nd Party Congress, held in April 1952, where the cultural work of the Party was a topic of discussion. All Party organisations were urged 'to develop the cultural struggle as a part of the political struggle'.[37] This in turn was the result of the work of the NCC, which had organised a series of widely publicised annual conferences. At the 1951 conference, devoted to 'the American Threat to British Culture', several of the speakers mentioned 'the vicious and corrupt influence of so many Hollywood movies'. But it was up to veteran Ralph Bond to point out that it was not enough to agitate against them, but that it was just as important 'to ensure that our people see the best works of film art from all countries'.[38] This was also the assumption behind a resolution adopted by Congress, which called on the one hand for 'more film shows' and on the other for 'more activity against the Americanisation of Britain's cultural life'.[39] What better way to fight Americanisation than by showing 'the sunshine of Socialism', as Colin Siddons so aptly coined the films from the Soviet Union, China and Eastern Europe?

There was another reason for the Party to boost the cultural life of the branches. Offering attractions like film, music or singing was a way of keeping intact that part of the membership which was not highly politicised and would only reluctantly attend regular meetings. Moreover film shows and musical performances were occasions when male members could take their wives along. The 'What's On' columns in the *Daily Worker* offer ample evidence that Party branches did make efforts to implement the Congress resolution. In order to do so the London District for example even appealed directly 'to *Daily Worker* readers with 16mm film projectors in the London area' to come forward in order 'to help increase use of progressive films'.[40] It meant that there always was a film show for communists to attend – at weekends they even had a choice of several – not only in London but also in the provinces.

For a while even such well-known and beloved speakers as Harry Pollitt or Willie Gallacher had to share the bill with one or the other film. As John Gorman has recalled in his autobiography, film shows organised by Party branches – 'in a blacked-out school hall, with uncomfortable wooden chairs' – would be preceded by 'a drive to sell shilling tickets'. These shows – in Gorman's recollection usually attended by 'twenty or thirty people' – inevitably ended with a few words about the Party, 'appealing for non-members to join, taking a collection, and advertising our next meeting.'[41] However, crowds of up to a thousand would turn up at the locations noted for their luxury (local cinemas) or civic status (town halls) that were booked by the friendship societies. For a time the New Era Film Society in co-operation with Contemporary even ran a film show every Tuesday night in Unity Theatre.[42]

New Era also continued its production activities. With financial support from the LTC further newsreels were shot of May Day demonstrations in London. Now that the ban had been lifted, it proved more difficult to make something special out of these May Day films. More ambitious was a series of films about youth festivals in Berlin (*Festival in Berlin*, 1951), Sheffield (*We who are Young*, 1952) and Bucharest (*One Great Vision*, 1953). Although still relying on the free labour provided by (remarkably talented) film technicians sympathising with the cause, these productions were turning more professional by the year. New Era, for example, had managed to get hold of four cameras, sound recording equipment and colour film stock for *We who are Young*.[43] Because of their subject matter these New Era films (distributed by Contemporary and Plato) appealed in the first place to 'converted' audiences: the youth festival participants themselves, their parents, their YCL-friends, or, in the case of the May Day films, the marchers and their friends.

Trade Unions

One thing that the managing director of Plato Films, Stanley Forman, still remembers vividly from his dealings with Emile Burns was that time and again the NCC chairman urged him to win over trade union audiences for 'his' films.[44] Already in the 1930s left-wing film groups had set their eyes on the trade unions: after all they had capital (always in short supply in the film business) and they had ready-made audiences consisting of ordinary members of the working class, namely the proletariat in its 'purest' form. The 1949 memorandum presupposed 'a universal interest throughout the Labour Movement in films, particularly films from the USSR and the New Democracies'.[45] Following this line of reasoning trade unionists only needed to be put on a diet of those films and their eyes would be opened to the communist point of view: 'If as many people in Britain had seen the Polish film *The Last Stage* as have seen Hollywood's *Salome*, nobody would be hoodwinked into giving as much as a toy pistol to the new Nazis in Germany.'[46]

This opinion was expressed in Birmingham at a conference on 'Film and the Labour Movement', organised by Plato. Early in 1952 Stanley Forman tried to interest trade union branches into booking films like *The*

Broad Highway, a Polish documentary about the reconstruction of Warsaw. He even suggested that they should have 'a "whip round" amongst their members to pay the modest cost of hiring the film'.[47] In July 1952 Plato organised a week's tour of County Durham showing the Czech feature film, *New Heroes Will Arise*, to three miners' lodges.[48] But a real breakthrough failed to materialise. Plato then developed the strategy of organising in close co-operation with local Trades Councils, Co-operative education committees, film societies and the like conferences on 'Film and the Labour Movement'. Through an extensive mailing every working-class organisation in a particular region was called upon to send a delegate. The programme included films from Plato's library plus a trade union film (usually chosen from the ETU's *A Power in the Land*, the Tailor and Garment Workers' *Through a Needle's Eye* or the Bakers' *A Call to Action*), a keynote speech by Ralph Bond, Sidney Cole or another left-wing film activist and talks by local representatives. In order to commit them to the conference local organisations were asked to supply the chairmen for the sessions.

It was hoped that those present at the 'Film and the Labour Movement' conferences would either not notice Plato's political affiliation or at least not be offended by it and then would let themselves be convinced of the need for film propaganda within the movement. However the first aim was not always achieved. Two representatives of the National Union of Agricultural Workers for example complained that 'it was all "Moscow" and "China"' at a conference they had attended in Gillingham and wanted to know if their suspicion that Plato was a communist organisation was correct. The TUC did not hesitate to confirm this. It received a number of enquiries regarding the 'Film and the Labour Movement' conferences and the nature of its sponsor, Plato Films. Although the film distribution company was not on the blacklist of proscribed organisations, the TUC's advice was invariably that it was 'not in order to associate with it'.[49]

It was not the TUC's opposition however that made Plato realise that the conference strategy was a dead end. It was difficult enough to sell the idea of using films to trade unions, but to convince them to take films made in Eastern Europe or the Soviet Union was just impossible. Stanley Forman recalls how upset and angry he was at the time, when the communist Leeds University lecturer Arnold Kettle confronted him with this home truth.[50] Surviving Plato booking sheets for 1953–54 bear out how right Kettle was. Out of more than 120 bookings for Polish films in January–May 1954 the only trade union booking was made by USDAW Birmingham (hiring *New Heart of Warsaw*), with the CP, YCL and, inevitably, the British-Polish Friendship Society taking up the lion's share.[51] For Plato's three Hungarian features there were no trade union bookings at all between January 1953 and May 1954.[52] By the end of 1955 Plato stopped organising the conferences. It was not until the early 1960s that the company (now operating under the name ETV) started again systematically approaching trade unions.[53]

The kind of long-term work of persuasion that Plato had in mind with the 'Film and the Labour Movement' conferences, was perhaps more successfully achieved by the Film Panel of the Authors' World Peace Appeal. The latter had its origin in the Stockholm Appeal of 1950. In January 1952 the Film Panel started its activities, which included an annual conference and the publication of a broadsheet, *Preview*, in January 1952. The panel's aim was to condemn 'films which sharpen existing dangers and hatred in the present world situation' and to welcome 'films which help to lessen world tension'.[54] In short reviews it judged films currently on release on their contribution 'towards peace or towards creating a war mentality'.

In 1953 the Film Panel scored its first success, when the Trades Union Congress adopted a resolution moved on behalf of the ACT by Ralph Bond condemning films of brutality and violence.[55] For a time communist film critic John Alexander acted as the Film Panel's secretary, while another communist, film technician and ACT activist Chris Brunel, masterminded many of its campaigns, involving trade unions, educational bodies, peace groups and the British Film Institute. In the late 1950s, long after the demise of the Authors' World Peace Appeal, it changed its name to Screen Viewers Panel and made its voice – quite influential among educationalists – heard until well into the 1960s.[56]

Changes

By the mid-1950s the novelty of Party branches organising their own film shows had worn off, as witnessed by their gradual disappearance from the *Daily Worker*'s 'What's On' column. Speakers were no longer billed as support act to a film. Around 1954 the New Era Film Society had put an end to its activities.[57] Bond Films too had stopped trading. Moreover, those films which had once been hailed as 'the sunshine of Socialism' were now under a cloud of suspicion as a result of the Thaw after Stalin's death. Communist films could be a liability too. In May 1956 Plato's managing director, Stanley Forman, had to admit that there had been a 'sad decline in the artistic quality of the Soviet postwar film'. He confessed that Soviet films had a lot of catching up to do with Soviet reality.[58]

Early in 1956 Plato found it more and more difficult to break even. Therefore when King Street offered to pay for the print costs, it eagerly accepted a ten-minute film, made by the newsreel studios in Peking, of Harry Pollitt's visit to China. It presented the CPGB secretary as a statesman of international stature, as *the* representative of the British people. Although Pollitt was not the man to promote actively the cult of his own personality, this short film came pretty close to it. In May 1956 Pollitt had to relinquish the Party leadership for health reasons. His successor John Gollan – 'whose Scottish voice is particularly well suited to the microphone,' a detail the *Daily Worker* was keen to emphasise – assured Robin Day in a rare television appearance that the Stalin cult could never happen again.[59] But as the contents of Khrushchev's Secret Speech became known, an increasing number of Party members doubted just that. The Soviet invasion of Hungary in November 1956 acted as a further catalyst. Among those who left the Party were Paddy Goldring and the paper's radio and television critic Alison Macleod.[60]

After the traumatic period of 1956–57 film slowly made a comeback in the Party. Some of the commercial success of the Soviet feature films of the Thaw, culminating in the first prize of *The Cranes are Flying* at the Cannes Film Festival, reflected on the Party. With Japanese anti-nuclear documentaries such as *The Shadow of Hiroshima*, Contemporary was reaching new audiences. Its director, Charles Cooper, was to play an important role in the distribution of the *March to Aldermaston* film (1958), a co-operative venture of a group of ACTT members.[61] Prompted by communist cameraman Lewis McLeod a group within this union (which now comprised television technicians too, hence the extra T in the acronym) made efforts to revive the art of social documentary.[62]

Plato too forged new alliances, particularly with the National Film Theatre where it presented seasons of Soviet and East German films. But it was a close collaboration with the German Democratic Republic which would mark the company in more than one sense during the coming decade. It led to highly acclaimed tours in Britain of the 'Brecht matinee' of the Deutsches Theater and Yiddish singer Lin Jaldati, but also to an outright ban by the BBFC of East German films distributed by Plato (*Holiday on Sylt*, *Operation Teutonic Sword* and *A Diary for Anne Frank*), not to mention a libel suit by General Speidel which put the company on the verge of bankruptcy and forced it to change its name into Educational and Television Films Ltd.[63]

Ironically, of course, just as communist film culture came in from the cold and regained some of its pre-war liveliness and credibility, cinema lost its place at the heart of the national culture to television. Before Alison Macleod left the Party she provoked a controversy in the *Daily Worker* by advising 'all Left Wingers' to 'forget whatever else you were saving up for, and save up for a television set'. Macleod's argument was simple: if one did not see what the majority of people were seeing, then one was 'not able to talk to them on equal terms'.[64] In a letter to the editor a housewife disapproved: to her it was much more important to have a fridge![65] But there was support from Stella Jackson who stressed 'the sense of being cut off, out on a limb, sectarian, that non-viewing gives'. She admitted that 'the working class has taken the telly to itself on a massive scale' and warned: 'Ignore it at your peril.'[66] Untouched, however, remained the underlying problem: to what extent could communists as the vanguard of the working class still speak on behalf of that same working class? Especially if they lacked the means to talk *to* the working class through the medium of television.

In the 1955 local and Parliamentary elections a number of short campaign films on topics like housing and German rearmament had been made to be screened by mobile cinema vans at street corners.[67] They were silent so that a Party speaker could add the commentary required for the situation. But the talk of the Parliamentary elections were not the street corner meetings but the television broadcasts held by the Conservatives, Labour and Liberals. The CPGB had been banned from the 'box', both for the special election broadcasts (which started in 1951) and ordinary party political broadcasts (from 1953). Although Alison Macleod argued that voters were not influenced by what they saw in the election broadcasts, it was clear that the communists had to gain access to this new and powerful mass medium if they wanted their message to get through to the population at large.[68] Despite mounting a vociferous campaign for access to television, the Party had to wait until 1966 for its first five minutes of television.[69] And few people by then wanted to stare into the sunshine of socialism.

Notes

1 *Daily Worker*, 15 April 1952.
2 See *The Film Factory. Russian and Soviet Cinema in Documents 1896–1939*, edited and translated by Richard Taylor, co-edited with an introduction by Ian Christie, (London: Routledge & Kegan Paul, 1988), p. 57.
3 For Kino and the Progressive Film Institute see Bert Hogenkamp, *Deadly Parallels. Film and the Left in Britain, 1929–39* (London: Lawrence & Wishart, 1986).
4 See two reports on the Soviet Film Agency (1941–42) kept in the Ivor Montagu papers, British Film Institute, London, files nos.178 and 179 (hereafter IM/BFI).
5 *Kinematograph Weekly*, 23 June 1949; letter from Ivor Montagu to editor of *Kinematograph Weekly*, 4 July 1949, in Ivor Montagu papers, National Museum of Labour History, Manchester, file CP/IND/MONT/9/1.
6 Montagu started his search just after the war and continued looking until the early 1950s. See letter from Ivor Montagu to G. Zakonchikov, 15 March 1950, in IM/BFI no. 218; letter from Ivor Montagu to Mr Solovey, 21 June 1951, in IM/BFI no. 225.
7 In this respect the demise of the cultural magazine *Our Time* is highly revealing. See Andy Croft, 'Writers, the Communist Party and the Battle of Ideas', in *Socialist History*, no. 5 (Summer 1994), pp. 2–25.
8 Sam Aaronovitch, 'The Communist Party and the Battle of Ideas', in *Communist Review*, (May 1948), pp. 148–157.
9 The pamphlet was written by Ivor Montagu, incorporating comments by Bert Batchelor, Montagu Slater, Jack Eighteen, Dicky Bird, W. Barnett and Ralph Bond. See IM/BFI no. 246.
10 *The Great Film Lock-out* (London: CPGB, 1949), p. 23.
11 The big cinema chains had refused to exhibit this film, directed by Bernard Miles, about workers taking over the management of a factory from their boss. Only after pressure from the President of the Board of Trade, Harold Wilson, could a release be secured.

The *Daily Worker* took an engineering shop steward to see the film (11 May 1950) and later asked its readers for comments (27 May 1950).

12 'Memorandum for Discussion. The Development of the Use of Films and Film-strips by The Party and the YCL', 4 pp., (1949), in IM/BFI no. 416.

13 Peter Sutton (Peter Brinson), 'Reflections of a Cultural Worker', in *Communist Review*, (April 1950), pp. 126–128, here p. 126.

14 Letter from Peter Brinson to Ivor Montagu, 25 February 1950, in IM/BFI no. 224.

15 *Daily Worker*, 25 February 1950.

16 *Daily Worker*, 20 July 1950.

17 Sam Napier-Bell was a well-known documentary producer and director, working with Basic Films. He and his assistant Clement Gayton were charged with 'obstructing the police'. Their cases were dismissed. See *The Times*, 17 May 1950.

18 Minutes of the Executive Committee of the London Trades Council, 25 May 1950, in TUC Library, London; minutes of the Delegate Meeting of the London Trades Council, 8 June 1950, in TUC Library, London; *Labour Monthly*, (July 1950), p. 336.

19 Report for June 1950, Executive Committee, Association of Cine-Technicians, p. 9, in IM/BFI no. 362.

20 See Bert Hogenkamp, *Deadly Parallels*, Chapter Two.

21 Letter from Tony Simmons to Ivor Montagu, 2 April 1951, in IM/BFI no. 225.

22 Letter from Tony Simmons to Miss Hellstern (Mrs Montagu), 12 September 1951, in IM/BFI no. 263.

23 'PFI to be stricken from the Register of Companies', note by Ivor Montagu, October 1951, in IM/BFI no. 263.

24 Company registration file, Plato Films Ltd., in ETV-archive, London.

25 *Daily Worker*, 3 May 1951.

26 16mm prints of this film were distributed by Plato. See file on *The Last Stage*, IM/BFI no. 303.

27 Files on *Council of the Gods* in IM/BFI nos. 225 and 287.

28 Plato Films, catalogue, ca. 1954, in ETV-archive, London.

29 Letter from Pat Sloan to Ivor Montagu, 4 March 1953; letter from Ivor Montagu to Charles Cooper, 10 March 1953; in IM/BFI no. 226.

30 The National Union of Students had requested an import licence for the East German colour documentary about the 1950 Whitsun Berlin Youth Festival, *Always prepared*. A NUS delegate had received a print of this film directly from Erich Honecker, then leader of the East German youth movement: F.D.J. Morrison was worried about the effect of the film on 'immature persons who have not the political wisdom to see through it'. See memoranda and correspondence on *Always prepared* in file PREM 8/1411, Public Record Office, London.

31 *Daily Worker*, 25 March 1952.

32 *Daily Worker*, 25 August 1951.

33 'Memorandum for Discussion. The Development of the Use of Films and Film-strips by The Party and the YCL', 4 pp., (1949), in IM/BFI no. 416.

34 *Daily Worker*, 1 January 1953.

35 *Daily Worker*, 8 March 1952.

36 *Daily Worker*, 20 October 1951.

37 *Daily Worker*, 15 April 1952.

38 Ralph Bond, 'Films', in *Arena*, vol. 2, no. 8 (June–July 1951), pp. 48–49, here p. 49.

39 *Daily Worker*, 15 April 1952.

40 *Daily Worker*, 26 July 1952.

41 John Gorman, *Knocking Down Ginger* (London: Caliban Books, 1995), p. 218.

42 *Daily Worker*, 22 November 1952.

43 *Challenge*, 20 December 1952.

44 Stanley Forman, interview with the author, 20 November 1995.

45   'Memorandum for Discussion. The Development of the Use of Films and Film-strips by The Party and the YCL', 4 pp., (1949), in IM/BFI no. 416.

46   *Daily Worker*, 5 October 1953.

47   Stanley Forman, 'Films a Weapon for Peace', in *World News and Views* (1952), p. 215.

48   *World News and Views* (1952), p. 334.

49   File 'Plato Films' in TUC archive, MSS 292/675.94, in Modern Records Centre, Warwick University.

50   Stanley Forman, interview with the author, 20 November 1995.

51   File Polish Films, in ETV-archive, London.

52   File Hungaro-Film, in ETV-archive, London.

53   See the correspondence from various trades council to the TUC for the period 1961–62. File 'Plato Films' in TUC archive, MSS 292/675.94, in Modern Records Centre, Warwick University.

54   *Preview*, vol. 1, no. 6 (1953), p. 2.

55   Trade Union Congress Annual Report 1953, pp. 319–324.

56   The name of its organ was changed too and became *Screenview*.

57   Some of the local New Era branches, like the one in Ilford, as well as the Clydeside Film Society continued their activities until the end of the 1950s.

58   *Daily Worker*, 30 May 1956.

59   *Daily Worker*, 18 July 1956.

60   See Alison Macleod, 'Witness: The Death of Uncle Joe', in *Socialist History*, no. 10, (1996), pp. 43–73.

61   See Morton Lewis, 'The Road to Aldermaston', in *Film & TV Technician*, (May 1958), pp. 274–275.

62   *Film & TV Technician*, (January 1958), p. 183; (June 1958), p. 305; (July 1958), p. 319; (December 1958), p. 399.

63   Stanley Forman, interview with the author, 20 November 1995.

64   *Daily Worker*, 4 January 1957.

65   *Daily Worker*, 8 January 1957.

66   *Daily Worker*, 10 January 1957; see also *Daily Worker* 10 January 1951.

67   *Daily Worker*, 7 February 1955.

68   *Daily Worker*, 27 May 1955.

69   A history of the campaign is given by Bert Baker in his pamphlet *The Communists and TV* (London: Communist Party, 1965); the Party's first television broadcast, by John Gollan, was shown on 23 March 1966.

Paul Hogarth

Afterword

Looking back on the period covered by these admirably informative essays has made me realise that we *did* create a radical culture despite the odds. But it did not last; at least in the spheres of literature and the graphic arts. One should blame the bureaucrats of King Street. So much was aborted because it was thought to be politically incorrect. Their active hostility towards the more creative spirits and protégés of the party's literary intelligentsia, led by Randall Swingler and Edgell Rickword, reflected a struggle that was going on in the Communist Parties of Europe and America at that time.

For me that hostility first became apparent while I worked on *Our Time* as its art editor during the final phase of its boom and bust existence. There was never a dull moment but it was an uphill task to get the magazine out on time. Before each issue could be printed and distributed, proofs had to be checked and double-checked and, if need be, Swingler himself called to account by King Street's cultural commissar, Emile Burns. It was obvious that Burns was attempting to wrest control of the influential *Our Time* out of the hands of Swingler, simply because it represented the *national* idealism of an intelligentsia transformed by wartime experiences. *Our Time* could only reach its readers through a national network of Party-controlled bookshops and sales outlets. Publication, therefore, was often delayed because King Street disapproved of any editorial reluctance to endorse Zhdanov's various campaigns against 'decadent' bourgeois culture or Lysenko's half-baked theories. Not surprisingly, *Our Time* ceased publication in October 1949.

All involved were stunned by the news. Shortly afterwards, James Boswell left the party. For him, it was the last straw. He advised me to stay clear of King Street and go my own way. 'Travel and draw,' he said, 'and work with Party activists grappling with real issues.' This was possible as I was also art editor of the monthly *Spain Today*, published by the International Brigade Association, edited by Lon Elliot, a former International Brigader then a *Daily Worker* sub-editor. But the real driving force behind the paper was the indomitable secretary of the IBA, Nan Green, widow of George Green, killed on the Ebro, and who herself had served in a Spanish Medical Aid Unit. Both suggested that I visit Franco's Spain as a tourist and make drawings.

The journey took place during the summer of 1949 and took me from Irun to the Asturias and down through Castille to Catalonia. It was an adventure in itself as my old second-hand Hillman kept breaking down on roads still pitted with half-filled shell and bomb craters. The entire country looked as if it had suffered from thirty, not three, years of civil war. Alas, I was no Jacques Callot to chronicle such tragic destruction with the artistry it so obviously required. But I learned a great deal and my drawings were widely reproduced in the communist and left-wing press throughout the world.

In 1952, fate again intervened. This time in the person of Betty Ambatielos, the indefatigable schoolteacher wife of Tony Ambatielos, the Greek seamens' union leader who faced execution with other communist union leaders at the hands of the military tribunals of Marshall Papagos who ruled Greece in those days. Betty asked me to depict Tony's trial and that of his comrades against the background of a country exhausted by five years of civil war. Under such circumstances I began to acquire the resources needed to create the quality of imagery that really would be a 'weapon in the struggle'.

Perhaps the most impressive of the activists I worked with was Ruth First (assassinated by a letter bomb in Mozambique in 1982). She was impressive because she possessed intelligence and courage to a remarkable degree. Anxious that I got 'my bristles up' she arranged eye-opening sorties into African townships which looked like the shell-wrecked landscapes of the First World War. Those two months in 1954 spent exposing apartheid in South Africa proved to be the peak of my agitprop travels.

From time to time I would attend meetings of the Party's Artists Group. I found them totally unreal. There was no effort made to examine past traditions of social and political art, such as the work of Grosz and other artists of the Weimar Republic or that of the Soviet scene of the 1920s in the Futurist-Dada-agitprop reporting of Alexandr Deineka in Lunacharsky's *Krasnaya Niva* an the Moscow *Prozhektor*. Through its stooges King Street peddled Socialist Realism based on nineteenth-century Russian academic naturalism. Inspired by Picasso, Guttuso and the Milan painters, headed by Mucchi, briefly mounted a challenge which in turn inspired Harry Baines and Ern Brooks but that was all there was.

I recalled the story that was going around Warsaw, told by the irrepressible Polish caricaturist Jerzy Zaruba (a near contemporary of James Boswell) whom I had befriended in 1953. There once lived an old king whose last wish was to have his portrait painted. So the most distinguished painter in the land was commissioned and the portrait duly painted. But the old king was not an easy subject to paint. He was blind in one eye, had a withered arm and was lame in one leg. The portrait revealed these physical defects all too clearly. The artist was shot at dawn. A second artist was summoned and he painted much of what he saw before him, rendering the old king's physical defects in a more romantic manner. But he, too, was shot. A third artist, an American, was given the commission and his picture received royal acclaim. For he had depicted the king shooting a deer, kneeling on one knee in profile, thus concealing his lame leg. His blind eye, closed up as if to sight his rifle, also concealed his withered arm. This, said everyone, was pure Socialist Realism!

Ironically, I too, like the American mentioned in the story, was now turning out drawings which concealed what was really going on in Poland, the GDR, Czechoslovakia and other Eastern Bloc countries. Minders dutifully produced statuesque heroes of socialist labour for me to draw in industrial enterprises from Anshan to Bucharest, from Kladno to Cracow. If I occasionally depicted a historic old town without any apparent political significance, they would be most upset.

Such graphic art, was by its very nature, essentially ephemeral and downright misleading. After October 1956, I turned my pencil the other way and depicted the huge demonstration of solidarity with the Hungarian Freedom Fighters in the centre of Warsaw, and I then turned to drawing people and places for what they were.

Radical art is more than a highly personal desire to protest, improve and reform in the interests of political ideology. As these essays so clearly reveal, communist writers, editors, musicians, artists and *artistes* strived with incredible dedication to create the literature, the periodicals, the pageants, the music and the festivals which have since become and inseparable element in the mainstream of a popular culture committed to the heightening of human awareness.

This does not mean that another Goya, another Daumier, or another Grosz will not emerge. As long as politicians exist there will be the need for radical attitudes and radical artists.

Notes on Contributors

Hanna Behrend, who spent a decade in Britain as a refugee from Nazi oppression, taught English Literature and Women's Studies at Humboldt University in Berlin and was one of the founding mothers in 1989 of the feminist Independent Women's Federation in East Berlin. She lectures and widely publishes on German history and politics and on feminist subjects.

Richard Hanlon lectures in Psychology and Social Policy at Blackburn College. He is a contributor to *Socialist History* and *New Times* and currently researching for an M.Phil on music and communism.

Hamish Henderson is Scotland's greatest collector of tales and songs for the common people and the founding father of the Scottish folk revival. He is editor of Gramsci's *Prison Letters* (Pluto Press, 1997); his *Elegies for the Dead in Cyrenaica* won the Somerset Maugham Award.

Bert Hogenkamp is Head of Research at the Netherlands Audiovisual Archive, Amsterdam and Professor of the History of Film, Radio and Television in the Netherlands at the University of Utrecht. He has published several books and numerous articles on the history of documentary film and film and the labour movement.

Maroula Joannou is Senior Lecturer in English at the University of Eastern England. She is the editor of *Women Writers of the 1930s: Gender, Politics, History* and co-editor (with David Margolies) of *Heart of the Heartless World: Essays in Cultural Resistance in Memory of Margot Heinemann* (Pluto Press 1996).

H. Gustav Klaus is Professor of the Literature of the British Isles at the University of Rostock, Germany. He takes a special interest in working-class and socialist writing and his books include *Tramps, Workmates and*

Revolutionaries (Pluto Press, 1993) and *Factory Girl: Ellen Johnson and Working-Class Poetry in Victorian Scotland* (1998).

Kevin Morgan teaches politics at the University of Manchester. He is co-editor of *Opening the Books: Essays in the Social and Cultural History of British Communism* (Pluto Press, 1995) and is currently writing a book on Bolshevism and the British left.

Gerald Porter is Senior Lecturer in English at the University of Vaasa, Finland. He has published widely on political and occupational songs, including the first full-length book on the subject, *The English Occupational Song* (1992).

Robert Radford is an artist and writer and a lecturer at Winchester School of Art, University of Southampton. His research into the Artists' International Association resulted in a commemorative exhibition and a book, *Art for a Purpose*; his most recent book is a monograph on Salvador Dali.

Mike Waite helps to edit the journal *Socialist History*.

Mick Wallis teaches Drama at Loughborough University and has published on sexuality and theatre pedagogy, as well as mid-twentieth-century performance. He is co-editor of *Coming on Strong* (1989) and co-author of *Studying Plays* (1998), both with Simon Shepherd.

Index